WOMEN'S MIGRATION NETWORKS

IN MEXICO AND BEYOND

Women's Migration Networks in Mexico and Beyond

TAMAR DIANA WILSON

UNIVERSITY OF NEW MEXICO PRESS ◆ ALBUQUERQUE

LIBRARY OF CONGRESS CATALOGING-IN-PUBLICATION DATA

Wilson, Tamar Diana, 1943–
Women's migration networks in Mexico and beyond /
      Tamar Diana Wilson. — 1st ed.
      p. cm.
Includes bibliographical references and index.
ISBN 978-0-8263-4720-6 (paperbound : alk. paper)
1. Women immigrants—United States—Case studies.
2. Women—Mexico—Economic conditions. I. Title.
      JV6602.W56 2009
      305.48'969120973—dc22
                              2009012484

Designed and typeset by Mina Yamashita.
Composed in Adobe Garamond Pro, bringing together elements of
Claude Garamond's Garamond and Robert Granjon's Granjon
in a contemporary typeface by Robert Slimbach.

To doña Consuelo and her family

Contents

Acknowledgments

I would like to thank Lisa Pacheco, acquisitions editor at the University of New Mexico Press, for her unending efforts on my behalf. I would also like to thank an anonymous reviewer for the suggestions that made the manuscript stronger. I am grateful to Sheilah Clarke-Ekong for her enduring friendship and her e-mailing of a number of articles I was unable to acquire elsewhere; to Cheryll Powers for her reading of the first four chapters; to Barbara Metzger for her line-by-line editing; and to Jo Griffith for diagramming the map and genealogies.

I would like to thank as well the editors of the *Journal of Borderlands Studies* for allowing me to publish most of my article, "Micro-, Meso- and Macro-Patterns of Women's Migration to Colonia Popular, Mexicali, Baja California," as chapter 4 of this book.

And I would like to give my overwhelming thanks to doña Consuelo, Anamaría and Roberto, and Irma and Raúl, as well as their network members, for letting me intrude upon and portray their lives. Doña Consuelo and her sons and daughters have been among my best friends, and I hope this book will do them justice.

Introduction

This book is a book of stories, stories that historians, geographers, sociologists, and anthropologists have told about women's work, gender relations, and the patterns of Mexican immigration; stories that people have told me about portions of their lives; and stories that I tell about them. It does not pretend to be the whole story about the lives or even the migration histories of these people. The whole story is always too complex to be told or sometimes even to be remembered. People selectively told me the stories of their lives and their migration and work histories, and I selected snippets and fragments from that material to report in these pages. My own stories, based on the art and science of participant observation guided and supported by the work of others, are snippets and fragments about migration and gender, about internal and transnational migration, about adaptation in two destinations in the United States through friendships made at work sites, and, in one destination, reinforced through ties of compadrazgo (ritual kinship relationships). They are about networks, their principles, and dynamics. Even though they are stories—slanted by selective perception and selective editing—they can throw light on reality: the reality of women's migration within Mexico, of women's acceptance of a double standard of morality, of women's (and their menfolk's) migration to the United States, and of their migratory and adaptive networks.

This is also, in large part, the story of doña Consuelo (a pseudonym, as are all personal names throughout), who has lived in various *ranchos* (unincorporated rural settlements), small towns, and a small city in the state of Jalisco; who spent many years in Mexico City, with side trips of temporary residence in the city of Zacatecas and back to Jalisco; and who migrated twice to the border city of Mexicali, Baja California, where she now lives. In telling her story, she focused on the men who had passed through her life, seldom talking about either her parents, who separated when she was fifteen, leaving her younger siblings in her care, or her offspring. I, by contrast, focus on her migration history and income-generating activities to call attention to the way women with few economic resources manage to survive and raise their offspring. The stories of two of her daughters, their husbands, and their friends at destination in Waters, Arizona, and Lake Tahoe Town, Nevada (invented names, as are all those of businesses employing the people I interviewed throughout), also focus on their migration and work histories. All interviews were conducted in Spanish and translated by me.

I got to know doña Consuelo, her daughters and sons, and two of her brothers some months after I began my PhD research in "Colonia Popular," a squatter settlement in Mexicali, in 1988 (Wilson 1992). With the help of six sociology students from the Universidad Autónoma de Baja California, Mexicali, I conducted initial interviews mapping migration histories and employment with household heads (sometimes both husband and wife) permanently settled on the *colonia*'s 155 house lots. From these interviews it became apparent that the highest percentage of people from the seventeen states of origin, plus Mexico City, had been born in Jalisco (16.7 percent). I then conducted thirty-eight in-depth interviews focused on migration and work history, sixteen of them with people from Jalisco. Following in the footsteps of Oscar Lewis (1975), I chose five families from these thirty-eight for in-depth study on the basis of their interesting migration and work histories and because of their exceptionally wide or exceptionally narrow networks. Doña Consuelo and her extended family were one of these five. Her sons and daughters and two brothers had followed her to Mexicali, as she had followed her mother. In the course of my fieldwork, besides doña Consuelo and her last husband (they had not yet separated), I interviewed her married sons and daughters and their spouses, a widowed younger brother, her eldest brother and his wife, and her father.

Doña Consuelo often invited me for lunch or dinner or just coffee at her house and after I had helped pay tuition for secretarial school for her daughter Anamaría and a niece of Consuelo's who was living with her, these meals became customary—doña Consuelo's way of reciprocating. I was always invited to family baptism, birthday, and *quinceañera* (whether for daughters or granddaughters) parties; one of the quinceañera (a fifteen-year-old girl's coming-out party) celebrations I attended was that of Anamaría, whose migration history to and in the United States will be recounted in chapters 6 and 7. I also accompanied doña Consuelo in her day-to-day activities: going to the dump with her to collect discarded clothing for resale, visiting and staying in the small shack she put up in a newly invaded squatter settlement on a lot she hoped to acquire for a son, attending her mother's and father's wakes when they died, and accompanying her to parties and gatherings government officials hosted seeking votes from colonia residents. The house lot with its little room that I bought in the colonia was only a block and a half from her house.

In conversing, we exchanged stories about our lives, and since I admitted to several marriages and long-term affairs (I was forty-six when I met her), she opened up to tell me what she had hidden from neighbors—and even her offspring—who might have judged her an immoral woman: that she had had three "husbands" (by which she meant, apart from one legal marriage, the men who had fathered her children). After some years of knowing her I mentioned that I would like to do a book about her life, and she greeted this suggestion with enthusiasm. The book would wait to be written for almost another decade.

My marriage to a man from the colonia in 1995 took me away from Mexicali and to Los Cabos. We returned to the colonia every year or so, however, and I always got together with doña Consuelo on my visits. When my husband and I separated early in 2002 I returned to my small house in Colonia Popular on many occasions from my base in San Diego, California, a two-and-a-half-hour drive away. It was in that year that doña Consuelo and I decided to begin writing "her" book—now envisioned to include the stories of her immigrant daughters and their spouses and network members. We agreed it was best for her to come and stay with me in San Diego where she could give me her undivided attention. As she pointed out, in Mexicali her family members, those who lived with her and those who lived nearby, would be dropping in and interrupting her telling of her story. From San Diego we went on to Lake Tahoe Town for several weeks with Irma and her husband and children on the occasion of their eldest daughter's quinceañera party and their long-delayed wedding. Later, we twice visited Anamaría in Waters for several weeks each time. I conducted interviews with the women, their spouses, and their network members in both places. Anamaría and Irma brokered interviews for me with their network members, some of whom had come to visit them for other reasons, while others had been asked to visit for that purpose, and still others we visited in their homes. In sum, it was under the auspices of Consuelo, Anamaría, and Irma that I was able to conduct this study.

Doña Consuelo's story and those of her migrant daughters are of interest for several reasons. First, she and her brothers and eldest son were born in Jalisco, traditionally one of the five major sending states of immigrants to the United States (e.g., Jones 1982, 1988). Because of their lack of transnational networks, however, none of her siblings or offspring crossed the border until after they had found themselves in Mexicali, or, as in Anamaría's case, had been born there. Second, it was two of her *daughters*, rather than sons, who became enmeshed through marriage, thus leading them to reside in the United States. Despite their presence in migration streams since the United States-Mexican War of 1846–48, research on Mexican women's migration has a shorter history than research on that of Mexican men.

A theme running throughout the book is that of networks: their characteristics, their development, and their dynamics. At the center of attention in these stories are the kinship networks that led doña Consuelo to Mexicali and a number of other women to Colonia Popular, Mexicali, the networks that enabled two of doña Consuelo's daughters to migrate to the United States, and the networks that these daughters and their husbands developed at destination. There is also an attempt to hypothesize the existence of certain principles of network expansion, both at origin and at destination, with special attention to urban-based emigration, such as that from Mexicali. The social capital these networks bear is seen to exist at individual, family, and community levels and expand or contract over time. Expansion is not unilinear; the experiences of doña Consuelo and her daughters make it clear that weak ties may be strengthened and strong ties may be weakened. This is shown by the presence of some network members, and the absence of others, at Irma and Raúl's wedding in the Lake Tahoe area in August 2003, fifteen years after the birth of their eldest daughter, Erlinda. It is also shown by the expansion and contraction of individual, family, and community social capital doña Consuelo and her family possessed in Colonia Popular.

A number of questions will be asked about these migration networks. Under whose auspices do women migrate internally? What part do women play in migration networks, internal and transnational? How is migration from urban centers different from migration from rural communities with regard to transnational (and gendered) migration networks? To what extent are Consuelo's two daughters and their husbands, immobilized by lack of documents enabling them to recross the border, to be considered "transmigrants" who "take actions, make decisions, and feel concerns, and develop identities within social networks that connect them to two or more societies simultaneously . . ." (Glick Schiller, Basch, and Blanc-Szanton 1992, 1–2)? I hope this book will contribute to the erosion of the male bias in migration research and the emerging consensus that individuals' access to networks and individual network exchanges are rights and responsibilities informed by kinship and gender "norms" (Pessar 2003, 84; see also Pessar 1999).

In the pages that follow, chapters consisting of interviews, conversations, and observations encapsulated in field notes are interspersed with chapters presenting the theories I developed over the years and on the basis of extensive interviewing in Colonia Popular. When I make generalizations about doña Consuelo and her family, they are clearly marked as such. I have purposely let people speak for themselves in a number of chapters—there is no reason I should speak for them in their stories when their voices are stronger than mine should be. I let some of my field notes stand as I originally wrote them, so that the reader can see on what data some of my generalizations are based, as well as obtain a better picture of

Consuelo's daily life and achievements, and those of her daughters, their husbands, and some of their network members.

In chapter 1 I summarize the history of Mexican migration to the United States since the U.S.-Mexican War of 1846–48. I also explore the many reasons for Mexican women's increasing participation in the migration stream to the United States.

Chapter 2 gives an abbreviated history of Mexican women's paid labor since the mid-nineteenth century and looks at the changes in gender relations over the past few decades associated with a cluster of factors, including lower birthrates and increasing educational and job opportunities for women.

Chapter 3 introduces key concepts in migration theory, including migration networks, social capital, and transnational migration, and includes a short discussion of issues in gender and migration. These concepts will be revisited in various chapters throughout the book.

In chapter 4 I address women's migration to Baja California, to Mexicali (the capital of that state), and to Colonia Popular, showing how network-mediated migration has led to the concentration of migrants from the same state of origin in particular cities and to particular neighborhoods in those cities. Female migrants to Colonia Popular migrated under the auspices of parents or husbands or as female heads of household accompanied only by their children. In this chapter, based on quantitative data, the typicality of doña Consuelo's move to Mexicali and to Colonia Popular is underscored.

In chapter 5, I report what doña Consuelo wished to tell me, prompted only by an occasional question, about her childhood; her *novios* (sweethearts); and the four men who fathered her children, how they treated her, and how they disappointed her. She told of her movement from rancho to rancho, from city to city, from state to state, sometimes accompanied by a man, sometimes fleeing one. Part of her openness with me, apart from the length of our friendship, was because—as mentioned previously—she knew I had been married several times and had also been subjected to domestic abuse.

In chapter 6 I describe the income- and "wealth"-generating activities that doña Consuelo has engaged in since her last arrival in Mexicali in the early 1970s—including anecdotes about her work in a shrimp-packaging plant, as a domestic servant and as a cook in a country club, selling ceramics door to door, and recycling clothing collected from the municipal dump. I also give an account taken from my field notes of her invasion of a new squatter settlement in 1990 in order to acquire a lot for one of her sons. I note as well her raising of livestock and poultry on her lot in Colonia Popular in order to augment her income—a rancho woman's adaptation to the city. Finally, I compare some of her life with that of Esperanza, the woman Ruth Behar (2003) has made famous.

Chapter 7 contains the migration histories of Anamaría (doña Consuelo's seventh daughter), her mother-in-law, Miriam, and her husband Roberto—both of whom preceded Anamaría to Waters, Arizona. Whereas Anamaría and Roberto crossed into the United States with border-crossing cards—later invalidated—Miriam crossed in a number of ways, with documents, and after she lost them, without documents. Following Brettell and deBerjeois's (1992) insights, I separate this chapter addressing migration networks, spanning origin and destination, from the following chapter on adaptation networks at destination.

Chapter 8 is concerned with Anamaría's and Roberto's adaptation network members, based largely on work-site friendships they developed in Waters. I present interviews with a number of Anamaría's closest friends, most of whom are from or have resided in Mexicali—where Anamaría and Roberto were born—though they did not know one another or become friends until arriving in Waters.

Chapter 9 recounts the migration histories of doña Consuelo's fourth daughter, Irma, and Irma's husband Raúl, first to Los Angeles, and then to Lake Tahoe Town, Nevada, under the auspices of the sons and daughter of Raúl's mother's brother. These cousins had left from a rancho near Tepatitlán, Jalisco. Tepatitlán, rather than Mexicali, is the source for establishing commonalities among several members of Irma's and Raúl's network in Lake Tahoe Town, despite the fact that they both lived in Mexicali with their families of procreation for many years and migrated from that city the United States. Injured by a fall from the roof while working at

Lake Tahoe Hotel, Raúl very much wants to continue living in the United States. Both he and Irma see their children's future as better secured in Lake Tahoe Town than in Mexicali. They related to me the onerous border crossings they had suffered in getting to the United States, which I present in this chapter along with an account of their migration network.

Chapter 10 is concerned with the expansion of Irma and Raúl's network at destination, fueled by the establishment of ritual-kinship ties. Besides interviewing compadres (ritual kin) and cousins, I explore which network members, some tied weakly, some strongly, were present (or absent) at Irma and Raúl's church wedding and party in August 2003 and on the same day as their eldest daughter's quinceañera (fifteenth-birthday) party. I found that weak ties can indeed be strengthened, and strong ties reinforced, but also that strong ties can be weakened by absence from important life-cycle events.

Chapter 11 describes the ways in which women can facilitate male transnational migration. Drawing on concepts from network and social-capital theory, I point to the importance of sisters in enabling the migration of their brothers, a phenomenon strengthened in urban centers, and the role of marriage in creating new transnational migration networks. The expansion and contraction of social capital on individual, family, and community (Colonia Popular) levels is also explored. In chapter 12, I advance some principles for understanding urban-based transnational networks as opposed to those found in more encapsulated rural communities.

Herstories

Women and Work

The stories of Consuelo, of her daughters who migrated to the United States, and those of their network members are embedded in complicated, overlapping histories of Mexico, the United States, women's work, and gender relations. In this chapter I will summarize some of these issues, beginning with the history of Mexican women's income-generating activities, including waged work, and then move on to map the contrast between traditional and more contemporary gender relations and expectations.

Notably, doña Consuelo and her daughters are among the poor women who have had to generate an income by working. Consuelo had to do so first as the guardian of her younger siblings, then as an unwed mother, and periodically as a female head of household. She also contributed income to the household when her successive husbands' wages were inadequate. Even when they were not, she felt it her duty to help out with household expenses. Her daughter Anamaría also worked to help out her mother's household and, after she was married and had immigrated to Arizona, to contribute to a higher standard of living for her own. Consuelo's daughter Irma also entered the labor force in Nevada after her husband's disabling accident in Nevada. Consuelo, Irma, and Anamaría are women who migrated, not always under the auspices of men. Consuelo moved to Tepatitlán, Jalisco, then to Mexico City on her own; later she moved twice to Mexicali, to where her mother had migrated earlier. Irma followed her husband to Los Angeles, planning and executing the trip without his prior knowledge. Only Anamaría crossed the border under her husband's auspices.

Mexican Women at Work

Until relatively recently, many ethnographers and historians claimed that it was unusual for Mexican women to work outside the home. In part this was because women's work was often invisible to the census takers—involving, for example, sewing garments for relatives or friends, running a small store from the house, selling various items door to door in the colonia of residence or nearby colonias, raising chickens or small livestock, and engaging in other income-generating activities belonging to the informal economy. In part it reflected a stereotyped vision of women's place both Mexican families and those who studied them embraced. Women themselves, as well as their husbands, stressed women's role as *amas de casa* (housewives); their husbands tended to consider their wives' employment as reflecting unfavorably on their own idealized role as the household breadwinner. In fact, however, despite the traditional prescription "women in the house, men in the street" (e.g., Behar 2003, 281), Mexican women have a long history of working outside the home, even before Mexico's independence in 1821. In 1811, women eighteen years of age or older constituted 30.9 percent of the capital city's labor force; by 1848 this percentage had risen to 36.6 percent and may be underestimated since indigenous women coming into the city to vend their wares may not have been counted (Arrom 1985a, table 14, 158). Women made up at least a third of Mexico City's labor force from the mid-eighteenth century to the beginnings of the twentieth (Thompson 1992, 150). Women worked as domestic servants, shopkeepers, artisans, seamstresses, street vendors, and "wage laborers in restaurants, small workshops or factories, which were usually unmechanized until the 1830s, but boasted a complex division of labor" (Arrom 1985a, 187).

A survey of the period from 1876 to 1970 (Thompson, 1991) reveals "wave-like rhythms" in women's participation in the Mexican labor force. There was a peak from 1850 to 1882, a trough from 1920 to 1940, and then a continual increase in women's labor-force participation thereafter, becoming marked in the 1970s (Thompson 1991, 406). In 1879, women were 28 percent of the work force in Mexico City's factories and workshops; in 1895, they constituted 27 percent of that work force (Thompson 1992, 150). In contrast, women's work-force participation in the late 1930s and early

1940s was especially low and related to high wages for men: these years "were probably the best and most optimistic years in the entire history of the [Mexican] industrial proletariat" (Thompson 1991, 403). With real wages for the designated male breadwinner at "an unprecedented high," married women were able to exit the work force and retreat into domesticity (Thompson 1992, 150, 153, 166). Women's, especially married women's, labor-force participation was, and still is, partially related to economic trends that have helped or hindered a male breadwinner perform his role.

Whereas working women in Mexico City were generally segregated into female-dominated cigarette and textile workshops and factories in the early nineteenth century, by the end of that century new industries, which Pres. Porfirio Díaz encouraged to locate in Mexico, began hiring women in factories that also employed men (Porter 2003, chap. 1). During the Porfiriato (the dictatorship of Pres. Porfirio Díaz, 1876–1910) women were increasingly employed as secretaries and store clerks; in 1885, women were 26.5 percent of the economically active labor force (Tuñón Pablos 1999, 75). During this period women were employed in all aspects of office work, as home-based artisans, and overwhelmingly, among poor women, as domestic servants (Ramos Escandón 1992, 156–57).

During the Mexican Revolution (1910–17), soldaderas (camp followers) accompanied troops on all sides. Many were married women fulfilling traditional domestic responsibilities for husbands. Others had been raped and abducted. Single, abandoned, and widowed women joined the soldiers to earn a livelihood or for idealistic reasons. They procured and prepared food, laundered, and mended clothing and uniforms, often taking up arms while the soldiers ate (Salas 1990, 39–44). Furthermore, women took part in the Revolution "as couriers, spies, employees, arms and munitions runners, uniform and flag seamstresses, secretaries, journalists, nurses—all decision-making roles. Many women teachers sought to educate the troops, while others learned to use the telegraph. Women helped draft plans and manifestos" (Tuñón Pablos 1999, 90–91).

After the Revolution article 123 of the 1917 Mexican Constitution—which "contained the most advanced labor law in the world at that time, recognizing worker's rights to organize unions, bargain collectively, and strike," as well as offering profit sharing and protections to workers—eventually became the Federal Labor Law of 1931 (LaBotz and Alexander 2005, 16). By the mid-1930s, pressures from unions had led to the establishment of a living wage for all but the most marginalized families, and except in these families, fewer women worked outside the home (Thompson 1991, 1992). By 1940, women formed only 7.3 percent of the economically active population (though this may underestimate women's agricultural work as part of the family labor force and their informal income-generating activities). After that, however, there was a continuous increase in women's labor-force participation, rising from 13.6 percent in 1950, to 17.9 percent in 1960, to 19.0 percent in 1970, to 27.8 percent in 1980, and to 32.0 percent in 1990 (Tuñón Pablos 1999, 75, 108). The number of domestic servants, almost all of whom were women, increased from 310,165 in 1950 to 541,063 in 1970, a difference of 230,898 (Leobardo Arroyo 1981, table 4, 424).

Although import-substitution industrialization, with its high tariffs and government subsidy of local businesses, began in the 1930s, it was not until the 1950s that it became a "comprehensive strategy" (Potter 2007, 7). These domestic industries hired women, who were later targeted for employment in the *maquiladoras* instituted by the Border Industrialization Program of 1965, under which materials imported from the United States were assembled or transformed for export. Some of these assembly plants, such as electric and electronics firms, showed a preference for young, single women, usually the daughters of the household; others, such as the apparel plants, tended to employ female heads of household and legally or common-law married women with children, an older and less well-educated group and one more recently settled in the border cities (Fernández-Kelly 1983). The high point of women's employment in the maquiladoras occurred in 1975, when 78.3 percent of the line operators were female; this had fallen to 55.2 percent by 2000, when lack of alternative employment drove men into the maquiladora work force (Wilson 2002, table 1, 6). Absolute numbers of women workers increased, however, from 78,880 nationwide in 1980 to 574,073 in 2000 (INEGI 2001, 8).

Mexico's economic crisis of 1982, brought about by the decline in the price of oil (Mexico's primary export), the stagnation of the industrial sector, and the inability of the Mexican government to pay its national debt to international moneylenders, pushed more women, especially married women, into the labor force. This development received impetus from the structural adjustment policies the World Bank and the International Monetary Fund (IMF) imposed, which involved privatization of state-run enterprises, including banks, cutbacks in federal subsidies to both rural and urban social programs, and the opening of the Mexican economy to international investment (see, e.g., Benería 1992; Chant and Craske 2003). The crisis promoted both internal and international migration as well as the increased entry of women into the labor force (Staudt 1999). The signing of the General Agreement on Tariffs and Trade in 1986, integral to the structural readjustment regime, caused the bankruptcy of small firms producing consumer goods such as shoes and clothing as cheaper imports from China, Hong Kong, and Brazil among other countries, undercut their prices (González de la Rocha 1995, 394).

The establishment of the North American Free Trade Agreement (NAFTA) and a renewed peso crisis in 1994 also had important effects on women's work in Mexico (e.g., Chant 1994; González de la Rocha 1988a, 1991, 1994, 2001; García and de Oliveira 1994). Most researchers agree these decades saw an increase in poverty, as high inflation and the devaluation of the peso eroded wages and male unemployment and underemployment increased; cutbacks in consumption, including expenditures on health and education; the entry of formerly unemployed household members, especially wives and teenagers (both girls and boys), into income-producing activities; and the extension of the household to include kin who could either contribute income or take over domestic chores (and sometimes both) for the newly working wives.

In most of the developing countries worldwide, the crisis associated with structural adjustment policies led to an increase in the numbers of women entering the informal economy (Lingam 2005), which the social and legal institutions that regulate formal employment do not oversee (Castells and Portes 1989, 12) and therefore provide no worker's benefits,

protections, or rights. For women in Mexico these informal or informal-
ized activities involved, overwhelmingly, domestic service (Arizpe 1977)
but included street vending, running small restaurants or stores, sewing
garments for friends and neighbors, outworking for subcontractors for
international and national companies in their homes, garbage picking and
recycling, and other home- or street-based activities that provided flexible
hours and did not interfere with child care (Benería 1989; Benería and
Roldán 1987; Chant and Craske 2003; Cunningham 2001; García and de
Oliveira 1994; González de la Rocha 1994; Wilson 1998c). At the same
time women increased their presence in all other sectors of the labor market. Whereas in the early 1970s most working women had been young,
single, and childless, between 1976 and 1987 older women, married or
in common-law unions and with children, increasingly entered the labor
force (García and de Oliveira 1994, 227). Although some of these were
middle-class career women, others were poor women seeking any type of
employment at all.

NAFTA, signed into law on the Mexican side under neoliberal Pres.
Carlos Salinas de Gortari (1988–94), led to an increase in unemployment
in both rural and urban areas. Mexican crops had to compete with subsi-
dized U.S. corn as tariffs against Canadian and U.S. agricultural produce
were lowered or eliminated. An estimated two million Mexican farmers
were forced out of agriculture as a result of this free trade, promoting both
internal and international migration or marginalization into a "desperate
poverty" (Bybee and Winter 2006, 1). Furthermore, "NAFTA's service-
sector rules allowed big firms like Wal-Mart to enter the Mexican market
and, selling low-priced goods made by ultra-cheap labor in China, to dis-
place locally-based shoe, toy, and candy firms. An estimated 28,000 small
and medium-sized Mexican businesses have been eliminated" (Bybee and
Winter 2006, 1). The resultant loss of jobs, in both agriculture and commerce, swelled the informal economy and women's presence in that economy as the household came to depend on the income-generating activities
of multiple members.

Between 1998 and 2003 the percentage of women employed in manufacturing (including sweatshops and outworking), commerce (including

running small stores and street vending), and in services (including domestic service) rose from 39.2 to 41.2 percent of the labor force (INEGI 2004a, fig. 1, viii). Throughout the economy, including construction (in which women composed 6 percent of the remunerated labor force), women's percentage of the work force increased from 35.4 percent in 1998 to 37.8 percent in 2003 (INEGI 2004a, table 57, 76, 4). They made up 35.3 percent of the labor force in manufacturing, 45.1 percent in commerce, and 42.2 percent in services (INEGI 2004a, figs. 2, 3, 4, ix–x).

Women's work outside the home has had mixed results for their status in the household and in society. Women workers in nineteenth-century Mexico City were often stigmatized, with the exception of middle-class women who opened a store or ran a school (Arrom 1985a, 201, 261; see also Porter 2003). For lower-class women the situation was different:

> Lower-class women, forced to take work that contemporaries considered degrading [e.g., domestic service, street vending, or waitressing, as well as prostitution] and that called their honor into question, hardly raised their status through their labor . . . The ill-repute of women's work, reinforced by limited job opportunities and the absence of economic incentives, made domesticity and patriarchal protection attractive. (Arrom 1985a, 201)

Women who worked in factories and workshops alongside men were considered outside the normative moral order and essentially morally stigmatized (Porter 2003, chap. 2). Employment of wives, mothers, and children in the multinational assembly plants does not necessarily lead to women's empowerment; this is partially because it is their family's economic vulnerability that drives them into the work force (Fernández-Kelly 1983, 137, 192).

In the 1970s, working women were "concentrated in occupations of low or medium remuneration that demanded few qualifications," including work in the informal economy, and such jobs were held not to be empowering (González-Salazar 1980, 188). Since women's work is often less prestigious than men's and viewed mainly as a supplement to the wages of a male head of household, it is often associated with low wages and low status (Chant 1997a, 128). Men whose wives work may cut back on their contributions to the household or even use their wives' earnings "to play cards or go out drinking with their male friends" (Chant 1997a, 142). At the same time, in some cases work brings increased status for women: middle-class women with careers are more obviously empowered, whereas poor, lower-class women forced to work for household survival may or may not be (García and de Oliveira 1994). Thus, depending on women's class position and level of education and opportunities the local labor market offers, some women may be empowered, whereas others will merely scratch out a living or a supplementary income for their families while holding down low-status jobs marked by drudgery.

In addition to economic crises, structural adjustment policies, and neoliberalism—with its globalizing emphasis on lowering trade barriers and promoting international investment—other social changes have led to a linear increase in Mexican women's employment. One of these is the demographic transition—an evolution from high mortality and high fertility to low mortality and low fertility. As a result of family planning, which the federal government of Mexico promotes, the average number of births per woman fell from 4.5 in 1980 to 3.2 in 1994 (Chant and Craske 2003, 72, 74) and by 2006 to 2.2 (INEGI 2007). There are regional differences, however, and rural women still tend to have more children than urban women and younger cohorts of women fewer children than their mothers (Chant and Craske 2003, 74, 76).

The lower fertility rate for younger women is related to later marriage among recent cohorts, and this in turn is related to both men and women spending more time in school. Women's educational attainment has risen steadily over the past several decades, encouraged by the 1992 law that made secondary education (grades seven through nine) mandatory (Parker and Pederzini 2001, 11). Previously, only primary education (grades one through six) had been mandatory. Arguing that the gender gap in education has decreased over the past thirty years, Parker and Pederzini (2001, 13–14) attribute this to the building of more schools— some in remote areas—that facilitated physical access to schooling and increasing employment of women outside the home, which made educating daughters a wise investment. Interestingly, by the end of the 1990s more female workers (23.5 percent) than male workers (9.6 percent) had a technical-school education, involving one to three years after primary, secondary, or high school in subjects such as computing, nursing, electronics, or secretarial skills (Parker and Pederzini 2001, 11). Thus, women's employment has expanded in tandem with falling birthrates and increasing educational opportunities.

In summary, apart from economic crises that make wives' and daughters' employment necessary to sustain household income, women's increased participation in the labor force throughout Latin America since the 1950s is a consequence of several circumstances. These include rising levels of education; higher age at marriage or first birth (or both); declining fertility; internal migration from rural to urban areas, where fertility rates drop as children become more costly; a rising proportion of female-headed households, in which the woman head is responsible for family survival; and "changing ideologies of motherhood in which financial contributions to the household are increasingly regarded as integral to maternal obligations" (Chant and Craske 2003, box 8.1, 207).

Gender Relations in the Past and Today

Women have increasingly, if sporadically, gained social and legal rights in Mexico since the colonial period, when the Spanish *patria potestad* (paternal authority) was the rule. Under patria potestad, fathers had full control over their wives and single children of both sexes; widowed women might exert authority over their minor children only if the husband had not appointed a guardian for them. Women were subjected to disinheritance, imprisonment, and even justifiable homicide at the hands of their husbands were they to commit adultery, while men's adultery was treated lightly and subject to few restrictions. Wives owed husbands obedience to the point that husbands could physically discipline them if they rebelled in any way (Arrom 1985a, chap. 2; 1985b). The Civil Codes of 1870 and 1884 eroded patria potestad somewhat by recognizing offspring's majority when they reached the age of twenty-one (though single women still had to seek permission to leave the family home up until the age of thirty); by granting a new authority over children to widows, to abandoned women, and to legally separated women whose husbands' behavior had given cause for the separation; by expanding the grounds for legal separation (there was no divorce until 1917); and by permitting a choice of community property at marriage—as under Spanish and colonial law—or separate property (Arrom 1985b).

In 1917, the Family Relations Law legalized divorce by common consent and on a number of grounds: women's adultery was always cause for divorce, but men's was only under certain circumstances, and married women still needed their husbands' permission to seek work outside the home (Tuñón Pablos 1999, 96). Thus, even in post-Revolutionary Mexico, which did not grant women the vote until 1953, the legal system continued to reinforce a double standard.

Although patriarchy, as enshrined in law and custom, persists among the better off and in some peasant communities (Lomnitz-Adler 1992, 205; Nash 2001; Wilson 2005, 101), women have contested it since the colonial era when they considered the actions of the patriarch to be unfair or unjust (Stern 1995). With the increasing penetration of capitalism, traditional patriarchal forms, in which elder males rule over an extended family of women and married and unmarried offspring, extracting their submission, obedience, and labor in the interests of the family household, have largely given way to "neo-patriarchal" households, in which the male head has authority only within the nuclear family (Wilson 2005, 101–7; 2003). This is especially the case where neolocal residence after marriage has become the norm for sons and daughters and is especially prevalent in cities.

Under both patriarchy and neopatriarchy, men and women agree upon certain principles with regard to gender relations: that wives and daughters should be virgins at marriage; that there should be a strict division of labor between men's tasks and women's tasks; that a woman's place is in the home and her primary responsibility that of motherhood; that a man's primary role in the household is that of the breadwinner and only he has the right to occupy public space; and that any kind of immorality, especially adultery, is far worse if committed by a woman than if engaged in by a man; that men can physically discipline rebellious wives (within reason); and that women should respect their husbands' wishes. The principle of respect for her husband shapes a woman's behavior, both within and outside the home. Poor women, especially, are held to a rigid standard of respect for their husbands. In a sample of women from 1980s Mexico City (Benería and Roldán 1987, 147–48):

> Wives defined "respect" as obedience to their husbands wishes or commands, and not doing anything without permission, such as going out, or visiting relatives; not engaging in any behavior he disapproves of (like talking to the neighbors). Respect also implied being ready to get up in the middle of the night and feed him if he happened to come home hungry; serve him and his friends . . . ; wait for him until he comes home; speak to him with deference, never resorting to foul language; never answer back in a loud tone; be ready to respond to his whims—"go and pay the bills," "go and borrow from Mrs. X" . . .

Linked with these principles is a widespread cult of the Virgin Mary, marked by a belief in women's "moral superiority" and "abnegation," defined as an "infinite capacity for humility and sacrifice" (Stevens 1973, 94). Under this set of beliefs, premarital chastity is idealized, though exceptions were made for poor women living in consensual unions as well as the "socially prominent young women" who, following a practice traceable to fifteenth-century Spain, have surgical replacement of the hymen in case of premarital coitus (Stevens 1973, 97). Hymen replacement is being practiced in some parts of Mexico today when virginity is lost through rape, incestuous or otherwise. Women and their kin believe that their chances for marriage are diminished or that husbands may subsequently mistreat them for not having been virgins at marriage (González-López 2007, 229), or at least at first intercourse with them. Even in the colonial period, some women had premarital sexual relations with the men who would become their husbands, but their virginity had to be proved at that point (Twinam 1998, 83).

Motherhood is considered the sine qua non of women's existence. Women endure male infidelity and abuse to ensure that their children have their father's monetary support and rationalize their own entry into the public space of the workplace as necessary for the good of their children (e.g., Chant and Craske 2003, box 8.1, 207; García and de Oliveira 1994, 188–91; González de la Rocha 1988b; 1994, 143; LeVine and Sunderland Correa 1993, chap. 3; Melhuus 1996, 243; Napolitano 2002, 151; see also Ehlers 1991 on the Guatemalan case). In some cases, motherhood is considered more important than marriage (Howell 1999, 120; see also Chant 1997b, 160). The cult of motherhood—strongly linked with Marianismo's stress on sacrifice for husbands and children—has a long history and is not only enshrined in state legislation, but is also exalted in Mexican unions nationwide. Despite the fact that women were often involved in union organizing, unions pushed for a living wage for male household heads while opposing women's presence in the work force in the name of their domestic role (Olcott, Vaughan, and Cano 2006; Gauss 2006, 190).

Machismo, the "cult of virility" (Stevens 1973, 90), by contrast "is associated with violence and aggressiveness, a particular form of self-assertion which more than anything implies being in control, being in command, having authority not only—or primarily—over women, but also over other men" (Melhuus 1996, 240). The most important reference group for men's machismo is their peers—other men—and it is often enacted through conquest of women and protection of one's own female relatives (wife, daughter, sisters, mother) from predation by other males (Melhuus 1996, 241, 243; see also Lancaster 1992, 236–37). Typical of macho friendships (though not all friendships between men) is spending time together in spaces outside the home, including public plazas, bars, and street corners, rather than with wives and children (Romanucci-Ross 1986, 236–37). Among machismo's more negative aspects are rampant infidelity; alcoholism; and physical, verbal, and emotional abuse of wives and sometimes children. These behaviors tend to be more prominent among the more economically insecure males and those who feel that their authority within the household is eroding: domestic violence is typical of machismo and a way of strengthening men's power within the household (García and de Oliveira 1994, 162; González de la Rocha 1988b; 1994, 31–32, 143–45; Gutmann 1996, 237; Romanucci-Ross 1986, 56; Roldán 1988, 233, 237; see also Hondagneu-Sotelo and Messner 1994). Spousal abuse is often provoked by a wife's bringing home more income than her husband; by a man's jealousy when his wife enters public space, for example, to find employment; by her asking him how much money he earns; or simply by her questioning his infidelities, absences, or activities. It frequently takes place when husbands are drunk "so women blame their behavior on their drinking" (González de la Rocha 1994, 144).

Being macho often involves contempt for one's wife. According to Roldán (1988, 239), whose study took place in the 1980s in Mexico City:

> Men expect and usually get obedience and deference. But they generally do not feel obligated to their wives' similar demands for respect, whether by recognizing or appreciating their contributions as housewives or through companionship and affection. Nor do they usually abstain from physical violence, verbal abuse, or contemptuous behavior toward their wives.

Domestic violence has historically been very common and remains so. In 2003, 46.6 percent of women who were married or in consensual unions reported emotional, economic, sexual, or physical abuse by their husbands or companions (INEGI 2004c, 29), and this figure may underestimate domestic violence in poor and working-class families.

Blatant infidelity is also associated with being macho. This sometimes takes the form of having a *casa chica* (small house), "an arrangement whereby a Mexican man keeps a woman other than his wife in a residence separate from his main (*casa grande*) household," constituting a "modern form of urban polygamy" (Gutmann 1996, 138). According to Lomnitz-Adler (1992, 128), the casa chica is a form of "urban machismo" that involves "not merely having a fixed lover or lovers, but actually establishing one or more parallel families, whose existence is ideally kept entirely separate from the male's primary legal family." He goes on to say, "This form of machismo does not merely involve having sex with many women, but entails having *children* with many women—in other words, having alternate families" that can be played off against one another (Lomnitz-Adler 1992, 128; italics in original). Women who marry a second time or move on to second or third consensual unions often explain why they want to have children with their consorts by saying that *el hombre quiere ver su sangre* (men want to see their blood). And of course, for men, having many children can be a sign of their virility.

In his study of a squatter settlement in Mexico City, Gutmann (1996, 140) found such arrangements typical only among the better-paid workers and upper- or middle-class men and contends that it is atypical among poorer men because they would be unable to support a second household. He overlooks at least two phenomena. First, it is not unusual for women in poor colonias such as the one he studied to be in a casa-chica situation with men who are better off. Furthermore, women in a casa-chica situation with poor men may simply live elsewhere, perhaps in other *colonias populares* (squatter settlements). Second, LeVine, Sunderland Correa, and Tapia (1986, 189) pose and answer the question as to how poorer men maintain casas chicas as follows:

> How does a teacher, a busdriver, or stonemason manage to support two wives, let alone, as in some cases, three? The answer is that women largely support themselves. Although the husband may have started married life supporting his first wife, he will contribute less once he establishes another household. For her part, the second wife does not expect to be wholly supported: it is a condition of the relationship that she generate an income of her own.

Since men's extramarital relationships often gain them the admiration of their peers (LeVine and Sunderland Correa 1993, 90–91), even poor men who cannot in any situation afford, or perhaps even want, a casa chica may engage in rampant infidelity, sometimes causing the temporary or permanent breakup of their households (Behar 2003; Grimes 1998; Howell 1999; Vélez-Ibáñez 1983). Women's increasing entry into employment outside the home has given men greater opportunity to find lovers. As LeVine and Sunderland Correa (1993, 90–91) point out, one type of extramarital relation

> is casual and may be pursued with any woman who is willing, often someone encountered in the workplace. In an earlier generation, women who worked outside the home were almost exclusively widows, abandoned wives, or girls from very poor families, but these days, young single women from all social backgrounds work in public situations where traditional norms of sexual conduct no longer have to be observed. A woman can have a relationship with a married man she meets at work without her family knowing anything about it. In a word, work and home lives may be kept quite separate, by women as much as by men.

This more liberal atmosphere is part of the reason men object to their wives seeking employment outside the home. In a rural village in Michoacán where women increasingly sought work in nearby strawberry-packaging plants, men opposed their wives' and daughters' employment because it "it challenged their manhood on two counts: their ability to support the family, and their ability to control 'their' women's movements . . . Innuendo suggested that away from the watchful eye of the male guardians of their honor, women would turn to illicit liaisons with strangers" (Mummert 1994, 196). In the 1980s, married women especially were constrained from working outside the household (Melhuus 1996, 245):

> Not only does a working woman show visibly that her husband is not man enough to provide for her (and their children); a working wife also brings to the fore a husband's jealousy. In fact "los celos" (jealousies) was the reason most often given, especially by young married women, for why they stopped working once they were married. Thus a married woman's work has a double implication: it detracts from her husband's honour and is associated with her being public, potentially available to other men.

At the same time, women who generated income by selling foodstuffs and soft drinks from the "ambiguous space of the threshold" of their homes were seen as protected from such male attention and as acting "properly" (Napolitano 2002, 46). Many women generate an income by working in their homes, for example, as outworkers for manufacturing companies, and thus avoid the "public-space" aspect of work that might provoke their husbands' jealousy.

Gender relations have recently begun to evolve more or less in tandem with women's increasing employment in both rural and urban areas, whether because of male migration and lack of adequate remittances, economic conditions that have made women's work necessary for household survival, or women's increasing migration to the United States. These phenomena can be considered the economic bases for gender changes. As González de la Rocha (2001, 93) points out as concerns women's empowerment, however, economic changes proceed more rapidly than social and cultural changes. Some of these latter changes are occurring because of the influence of tourists from the United States and Europe and women's transnational migration, both of which permit women as well as men to observe alternative forms of gender relations (e.g., Chant 1997a, 141; Hirsch 2000, 2003). They are also being promoted by media images and the desire to be "modern" (Hirsch 2003, 12–13, 82). American films are constantly shown in movie theaters and are available, along with European films, on television; they are also available on VCRs and DVDs in everything from mom-and-pop video stores in small towns to Blockbuster outlets in cities. As Hirsch (2003, 82) points out, these also include pornographic films.

Much of the change that has occurred in gender relations or that younger wives are calling for is related to women's higher level of education and consequent ability to hold salaried jobs (e.g., García and de Oliveira 1994, 212; Howell 1999, 118–19; see also Chant and Craske 2003). Even women with informal income-generating strategies are challenging their husbands' abusive behavior, however, especially if they make as much or more than their husbands (e.g., Benería and Roldán 1987; Roldán 1988).

Among the young women who work in the strawberry-packaging

plants in Michoacán, Mummert (1994, 207) found that "most young wives today are not willing to adopt a submissive role when faced with physical abuse or adultery on the part of their husbands. Young girls are adamant in their views, and they reject being victimized: 'I don't think as my mother did that one must put up with whatever kind of husband one might happen to marry.'" The mothers and even grandmothers of the young women maturing in the 1980s and later often support educating daughters and granddaughters so that they need not remain in an unhappy marriage (Howell 1999, 118–19):

> Parents who encouraged their daughters to study hoped they would use their education to become independent and *defenderse*. This viewpoint is seen in the words of a seventy-year-old mother who observed "not all marriages go well. If your daughter is educated, she can support herself. If she doesn't marry, she can support herself. If her marriage doesn't work out, she can support herself. So in all respects it is important that a daughter study."

At least three possibilities affecting gender relations arise from women's ability to earn an adequate income. First, wives may lose "respect" for husbands whose contributions to the household are seen as inadequate—this often in the context of his keeping back money for drinking, gambling, or womanizing. Second, wives' ability to support themselves and their children may be a lever in securing a more companionate marriage. Third, the number of female-headed households (even if only intermittently so) may increase as women abandon unhappy or abusive marriages.

Among home-based outworkers interviewed in Mexico City in the 1980s, women who contributed more than 40 percent of household income no longer waited on their husbands by washing, ironing, or cooking for them to the same extent as when husbands contributed more. They might leave the house to visit friends or take jobs outside the home even without their husbands' permission and might defend themselves against physical abuse and even "resort to foul language" (Roldán 1988, 243; see also Benería and Roldán 1987). This loss of respect is the result of the husband's failure to fulfill his role as primary breadwinner—a violation of the patriarchal or neopatriarchal pact. In Gutmann's (1996, 15) Mexico City study, some women are now behaving in ways traditionally associated with machismo, including infidelity, drinking, and abusive behavior. The occasional occurrence of infidelity on the part of women is, however, documented as early as the 1970s in a village in Morelos (Romanucci-Ross 1986). Intrafamilial violence perpetuated by men can be expected to increase in these "loss of respect" situations.

A generational change is observable in women's expectations in marriage, especially among Mexican immigrants to the United States (Hirsch 2000, 2003). Rather than a marriage based on respect, women (and often men) are seeking marriages based on *confianza* (trust). In this type of companionate marriage, wives take part in making decisions and feel free to express their opinions, while men do not interpret disagreements as a challenge to their authority and thus to their manhood. Husbands and wives spend time together either in the home or by going out together, thus challenging the man-in-the-street, woman-in-the-house paradigm. There has been some erosion of the traditional gendered division of labor as men help out with household chores and women take jobs outside the home. Furthermore, there has been a decline in fertility related to a greater desire for emotional and sexual intimacy between husband and wife (see Hirsch 2000, 373–76).

Hirsch (2000, 2003) relates these changes to migration to the United States, but the demonstration effect of these changes—when couples return from Atlanta to visit their hometowns in Michoacán—has influenced gender relations there as well. She points out that in the United States undocumented men are less able to openly display macho comportment (e.g., public drunkenness and aggressiveness) or engage in domestic violence. This is because 911 is just a call away—and either behavior could lead to attention from the authorities and deportation. Furthermore, they do not have fathers and uncles present to criticize them for being insufficiently macho (Hirsch 2000, 376, 380). A major difference that Hirsch (2000, 382; 2003, chap. 6) underscores, however, is that women's wages in the United States, even if just above the minimum, are adequate to support them and their children, especially if some of the children are U.S. citizens and qualify for Medicaid. In contrast, the jobs they could find in or near their hometowns in Mexico would not pay them enough to support themselves and their children. This gives U.S.-based women greater leverage in their demands for a companionate marriage (Hirsch 2000, 384). Women's work in Mexico is, however, having many of the same consequences. Among some families in Querétaro, "expanded roles for women in household survival in the 1980s may have given rise to recognition of the potential for female independence, and realization on the part of men that unless they comply more fully with their family obligations and allow women some measure of personal freedom, they may face a situation where their wives or children leave them" (Chant 1994, 225). And, in Mexico City, younger women who are better educated and hold salaried jobs maintain that they have the right to partake in decision making in their households (García and de Oliveira 1994, 212).

At least some Mexican women have long sought companionate marriage: in a 1920s Mexico City vocational school, the civics teacher, Dolores Ángela Casillo, was investigated for teaching the ideal of that type of marriage and the right of women to seek divorce if in an unhappy relationship (Schell 2006, 122–23). Before the greater involvement in generating at least some income among greater numbers of women, companionate marriage remained only an ideal.

Earning a wage has permitted many women to escape abusive marriages and thus increased the number of female-headed households (however transient). In Puerto Vallarta, where female-headed households were more common than in two other Mexican cities (Chant 1997a, 1997b), the propensity to form new female-headed households was also greater. The female-headed model is a socially available alternative, and both daughters and nieces of female-headed households as well as neighbors and friends who may be experiencing disagreeable marriages can observe this. In other words, the presence of numerous female-headed households may have a demonstration effect for other women in less than satisfactory marriages.

At the same time, the model is more economically feasible: material conditions permit its formation and survival. Jobs are more available in Puerto Vallarta, where a booming tourist industry employs women in restaurants, hotels, and elsewhere, than in other cities in Mexico (Chant 1997a, 1997b). That jobs permit women freedom to leave an unhappy marriage is also a point Safa brings out (1995) in her study of Caribbean women. The inability of the male head of household to fulfill his normative role as breadwinner, whether because of periodic unemployment, underemployment, an inadequate wage (structural factors), or the husband's diversion of the wage to leisure pursuits (personal circumstances) may lead to the formation of a female-headed household. In situations of economic crisis, when multiple wage earners are needed in the household, such crises may often cause the exit of the wife or the husband.

The formation of a female-headed household may be passive or active (Bradshaw 1995, 144; Chant 1985; Safa 1981). In the passive form, a woman's paid labor threatens the male head of household's traditional role as sole breadwinner, leading to contradictions in the expected gender order that often motivate him to abandon the household. As Safa (1995, 58) points out, men are often unable to earn a wage substantial enough to fulfill the breadwinner role given economic crises and structural adjustment policies—phenomena that have affected most Latin American and Caribbean countries, including Mexico (Alarcón-González and McKinley 1999; Chant and Craske 2003). Thus, an inadequate wage may lead husbands to abandon wives and children.

In the active form, women earning an income can envision the possibility of supporting themselves and their children alone and thus exit unhappy or disappointing marriages (Bradshaw 1995, 144; see also Safa 1995; Chant 1985, 1991, 1997a, 1997b). In locales where male underemployment and opportunities for female employment are common, some women refuse to marry at all (Chant 1997b, 160).

As job opportunities increase for women, more of them are likely to abandon unhappy marriages and set out on their own (Chant 1991, 1997b; Safa 1995). That is partially how Chant explains the greater number of female-headed households in the 1980s in the tourist town of Puerto Vallarta as compared to Querétaro and León, where there were fewer opportunities to for women to find employment. At the same time, the continual economic crises in Mexico that have forced women into employment may also have forced them to remain in unhappy marriages in order for them and their children to survive (González de la Rocha 1988b, 1994, 2001).

Female heads of households constituted 23.1 percent of all households in 2005, with states such as Baja California, with its many maquiladoras, and Guerrero and Oaxaca, where men have recently entered the transnational migration stream, having percentages higher than that average (24.2 percent, 24.5 percent, and 24.4 percent respectively); in the Federal District the figure was 28.9 percent (INEGI 2006a). In absolute numbers female-headed households increased from 926,426 in 1960 to 2,805,488 in 1990 subsequent to the first economic crisis in 1982. By 2005, after the second economic crisis of 1994, that figure had doubled to 5,717,659, of which 880,757 were made up of women living alone (INEGI 2006b).

The distinction between passive and active female-headed household formation challenges Oscar Lewis's (1961, xxvi; 1968, 191) observation, based on research in the 1950s, that there is "a relatively high incidence of the abandonment of mothers and children." Lack of reciprocity, companionship, or fidelity; inadequate income contribution whether the result of structural or personal reasons; or domestic violence all may lead women to abandon their partners. Female abandonment of men is, however, predicated on two conditions: adequate income-generating opportunities for women and the existence of a social network that will extend aid until the point at which a woman can establish herself as an independent household head or, alternatively, find a new mate. In sum, women's employment has permitted wives to renegotiate or break the marital contract.

Contrary to conventional wisdom, then, working women have long been common in Mexico and have become increasingly so as women have gained greater access to education, reproductive rights, and expanded employment opportunities. Similarly, while migration has always been an option for both men and women, the economic and social and cultural changes described here have contributed to a significant increase in the proportion of women among internal and transnational migrants.

CHAPTER 2

Gender and Mexican Migration

The U.S. war against Mexico, which began in 1846 under President Polk, ended in 1848 with the Treaty of Guadalupe Hidalgo. Together with the secession of Texas from Mexico and its annexation to the United States in 1845 and the Gadsden Purchase of 1853, the U.S.-Mexican War led to "the detachment of one-half of Mexico's territories, including California, Utah, New Mexico, Arizona, Texas, and portions of Wyoming, Colorado, Kansas, and Oklahoma" (Martínez 2001, 5). Now land-rich but labor-poor, U.S. employers in railroads, agriculture, mining, and construction began to recruit laborers from Mexico. The shortage of low-wage laborers was exacerbated when the 1882 Chinese Exclusion Act and the 1908 Gentlemen's Agreement ended further immigration from China and Japan, thus preventing employers from securing workers from those countries (Gutiérrez 1995, 43–44; see also Cardoso 1980, chap. 2).

Mexican and U.S. census data suggest that there were 84,000 Mexicans and people of Mexican descent in the United States at the end of the war; thereafter immigrants from what remained of Mexico increased from approximately 27,000 in 1860 to 71,000 in 1880 and 103,000 in 1890 (Corona n.d., table 3, 57). Between 1910 and 1930 the number of Mexican immigrants grew from 232,000 to 640,000 and then, primarily as the result of the deportations during the Great Depression, fell to 377,000 by 1940. Since then there has been a steady increase in permanently settled immigrants from Mexico, rising from 576,000 in 1950 to 4,447,000 in 1990 (Corona n.d., table 3, 57). (As it is notoriously difficult to count the undocumented, these figures may be an underestimate.) Despite periodic deportation drives and augmented border patrolling over the decades, the number of Mexicans crossing the border into the United States has steadily risen. Between 2000 and 2005 an average of 577,000 Mexicans migrated to the United States annually, 244,000 (42.3 percent) of them women; over the same period 41,000 Mexican immigrants returned to Mexico, 14,000 (34.1 percent) of them women (Bush 2007).

Besides the pull factors in the U.S. labor market, accompanied by active recruitment efforts, whether through agents going into Mexico to find workers; by spreading the word through immigrants already present in the United States; or by tapping centers where Mexican laborers clustered, such as El Paso, San Antonio, and Los Angeles (McWilliams 1968; see also Balderrama and Rodríguez 1995, 15; Vargas 1993; Vélez-Ibáñez 1996, 78), there were also push factors in Mexico that accounted for the search for work across the border. Immigration was facilitated when, in the 1880s, the Mexican National Railroad reached the northern border (Romo 1975, 174). Because of the difficult economic conditions associated with the expropriation of peasant lands by the hacendados (hacienda owners) and the marginalization of subsistence and small farmers by the export-oriented agricultural policies of the time, as well as by anti-Porfiriato sentiments, Mexicans looked to the United States (M. González 2000, 120), though many rural residents migrated internally (Gutiérrez 1995, 44). Many of those who crossed into the United States were peons escaping the oppressive conditions on the haciendas; others were migrant workers who continued their trek from within Mexico to north of the border (Cardoso 1980, chap. 1).

At first clustering overwhelmingly in the southwestern states of Texas, Arizona, New Mexico, and California, Mexicans had been pulled by railroad construction and maintenance as far away as Chicago by 1904, and by 1916 there was a Mexican settlement in that city (Taylor 1968a, 28). Los Angeles had continued to be a major magnet as it industrialized in the 1890s, but until the Mexican Revolution many immigrants returned to Mexico during the slack season in the fields and on the railroad (Romo 1988, 31, 58–59). Working on the railroads was particularly important in dispersing both Mexican-Americans and Mexican immigrants to areas outside the Southwest: both Kansas City and St. Louis, for example, began to be destination points after the completion in 1904 of the Brownsville-Kansas City Line (J. R. García 1996, 6). By the beginning of World War I, Mexicans had a presence as far east as New England and New York, and by the early 1920s they were being recruited into the Bethlehem Steel Company in Pennsylvania (Griswold del Castillo and de León 1996, 65; Taylor 1968b). Besides working in the cotton fields of Texas and in the agricultural fields of California, New Mexico, and Arizona, after 1897 Mexicans also worked in the beet fields of Michigan and Colorado and later in Utah and Idaho and elsewhere (M. González 2000, 133; see also Zamora 1993, 19). Entire families, including wives and daughters, took part in the cultivation and harvest of sugar beets (J. R. García 1996, 84), as they were to do throughout the twentieth century. Women also worked in the cotton fields and vegetable farms of Texas (Zamora 1993, 26) and as part of the family labor force in agricultural fields throughout the Southwest.

Although most Mexican immigrants were men, the dislocations caused by the Mexican Revolution of 1910–17 and the Cristero Rebellion of 1926–29—the latter centered in central Mexico, especially Jalisco—forced entire families out of the country. Male migration was marked, however. Before the 1900s there were 131.2 men for every 100 women; this fell to 116.8 for the 1915–19 period, then rose again, reaching a ratio of 152.8 men per 100 women in the years from 1925 to 1929 (Hernández Álvarez 1966, 481). Rural regions in the United States tended to have a higher ratio of men than urban centers: in 1940, for example, there were slightly more women than men in cities, with a ratio of 98.3 (rising to 101.2 in 1950), whereas there was a ratio of 134.5 in rural regions (rising to 179.7 in 1950, when the Bracero Program was in full swing) (Hernández Álvarez 1966, 481).

U.S. immigration legislation of 1917, with its eight-dollar head tax, literacy test, and prohibition of contract labor, was primarily aimed at halting the immigration of unskilled laborers from eastern and southern Europe. Under pressure from employers, first agricultural field hands, and then mining, industrial, and construction workers from Mexico were excluded from these provisions (Cardoso 1979, 18; Martínez 2001, 28; Romo 1975, 180–81). As Ngai (2004, 55) points out, however, crossing the border became regulated for the first time, and the hardship the head taxes imposed led many Mexicans to cross without inspection.

World War I had exacerbated labor shortages in the United States, when more than one million citizens were conscripted into the armed forces (Cardoso 1979, 7). Mexicans were recruited to fill the shortage under a temporary guest-worker program established in 1917; more than eighty thousand Mexican laborers came to work in agriculture, in the mines, and on the railroads (Martínez 2001, 28; G. González 2006, 33; see also Cardoso 1980, chap. 3). Mexican workers also "helped construct military bases and picked cotton used in gunpowder and clothing. Mexicans who worked in the mines of the Southwest also helped to provide a steady flow of copper, lead, and other minerals needed for the war effort" (Romo 1975, 181). Also during World War I, Henry Ford recruited several hundred Mexican students to learn production and repair with a view to setting up automobile factories in Mexico; lured by wages of five dollars a day promised in the Ford plants in the United States, thousands of Mexicans sought and found work in them, and by the 1920s approximately fifteen thousand Mexicans lived in Detroit (Valdés 2000, 41; see also Alvarado and Alvarado 2003, 11). They were also employed, to give just a few examples, in the meat-packing plants of Chicago, the steel mills of Milwaukee, and the Appalachian coal mines (Alvarado and Alvarado 2003, 11; Valdés 2000, 41). Mexicans also found work in the fish canneries of Washington, Oregon, and Alaska: more than fifteen thousand Mexican-Americans and Mexican immigrants were working in the Alaskan canneries by 1917, though numbers dropped thereafter because of the harsh working conditions (García 2005, 90).

After the war ended, a depression occurred in 1920–21. As they often would be over the next eighty years or more, Mexicans were scapegoated and workplace raids, forced deportations, and voluntary repatriation programs surged (Alvarado and Alvarado 2003, 19; Cardoso 1980, chap. 6). Once the depression was over, Mexican workers were sought once again, in a pattern that has come to be known as the "revolving door," and they flocked into the United States. As Manuel González (2000, 120) reports, "The decade of the 1920s, the years immediately after the revolutionary upheaval, witnessed the largest exodus from Mexico, particularly from the western states of Guanajuato, Jalisco and Michoacán." Mexicans returned to their traditional jobs in mining, agriculture, and railroading but now also had a foot in packing houses, steel mills, foundries, and the automobile industry; immigrant small businessmen catered to their conationals by running small stores, restaurants, poolrooms, and the like (e.g., Taylor 1968a; M. González 2000; Valdés 2000). When the 1921 and 1924 immigration acts were passed they put in place a quota on immigrants from Europe, but again, under pressures from employers of Mexican labor, they set no ceiling on immigrants from Latin America (Romo 1975, 188–89). Mexican immigration continued to grow until the Great Depression of 1929. Between 1910 and 1930 an estimated 10 percent of Mexico's population of slightly more than fifteen million came to the United States (Griswold del Castillo and de León 1996, 60).

Throughout the period up until 1930, immigrant women were employed not only in agriculture but also in manufacturing, light industry, and clerical work—among other occupations (J. R. García 1996, 84). Married women, other than those who were part of the family labor force in agriculture, were restricted by cultural norms to income-generating activities they could carry out in their homes: they took in boarders or engaged in "washing, sewing and ironing for other families" (Zamora 1993, 26). Most of women's work was low status and poorly paid, and men were concentrated in low-skilled or semiskilled employment as well.

With the coming of the Great Depression workers were laid off in the automobile plants, foundries, and steel mills; for example, "Between 1930 and 1932 steel production dropped from 90 percent capacity to 15 percent nationally, and Mexicans employed in the steel and iron foundries of Chicago, Gary, Toledo, and Bethlehem lost their jobs" (J. R. García 1996, 225). Because most Mexican immigrants in the Midwest were undocumented, they could not seek public assistance (J. R. García 1996, 227). Hostility toward Mexicans was common and perpetuated in the print media (Betten and Mohl 1973, 378). The reasons given for the subsequent repatriation drives ranged from saving welfare agencies money and getting rid of indigents to creating jobs for "real" Americans (Balderrama and Rodríguez 1995, 99).

Throughout the United States a number of newly unemployed Mexicans returned voluntarily to Mexico, but after 1932 they were coerced into doing so, sometimes through forcible deportation and sometimes through verbal threats and deception (J. R. García 1996, 230–38; Hoffman 1974; see also Balderrama and Rodríguez 1995; Betten and Mohl 1973). In Los Angeles County, for example, Mexicans who were repatriated were given "departure cards" with the assurance that they could return when they wished; stamped on the back, however, was "Los Angeles County/ Department of Charities/County Welfare Department," identifying them as recipients of aid for travel back to Mexico (Hoffman 1974, 91). Since becoming a public charge had been identified in 1930 as grounds for deportation, exclusion, or both, they had no hope of returning.

As Balderrama and Rodríguez (1995, 99) tell it: "Trains, cars, trucks and buses streamed southward from every corner of the land. Los Angeles, Phoenix, El Paso, Denver, Kansas City, Chicago, Detroit, Pittsburgh, New York, New Orleans, San Diego, San Francisco, Portland, Seattle, and Fairbanks, Alaska, spewed forth their human jetsam." Those with no transportation walked; others, coming from Mexico's Atlantic or Pacific coast, were sent back in empty cargo ships (Balderrama and Rodríguez 1995, 99–100). By the end of the 1930s more than a third of Mexicans in the United States, or about half a million people, had returned to Mexico (J. R. García 1996, 239). Among those deported were children in county orphanages, many of them born in the United States, and even the terminally or mentally ill (Balderrama and Rodríguez 1995, 84, 107, 110). Some adult children born in the United States decided to stay, thus splitting families; young children born in the United States were deported along with their parents (Balderrama and Rodríguez 1995, 103).

As we have seen, the 1930s were not depression years in Mexico: fewer women worked outside the home, and unions organized and successfully pressed for a family wage. Furthermore, under article 27 of the 1917 Mexican Constitution the government was empowered to distribute ejido (communally owned and often individually tenured) lands to villages and the landless (Simpson 1937, 54; Whetten 1954, 114). Although lands were distributed after the Revolution, most ejido grants occurred under the presidency of Lázaro Cárdenas (1934–40) (Esteva 1983, 35, 266), enabling many of the rural landless to become small farmers. The Mexican government also offered a hand to the returnees, with, among other things, agricultural colonization schemes. (Many of these colonization schemes failed because of the lack of organization, however) (Hoffman 1974, 135–46). Nonetheless, it was mainly Mexican towns and cities—especially those along the border—that were overwhelmed by the numbers of returning immigrants.

By the beginning of World War II, Mexican laborers were being recruited once again, this time under the aegis of the Bracero Program (1942–64.) The braceros, or "arms" (i.e., field "hands"), were exclusively men, since the Mexican government feared that women could become targets of abuse (Martínez 2001, 34). Though hired primarily for agricultural work, some of the braceros also manned railroads, worked in the forest service, and were employed in industry in the northwestern, Great Plains, and midwestern states (Martínez 2001, 36; see also Acuña 1988, 54; Galarza 1964, 54; Gamboa 1990; G. González 2006). The Bracero Program passed through several stages, with both the United States and Mexico offering amendments (though Mexico's requests were generally ignored). In the first phase, from 1942 to 1947, recruitment efforts took place under the auspices of the Department of Agriculture; from 1947 to 1951 growers contracted directly with workers in recruitment centers in Mexico and after 1949 also arranged to legalize undocumented workers already in the United States, converting them into contract workers: "Between 1947 and 1949 approximately 74,000 braceros were contracted from Mexico, while 142,200 undocumented workers were legalized and contracted directly to growers . . ." (Calavita 1992, 28). From 1951 to 1964, recruitment efforts were restored to the U.S. government though the Department of Labor. In 1956, 445,000 braceros were imported, and more than 400,000 came into the United States annually between then and 1960: "In 1959, nearly 50,000 farms employed braceros, with the vast majority concentrated in Texas, California, Arkansas, Arizona, and New Mexico" (Calavita 1992, 141). Approximately 4 million braceros were contracted under the program (Barajas et al. 2007, 28).

This temporary guest-worker program has been widely criticized for its mistreatment of workers, who constituted, in essence, a "captive" work force, denied the right to change employers (Calavita 1992, 75). They were forced to accept arbitrary decisions by the grower—who often paid wages lower than promised, colluded to put a ceiling on wages, and played the undocumented off against the contracted workers—and often had to live in deplorable housing conditions (see e.g., Calavita 1992; Galarza 1964; G. González 2006).

Undocumented workers, often unable or unsure how to qualify under the program, were employed by growers to undercut the wages and other guarantees that were supposed to be extended to the braceros. They began crossing the border from the inception of the program in 1942. In order to gain "control" over the border, Operation Wetback was initiated in 1954: it involved raids on workplaces, roundups, and massive deportations (Martínez 2001, 37). Having deported 875,000 Mexicans in 1953, in 1954 the Immigration and Naturalization Service (INS) returned 1,035,282 undocumented workers to Mexico (Acuña 1988, 267).[1] As during the Depression, many of those deported were long-time residents of the United States, some with U.S.-born spouses and children (Gutiérrez 1995, 163–64).

A year after the end of the Bracero Program in 1964, the Border Industrialization Program was established with an eye to giving work to returning braceros (Tiano 1990, 199). As we have seen, it was primarily women—young, single, and relatively well educated—who were employed in the assembly plants, undercutting the Mexican government's original rationale. Also in 1965, amendments were made to the Immigration and Nationality Act of 1952 (also known as the McCarran-Walter Act), which had continued the national-origins quota system the Immigration Acts of 1921 and 1924 had established. The Hart-Cellar Act of 1965 repealed the quota system, established a ceiling of 170,000 admissions annually, with no more than 20,000 to come from any one country unless spouses or children of citizens (though this provision was not applied to Mexico until 1968). It also established a seven-tiered preference system reinforcing the family-reunification orientation of past immigration legislation:

U.S. citizens could sponsor unmarried adult sons and daughters (first preference); married sons and daughters (fourth preference); brothers and sisters (fifth preference); and spouses and children of legal residents (second preference) (Gimpel and Edwards 1999, 102–3). These preference categories were not to be charged against the country ceiling. Nonetheless, undocumented immigration accelerated after the Hart-Celler Act that imposed, for the first time, a quota on immigrants from Mexico.

Many of the braceros who had achieved legal residence through the intervention of sympathetic employers, who wished to keep them on, began to bring over wives and children—often at their wives' insistence (Hondagneu-Sotelo 1994, 70–71). Undocumented immigration accelerated after 1965, and unlike the pre-1965 migrants, who had come overwhelmingly from rural areas and were nearly all concentrated in agricultural field work, the post-1965 immigrants were from both rural areas and urban centers, and many went directly to work in U.S. cities (Hondagneu-Sotelo 1994, 103–4). Whereas previously most immigrants had been "target earners" spending short periods of time in the United States to achieve an economic goal (e.g., building a house, buying a pickup or a tractor), "by the 1960s their perceptions and motivations had changed. Sustained access to high U.S. wages had created new standards of material well-being and instilled new ambitions for upward mobility that involved additional trips and longer stays" (Massey, Durand, and Malone 2003, 42). Massey, Durand, and Malone (2003, 45; see also Massey and Singer 1995) estimate that between 1965 and 1986 there was a net immigration of 5.7 million Mexicans who came to settle for longer periods of time; of these 81 percent were undocumented, and among them were women.

In 1986 the Immigration Reform and Control Act (IRCA) was passed after more than four years of wrangling in Congress. Besides instituting employer sanctions for the first time and augmenting the number of Border Patrol agents, it granted a general amnesty to undocumented immigrants, men and women, who had lived in the United States continuously since January 1, 1982, and to those who had worked in agriculture for a minimum of ninety days between May 1, 1985, and May 1, 1986 (Special Agricultural Workers, SAWs). By January 1989, when the amnesty program ended, slightly more than 3 million undocumented immigrants had applied for amnesty, 2.3 million of whom were Mexican (Massey, Durand, and Malone 2003, 90; see Gimpel and Edwards 1999 for the politics involved in the passage of this legislation). The family-reunification provisions of prior immigration acts were kept in place, and ceilings were raised; immigration soared as the newly amnestied brought in family members (Gimpel and Edwards 1999, 179). The newly documented began to migrate to new destinations within the United States; currently Mexicans live and work in all states of the union, including Alaska and Hawaii, where they are clustered in construction in Maui and coffee harvesting and processing on the Big Island (for research in some of the new destinations, see Zúñiga and Hernández-León 2005).

Beginning in 1978, the United States had begun to "militarize" the border in the hope of cutting back on undocumented immigration. During the Reagan administration (1980–88), military technology was increasingly used in the interest of deterrence. Among the examples Dunn (1996, 58) gives are:

the supplying of M-14 and M-16 military-issue rifles to the Border Patrol (under the rubric of drug enforcement), the greatly expanded use of helicopters . . . , the introduction of an extensive array of sophisticated vision equipment, the expanded replacement and apparent upgrading of intrusion-detection electronic ground sensor systems [used in Vietnam during the war] . . . , the introduction of low-light-level television surveillance equipment along the border in parts of six Border Patrol sectors, and the introduction of air-borne infrared radar.

Deterrence efforts escalated in the early 1990s under President Clinton with the establishment of Operation-Hold-the-Line (initially named Operation Blockade) in El Paso in 1993 and Operation Gatekeeper in San Diego in 1994 (Massey, Durand, and Malone 2003, 93–94). Undocumented immigrants were channeled to more hostile crossing points, where increasing numbers of immigrants died of hypothermia and thirst (Cornelius

2001, 2007; Operation Gatekeeper Fact Sheet, n.d.). Cornelius (2007, 3) tells us that "between 1995 and 2006, there were over 3,700 *known* deaths due to unauthorized border crossings. . . ." With this rerouting of immigrants the geographical area Operation Gatekeeper and Operation-Hold-the-Line covered was expanded; Operation Safeguard began in 1995 around Nogales, Arizona, and later expanded along the border, and in 1997 Operation Río Grande was established in Southeast Texas (Massey, Durand, and Malone 2003, 95). These operations also led to more permanent settlement among the undocumented (e.g., Cornelius 2007, 5; Massey, Durand, and Malone 2003).

Increasing numbers of immigrant women and children from Mexico, believed to be potential recipients of public services, motivated immigration and welfare legislation in 1996. Passed in that year, the Illegal Immigration Reform and Immigrant Responsibility Act and the Personal Responsibility and Work Opportunity Reconciliation Act deflected responsibility for the welfare of new legal immigrants from the government, whether state or federal, to sponsors of the immigrants. A potential immigrant's sponsor, whether relative—as in most cases—or employer, had to sign an affidavit of support showing that he or she earned 125 percent of the poverty line. If the immigrant applied for any federally funded benefit, the sponsor's income and resources were deemed to belong to the immigrant in calculating his or her needs (Fragomen 1997, 450; Gimpel and Edwards 1999, 79–80, 214). Closely following the provisions of California's Proposition 187, passed in 1992 but later declared unconstitutional on the grounds that it infringed on federal authority, these acts together barred both undocumented and recently arrived immigrants from programs such as Social Security (Massey, Durand, and Malone 2003, 96). The year 2007 was depressing for the undocumented, as two pieces of legislation that would have been beneficial for them and their undocumented offspring were voted down in the U.S. Congress. The first bestowed a limited amnesty on the undocumented, who, however, in a controversial provision, would have had to return to their country of origin in order to apply for it. The second, the DREAM Act, would have allowed undocumented children who went through high school in the United States to attend their state universities with in-state tuition. A number of states, notably Arizona, have passed anti-immigrant legislation. Meanwhile border walls continue to be reinforced and extended, the Border Patrol continues to be fortified, and anti-immigrant think tanks and groups like the Minutemen verbally or physically attack undocumented immigrants and Latinos.

Mexican Women's Increasing Migration

Estimates for 1996 show approximately 7.3 million undocumented Mexican workers in the United States, of whom 44 percent are women (Ávila, Fuentes, and Turán n.d., 163).[2] Since that time both legal and undocumented women have increasingly come to reside in the United States. Although more than half of the immigrants to the United States since the 1930s have been women (Houstoun, Kramer, and Barrett 1984), until the past two decades males were exceptionally predominant among Mexican immigrants (Donato 1993; Zahniser 2000), especially the undocumented. The numbers are converging, however, for a variety of reasons. First, on the U.S. national level, provisions of immigration legislation, such as that of the 1986 Immigration Control and Reform Act that provided amnesty to at least 2.3 million of the Mexican undocumented (Bean, Vernez, and Keely 1989), had family-reunification provisions paralleling other immigration legislation concerned with documented immigration. This facilitated women's (and children's) migration (Cornelius 1993; Wilson 2006a). Second, on a transnational level, the pattern of recurrent male migration, with multiple border crossings over a working career, has been replaced by a pattern of more permanent migration, partly because of the dynamics of migration-network maturation and the establishment of "daughter communities" abroad (e.g., Massey 1990; Massey et al. 1987; see chap. 2), but also, and perhaps more important, because tightening control of the border has made the border crossing both psychically and economically more costly and highly dangerous (Cornelius 2001, 2007; Dunn 1996; Massey, Durand, and Malone 2003; Nevins 2002; Zahniser 2000). The mounting death toll along the border as the undocumented moved toward crossing the Arizona desert, where formal vigilance had been less, has led to longer and longer time periods spent in the United States and a greater tendency toward permanent or semipermanent settlement. This more permanent settlement has led to a desire for family reunification (Massey et al. 2003), especially on the part of wives, who may migrate to join husbands even if not under husband's auspices (Hondagneu-Sotelo 1994).

Third, and on a more social-psychological level, is a changing family dynamic in Mexico, given the new stress on companionate marriage among women in their midthirties and younger (Hirsch 2000, 2003, Wilson 2006a). "Young women . . . make migration and marital togetherness an explicit negotiation point during courtship. Before they marry they tell their boyfriends that if they are planning to go north they should save or borrow to pay the coyote for both of them, because '*no me voy a casar para estar sola*' (I am not getting married to be alone)" (Hirsch 2003, 150).

A fourth contributing circumstance has been the increasing involvement of women in formal-sector wage manufacturing work and services since the initiation of the Border Industrialization Program in 1965 and with tourism development programs begun in the early 1970s; however, women's work-force involvement has spread throughout Mexico, even into some rural areas (Arias 1994; Mummert 1994; Wilson 2008a). As detailed above, this entrance of women into the labor force was accelerated because ever-higher proportions of Mexican women have entered, and been driven into, the labor force because of periodic economic crises in Mexico since 1982 (Cornelius 1993, 342; González de la Rocha 1991, 2001; Roberts, Frank, and Lozano Ascensio 1999, 241–43). As we have seen, successive peso devaluations, high inflation, and structural adjustment policies that cut urban and rural subsidies and privatized the economy have forced women and children into income-generating activities in the informal sector and wage labor in the formal sector at unprecedented rates in an attempt to maintain the value of the household wage. Wives and sisters have thus come to expect to work, and many have had work experience before migrating. As Cornelius (1993, 342) points out, "The higher propensity of females to migrate to the United States in recent years is also a consequence of Mexico's economic crisis, which has driven more wives, single women, and children into the work force. Especially among

Mexico's urban poor, the male family head's income is not nearly sufficient now to meet the family's needs. . . ." Thus, women have more experience in the labor force and may often have expectations of seeking an income in order for the family to survive (Wilson 2006a).

Finally, low-wage sectors of the U.S. economy have offered more jobs to women in recent decades in both services and manufacturing (Cornelius 1993, 343). For example, immigrant women have increasingly worked in hotels, hospitals, and restaurants as service workers and filled the garment, electronics, and food-packaging plants in the manufacturing sector. Thus, opportunities beckoned.

The above summary of the history of women's work in Mexico, recent changes in gender relations and expectations, and the increasing importance of women's migration from Mexico should help to dispel the stereotypes of women that underestimate their work, whether in the formal or informal sector, and their propensity to migrate across national borders. In the next chapter, concepts in migration studies and gendered migration will be introduced and explored as to how they relate to Mexican women's immigration to the United States.

CHAPTER 3

Concepts in the Study of Migration

To understand the patterns of migration in which doña Consuelo and her daughters participated, it is helpful to review the concepts of migration networks and social capital, the phenomenon of transnationalism, and issues in the study of gender and migration.

Migration Networks

Common to both internal and transnational migration is that movement and settlement are most generally network mediated—dependent on aid from kin, friends, and in the Mexican case, compadres (ritual kin) (Balán, Browning, and Jelin 1973; Durand and Massey 1992; Kemper 1977; Lomnitz 1977; Massey 1987; Massey et al. 1987; Portes and Bach 1985). This aid can include meeting migrants on arrival; providing them meals and shelter; helping them find housing and employment; orienting them to life in the town or city, including sites of services and entertainment; showing them how to tap available services; and, in the case of the undocumented, how to keep a low profile, extending financial assistance to pay for the coyote (human smuggler) if the migrant is crossing the border clandestinely, and constituting the primary source for social and reciprocity relationships and moral support once the migrant has established himself or herself at destination (Wilson 1992, 38; 1994, 271). If a single most important network function can be isolated, at least for men and often for women, it is that of helping migrants to find jobs in the local labor market; if this cannot be done, for example because of labor-market saturation or lack of adequate ties to employers, immigrants may move on to other locales where network members are present (Wilson 1998a).

Network-mediated migration has long been documented for internal migration within Mexico (e.g., Balán, Browning, and Jelin 1973; Butterworth 1962; Cohen 2004; Kemper 1977; Lomnitz 1977; Nutini and Bell 1980; Ugalde 1974; Rivero-Fuentes 2004; Wilson 1998b). For example, interviews with 904 migrants to Monterrey, Nuevo León, showed that 84 percent already had friends or relatives there when they arrived (Balán, Browning, and Jelin 1973, 159), and a study of a colonia in Ciudad Juárez showed that upon arrival 54 percent of migrants received food and lodging from relatives and another 10 percent received such aid from friends (Ugalde 1974, 39). This kind of aid is common in internal migration—migrants go where their social networks lead them—and especially in transnational migration to U.S. cities and agricultural communities (see, e.g., Chavez 1992; Cohen 2004; Haney 1979; Hondagneu-Sotelo 1994; López, Oliphant, and Tejeda 2007; Massey et al. 1987; Mines 1981; Mines and de Janvry 1982; Mines and Massey 1985; Portes and Bach 1985; Tienda 1980; Wilson 1992, 1993, 1994, 1998a, 2006b). A study of immigrants from a rural community in Jalisco showed that 70 percent of the documented and 88 percent of the undocumented found work through their social networks at destination and that undocumented immigrants were especially dependent on these networks (López, Oliphant, and Tejeda 2007, 84, 92). Where potential migrants have friends or kin partially determines whether they will move internally or across the border. As Cohen (2004, 75) relates in his study of migration from Oaxaca: "A rural Oaxacan migrant chooses between a national and international destination based upon the relationships he holds with already settled migrants or the networks he establishes through family or friends." This statement is generalizable both to women and to those moving internally or internationally from other states.

Network-mediated migration breeds more migration as each new migrant becomes a contact person who can provide aid and information to friends, relatives, and compadres. This "cumulative causation" has been described as follows (Massey, Goldring, and Durand 1994, 1499–1500; see also Massey 1990):

Every new migrant . . . reduces the costs and risks and increases the attractiveness and feasibility of migration for a set of friends and relatives. With these lowered costs and risks, additional people are induced to migrate for the first time, which further expands the set of people with ties abroad. This additional migration reduces costs and risks for a new set of people, causing some of them to migrate, and so on. Once the number of network connections reaches a critical threshold, migration becomes self-perpetuating because each act of movement creates the social structure necessary to sustain it.

The trajectory of migration is cumulative because the migrants aided by former migrants in turn extend aid to others. The result is that as more people enter the migration stream costs and risks are lowered for ever more potential immigrants (Massey, Goldring, and Durand 1994; Massey and García España 1987). This model predicts that once every member of a given community has network members in the United States, when an ever-increasing proportion of community members reside across the border, and when prevalence rates for migration reach approximately 80 percent among males, a saturation point is reached and "the process of migration loses its dynamic momentum for growth" (Massey, Goldring, and Durand 1994, 1502–3).

Massey, Durand, and Malone (2003, 20; emphasis mine) reiterate this saturation thesis in the following terms: "In any *bounded population* . . . processes of cumulative causation cannot continue ad infinitum. If migration continues long enough, networks eventually reach a point of saturation within any particular community." Immigration thereafter declines because "the stock of new migrants becomes very small and is increasingly composed of women, children, and the elderly."

Nonetheless, even when a saturation point seems to be approaching for any one community (i.e., rural community), networks may continue to expand there. This happens when people from outlying ranchos migrate to dynamic, immigrant-sending communities and as marriages occur between members of migrant- and nonmigrant-sending communities and when new members are incorporated into existing networks, i.e., the rural communities are not always so bounded (Wilson 2009). Yet, cumulative causation has been found to be typical of both internal and transnational migration (Rivero-Fuentes 2004).

The saturation cannot work the same way in cities as it may sometimes do in rural areas, and urban network dynamics also differ. Cumulative causation tends to be absent in urban sending centers "mostly because levels of migration experience rarely reach the critical point at which they might cause the self-feeding process of migration" (Fussell and Massey 2004, 165). The family-based dynamics of urban networks differ from those in rural areas. This is true because one's spouse and friends, in-laws, and neighbors are often from other states or from other communities within the state of family origin.

A study of a rural community in Jalisco with high rates of migration to the United States points to three network principles that can also be applied to internal migration (Wilson 1998b). First, networks are multilocal (i.e., network members may be scattered among a variety of geographical locations). The importance of a particular destination may change over time, with some destinations eclipsing others in importance. The deciding circumstance may be labor-market conditions at the destination. Second, once immigrants establish themselves at a work site or at several work sites they can use their networks to help members of their community and their families get jobs (e.g., Cornelius 1991, 177; Durand and Massey 1992, 34; Browning and Rodríguez 1985, 286). Third, networks expand over time through the "strength of weak ties" (Granovetter 1973, 1982) to encompass new geographic and new work-site locations as acquaintances pass on information about job opportunities. Acquaintances can evolve into friends, compadres, or even in-laws, thus converting weak ties into strong ties and expanding an individual's network and those of other members of that network (Wilson 1998a).

Although cumulative causation is the primary explanation for increased migration from Mexico to the United States, in some instances network aid may be unavailable. This is true within Mexico as well. As González de la Rocha (2001, 91) points out, during economic crises, many families can become social isolates because of a paucity of resources to exchange:

> Networks are not simply "there" for people to access but the outcome of participation in establishing and maintaining social linkages. They are social constructions that require . . . that some assets be invested. Individuals who have the resources to be part of a relationship of reciprocity . . . will be in a position to maintain that link, and those who lack resources to exchange will not.

U.S.-based immigrants may have too many people living with them to take on another, however temporarily. They may be unable to put together, even with loans from network members, enough money to pay a coyote and may lack adequate contacts with local employers to help newly arrived immigrants obtain jobs. Most Mexican immigrants do, however, have strong networks to aid their migration and adaptation. In contrast, Salvadorans on Long Island and in San Francisco, for example, often have insufficient resources to engage in reciprocity relationships in the United States (Mahler 1995; Menjívar 1997, 2000).

In her study of Salvadorans in San Francisco, Menjívar (2000, 156) found that networks may break down for people with inadequate resources: "People need a minimum of resources to help others; otherwise they have nothing to share." In part this is because Salvadoran migration networks, having begun with the troubles in distant El Salvador in the 1980s, are far less mature than Mexican migration networks that—though periodically disrupted, as in the deportations during the 1930s—have been expanding in a neighboring country for more than 150 years. Social and kinship networks are especially fragile for Salvadorans because of their undocumented status and because they lack the information channels and employment networks that reach into Mexican communities even at origin. In contrast to the Salvadorans, most Mexicans enjoy "a web of informal networks through which resources and information actively circulate [that] gives the newcomers access to vital information and benefits without overburdening their relatives in the U.S." (Menjívar 1997, 20). Because long-standing, informal employment networks exist for most Mexican migrants, a recent arrival can find a job almost immediately and begin contributing economically to the household that has offered him or her aid in the migration process. Salvadorans do not have this advantage and may spend long periods unemployed, with the result that in many cases they cannot reciprocate for the aid extended to them (Menjívar 1997, 20). Mexico's border with the United States and the long history of Mexican presence in and migration across that border have meant that network-mediated migration is especially important in their establishment in the territory of their northern neighbor.

Historically, most of Mexican migration to the United States was temporary, circular, and overwhelmingly male, though some immigrants settled in, even—we have seen—before the Great Depression of the 1930s. This settling in resumed during and especially after the Bracero Program and even more so after the 1986 IRCA granted amnesty to the undocumented. In keeping with the dynamics of network-mediated migration, over time a source community develops "daughter communities" in the United States, as some immigrants decide to settle permanently and bring their families (Massey et al. 1987, 161): "As people turn away from their former economic pursuits at home and specialize increasingly in U.S. wage labor, a life of seasonal commuting back and forth is difficult to sustain . . . At the same time, migrants become enmeshed in a web of social and economic ties in the United States that bind them increasingly to specific locations and employers."

Networks become anchored in these slowly evolving daughter communities and act as magnets to pull more people into the migration stream, in keeping with the principles of cumulative causation (Massey et al. 1987, 161). With the militarization of the border, settlement has accelerated, as risky border crossings discourage return migration or even visits to their communities of origin for the undocumented—unless it is a permanent return. Nonetheless, no matter how difficult the crossing, how many walls are built, or how many guards patrol the border, migrants will find a way to join friends and relatives on the other side: counterfeiting of documents will become more sophisticated, tunnels will be dug, and boats or aircraft may be employed. While these new means of crossing may increase smugglers' fees, making the condition of the border crossers even more economically desperate and subjecting them to increased danger, militaristic measures will not halt the migration of people without legal documents.

Two types of transnational migration networks can be distinguished: one facilitating the reuniting of an extended family (or, to expand on this, directly aiding in the process of migration for kinship and social network members) and one facilitating the adaptation of migrants to their new destinations (Brettell and deBerjeois 1992, 46–47). Though membership in these networks usually overlaps, the latter type can be expected to expand at destination as weak-tie acquaintances are turned into strong-tie network members through marriage or compadrazgo (Wilson 1998a). Both types of networks provide social capital to their members.

Social Capital

Several definitions of social capital have been advanced and expanded upon over the past two decades. Three of the most widely used in sociology and anthropology are those of Pierre Bourdieu and Löic J. D. Wacquant (1992), James S. Coleman (1988), and Alejandro Portes (1995). Both Bourdieu (1986) and Coleman contrast other kinds of capital with social capital: what is economic capital for Bourdieu is financial capital for Coleman, and what is cultural capital for Bourdieu is human capital for Coleman. While for Bourdieu the forms of capital are considered accumulated labor, for Coleman they are considered productive agents. Though both accept that social capital takes on institutionalized forms based on closed communities, Coleman (1988, S118) underscores that it can arise or disappear and that most forms of it are "created or destroyed as the by-products of other activities." It is, therefore, like other forms of capital, fluid and changing.

Bourdieu and Wacquant (1992, 119) define social capital as "the sum of the resources, actual or virtual, that accrue to an individual or a group by virtue of possessing a durable network of more or less institutionalized relationships of mutual acquaintance and recognition." Bourdieu (1986, 248) also stresses that the existence of a "durable network of more or less institutionalized relationships of mutual acquaintance and recognition—or in other words . . . membership in a group . . . provides each of its members with the backing of the collectively owned capital, a 'credential' which entitles them to credit, in the various senses of the word." In other words, as a member of a group, a person has access to certain resources, and that access constitutes social capital. Yet membership in networks or groups may expand or contract.

According to Coleman (1988, S98):

> Social capital is defined by its function. It is not a single entity but a variety of different entities, with two elements in common: they all consist of some aspect of social structures, and they facilitate certain actions of actors—whether persons or corporate actors—within the structure. Like other forms of capital, social capital is productive, making possible the achievement of certain ends that in its absence would not be possible.

Coleman's approach emphasizes the rational actor. Portes (1995, 12) defines social capital as referring "to the capacity of individuals to command scarce resources by virtue of their membership in networks or broader social structures . . . The resources themselves are *not* social capital; the concept refers instead to the individual's *ability* to mobilize them on demand." Portes (1995, 12–13) goes on to say that there is a sense of moral obligation to network members, and one foundation of social capital is the expectation of reciprocity.

All these definitions emphasize the role of the network in helping members to reach their goals. In contrast to Portes, I consider scarce resources, including time, labor, goods, and services that network members provide to one another, also part of social capital. I also underscore that weak ties may be strengthened (networks do not remain static) and that affective labor is also involved. Therefore I will define social capital as valued resources embedded in and accessed through networks that permit network members to avail themselves of the economic and affective goods and labor of others, whether through strong ties or weak ties in the process of being strengthened. Under "economic goods and labor" I include the provision of loans, shelter, jobs, and goods and tools for carrying out jobs. I also include aid in building self-built houses in squatter settlements and inclusion in work crews where remuneration may be in kind, in cash, or in other valued goods and services. (One such work crew may be a grassroots organization pursuing any of a number of goals.) Under "affective goods and labor" I include invitations to meals, social events, family life-cycle celebrations, and offers of ritual kinship, all of which can be occasions for the expansion of what Lomnitz (1977, 133) has called "ego-centric" networks. The social and life-cycle events at which affective goods and labor are provided can also be occasions for extending the contrasting "exocentric" networks, reciprocity networks characterized by "the fact that exchange is not centered on one individual but is practiced by all partners alike" (Lomnitz 1977, 134). Lomnitz (1977, 134–35) goes on to explain:

> Often an exocentric network is a formally constituted social group such as an extended family; in other cases, it is a group of relatives or neighbors whose social relation is one of economic cooperation. Each member of an exocentric network may maintain additional dyadic reciprocity relations with individuals beyond the network; such relations tend to be less intense and less stable than those practiced within the network.

Social capital can be held by individuals, by families, or by communities, and each of these types of social capital can expand or contract.

Migration networks, whether extending internally within Mexico or across the U.S.-Mexico border, provide social capital to their members. Social capital is realized (in economic terms) in successful establishment in the host country (or, in the case of internal migration, in the host city) or in obtaining employment through network-mediated entry into work sites, whether, for example, a restaurant, a hotel, a factory, a foundry, or a construction project (Wilson 2006b). Massey et al (1987, 170), describing social capital as access to jobs, housing, and financial assistance extended by previous migrants to later migrants, maintain that as the number of migrants increases, social capital increases and the costs and risks are reduced for an increasing number of potential migrants at origin. Network members can count on aid from previous migrants and, because of the stress on reciprocity inherent in networks, be counted on to extend aid to future migrants. Reciprocity is a culturally sanctioned way of treating kin and friends who have (as culturally expected) helped one out in the past and may (as culturally expected) do so in the future.

Thus, social capital increases with the expansion of migratory networks to include more and more migrants from the sending community (Massey and Espinosa 1997, 952) and with the expansion of social networks at destination through the conversion of people met, for example, on the job or in places of recreation into friends, compadres, and possibly in-laws. These initially "diffuse" (as opposed to "dense") network members can also aid one another in finding jobs, services, and housing (Wilson 1998a). The ties that bind origin and destination communities form a field that is "transnational."

Transnationalism

Transnationalism—dynamic flows and linkages between two or more countries—can be observed from "above" and from "below" (Guarnizo and Smith 1998). Transnationalism from above can include capital flows (e.g., U.S. and other nations' investment in Mexican maquiladoras), media flows (e.g., Hollywood films and U.S.-based TV network programming seen in Mexico and Mexican films in the United States), diplomatic flows (e.g., the creation of NAFTA and Mexican pressure on the U.S. government for fair immigration legislation), and technology flows (e.g., the presence of Ford and Chevrolet plants in Mexico), among others. What migration scholars usually mean by transnationalism from below is the crossing of borders by migrants who continue to have relationships with the communities, kin, and friends left behind.

The notion of "transmigrants" (Basch, Glick Schiller, and Szanton Blanc 1994, 7)—participants in transnational migration—stresses their tendency to "develop and maintain multiple relationships—familial, economic, social, organizational, religious, and political—that span borders" and to "take actions, make decisions, and develop subjectivities and identities embedded in networks of relationships that connect them simultaneously to two or more nation states" (see also Glick Schiller, Basch, and Blanc-Szanton 1992, 1–2). Transnational migration involves the building of "social fields" that link together the countries of origin and of destination. Glick Schiller (1999, 97) explains: "We use 'social field,' defined as an unbounded terrain of interlocking egocentric networks, as a more encompassing term than 'network,' which is best applied to chains of social relationships specific to each person." Elsewhere, she contends that a social field is a network of networks; it involves "socio-centric" analysis rather than the egocentric analysis based on the study of individual networks (Glick Schiller 2003, 107). (Notably, this distinction ignores exocentric networks and family or household networks.)

Mahler (1998, 74) takes issue with the earliest definition of transnational migration (initiated in Glick Schiller, Basch, and Blanc-Szanton 1992 and repeated in Basch, Glick Schiller, and Szanton Blanc 1994) by pointing out that it "offers little assistance for evaluating the content, intensity, and importance of transnational ties, for examining the interests served through these ties, and perhaps more fundamentally, for establishing a typology of transnational actors—individuals, families, households, hometown associations, governments, etc." Transnational households, families, and social or kinship networks must be distinguished from the "transnational communities" anchored in a rural village at origin and in daughter communities at destination on which much theorizing about transnational migration has been based (e.g., Guarnizo and Smith 1998, 17–18; Goldring 1998; Levitt, 2001, 2003; Rouse 1992; Smith 1998), but they are the building blocks of those communities.

Migrants are a heterogeneous group with distinct human and social capital endowments, and, depending on their labor-market positions and social resources at destination, some migrants can maintain transnational ties while others do so with difficulty, if at all (Guarnizo and Smith 1998, 14). The question has been raised whether to deserve the label "transmigrant" the migrant must move back and forth between origin and destination communities (and how often) or if sending remittances and other goods to network members left behind is sufficient (Mahler 1998, 77). Would network members who do not move back and forth but provide network aid to those who come afterward be considered "transmigrants"?

A partial answer to this question is to envision some migrants, usually those with legal documents, as transnational links who are able to keep up face-to-face interaction with family and community members on both sides of the border. On the family level, these transnational links are similar to Bott's (1957, 140) "connecting relatives," who "direct the flow of relationships between kin, sometimes helping to bring them together, sometimes discouraging them from seeing each other." Able to cross borders easily, such connecting relatives can carry gifts from one relative to another and provide information about conditions at destination, as well as encourage or discourage other family members' migration. Mothers, in Bott's (1957, 141) study of English families, are more likely to play the role of a connecting relative than fathers, and grandparents also had a hand. In the following stories of Mexican migration both fathers and mothers are connecting relatives and transnational links, though fathers' more constant appearance may be the result of men's historically greater presence in the transnational migration stream.

Gender and Migration

Much recent scholarship has shown that all relationships—from individual interactions to the constitution of the nation state—are gendered and that gender intersects with race, class, and ethnicity to form multiple hierarchies of power and domination (e.g., Chow 1996). As we have seen, gender relations are heavily involved in the migration process, and legislation concerning immigration has gendered consequences. For example, the Bracero Program recruited men only and "established gendered migration networks that have endured for decades, and crafted the stereotypical 'wetback' image of the Mexican migrant as rural, male, and poor" (Mahler and Pessar 2006, 47). The family-reunification provisions of immigration laws, by contrast, permit wives and children to join their spouses. Gender structures relations within the household, at both origin and destination, informs the construction of migration and adaptation networks and determines the types of goods and services that can be exchanged, conditions the ability to move about in public space in the destination (as well as the origin) community, and affects the process of crossing the border and the process of settlement (or return). Women's motivations for migrating—apart from economic push-pull factors—may differ from men's. Wives may simply wish to reunite the family; however, some migrant women are escaping abusive or unsatisfactory relationships with men or feeling the socially stigmatized status of abandoned woman or unwed mother (Chavez 1992, 31).

Wives left behind by migrant men assume more power in the household; they must make crucial decisions as well as manage the household budget in the absence of their husbands (e.g., Mummert 1988). In the absence of husbands (in urban areas) or if husbands' remittances are too low (in rural areas), women must seek an income either through wage work or in the informal economy in order to ensure the survival of the household (Aysa and Massey 2004, 139). When men migrate, wives may also take over what is traditionally defined as men's work. For example, when Zapotec men from a town in Oaxaca went north under the Bracero Program, their women took over their work in the fields and in weaving (Stephen 1991, 109–15). These changes in patterns of authority and household division of labor can cause conflicts in the household when husbands and fathers return (Mummert 1988, 285–86).

In the United States, immigrant wives gain power while immigrant husbands lose it. As seen earlier, wives have greater access to public space as they travel to their jobs, enjoy an anonymity and thus a privacy unavailable in their hometowns, and can call 911—or threaten to do so—in the event of domestic violence. Men, especially if they are undocumented, must refrain from public behaviors common in their communities of origin (Hirsch 2003, chap. 6; 2000). Thus, gendered hierarchies of power within the household are challenged in the context of immigration, at both origin and destination.

In many cases, women's migration networks (especially among the undocumented) are separate from or only partially overlapping with men's. Women's networks may sponsor only other women, and once at destination, women's networks may remain relatively autonomous from men's (Hondagneu-Sotelo 1994; Kossoudji and Ranney 1984; Hagan 1994). In the Mexican barrio in northern California that Hondagneu-Sotelo (1994) studied, women's migration networks aided women in at least four distinct ways. Women advanced money to other women for the trip across the border; familiarized newcomers with neighborhood facilities and social, medical, and other types of services available at destination; facilitated the job search, helping to place kinswomen and friends as domestic servants; and informed the new immigrants about community organizations such as those that developed during the amnesty program to help people take advantage of the IRCA provisions. Hagan's work among Guatemalan Maya women in Houston also found that immigrant women's information networks were not coterminous with men's. At the same time, women may indeed migrate under the auspices of male relatives and men under the auspices of female relatives.

Though both men's and women's adaptation networks can aid them in the job search, such networks usually channel migrants into gendered work types, with, for example, men often working in construction or as mechanics and women often working in domestic service. Other jobs, of course, are not so gender segregated, and men and women can use each other's networks to find employment. The resources offered to network members also differ between men and women; for example, it is more likely that men will aid in home repairs or fixing vehicles, while it is more likely that women will cook or clean house for a sick relative or friend or take care of a friend's or a *comadre*'s children.

Even crossing the border without documents is a gendered process: women are more vulnerable to assault, robbery, and rape. Because of their greater vulnerability, women show a greater tendency than men to use coyotes, to borrow legal documents from a look-alike relative, or, if residing in a border city, to use a border-crossing card (which does not permit taking employment or long-term stays) to gain access to work in the United States (Donato and Patterson 2004).

Once established in the United States, women often prefer to remain because of their newfound freedoms, their earning of a higher income than is available in Mexico, and their increased power within the household because of that income (see, for Dominican women, Pessar 1988, 1986; Grasmuck and Pessar 1991; Mahler and Pessar 2006 and for Mexican women, Hirsch 2003, chap. 6; Hondagneu-Sotelo 1994, chap. 5; Hondagneu-Sotelo and Messner 1994). Men often prefer to return if not to their communities of origin then to somewhere in Mexico—the country where their patriarchal or neopatriarachal privilege is recognized and ratified. These insights are bolstered by statistics the National Study of Demographic Dynamics generated that show that between 1987 and 1992 only 16.1 percent of return migrants were women—yet in 1996, 44 percent of undocumented immigrants from Mexico were female (Ávila, Fuentes, and Turán n.d., table 1, 152, 163).

CHAPTER 4

Women's Migration to Colonia Popular

Mexicali, the capital of Baja California, lies across the border from Calexico, California, and the agriculturally rich Imperial Valley. It is the second-largest city in the state after Tijuana and like Tijuana has become a major center for the maquiladoras in which components of textiles, electronic goods, car parts, furniture, and other items brought in from the United States and elsewhere are assembled, primarily by women workers (Fernández-Kelly 1983; Tiano 1994, but see Wilson 1999), into finished products and reimported. The population of Mexicali and the *municipio* (county) of the same name of which it is a part has continually increased since the turn of the century, when it was primarily an agricultural supply center. It held this status until the 1965 Border Industrialization Program was introduced and the maquiladoras began to burgeon. Between 1950 and 1960, the city's population more than doubled, from 124,362 to 281,333 inhabitants, and by 2000 the city had grown to 764,602 inhabitants (CONEPO 1997, 93; INEGI 1991a, 1; 2002,78; Wilson 2005, 3). Most of its growth was the result of in-migration from other states in the Republic of Mexico.

Patterns of women's migration to the U.S.-Mexican border have received less attention than patterns of men's migration. Even studies of male migration to the border often neglect theories developed in analyses of transnational immigration. Often, models of internal migration are bipolar, looking at rural-urban migration flows as though the first destination were the last destination. Alternatively, in several studies of migration to the border, a "stage-migration" pattern has been discerned. Stage, or step migration was first conceived and labeled as such by Ravenstein

(1885, 1889). In his studies of European internal migration during the nineteenth century, migrants were seen as moving successively from smaller- to intermediate-sized population centers and thence to larger localities. With respect to internal migration to the northern Mexican border, it has been suggested that rural out-migrants tended to migrate first to a city nearest them and only afterward to a border city. A more recent conceptualization of immigration is contained in the network-mediated migration model, which, as detailed above, asserts that migrants go where they have kin or friends.

As we saw in the last chapter, research has shown that male and female transnational migratory networks are not always identical. An important question is whether there are women's networks for internal migration to the border as well as for transnational migration. Since most immigration, whether transnational or internal, is network mediated, immigrants are "channelized" (Jones 1982) to one destination rather than to another—to Chihuahua or Baja California, to Tijuana or Mexicali, depending upon where potential in-migrants have kin or friends willing to offer them a helping hand. It must be kept in mind, however, that networks are not bipolar (Cornelius 1991; Ho 1993; Wilson 1994; Uzzell 1976).

My interviews between 1988 and 1992 in Colonia Popular with 149 women residing on the colonia's 157 occupied lots (a 95 percent sample) revealed that 114 (76.5 percent) had migrated to Mexicali from other states in Mexico. The patterns of these women's migration varied; there were distinct patterns for women's migration, depending on whether they were accompanied by husbands or whether they migrated without the aid of male relatives (husbands or fathers). Women's networks were a central influence in clustering women from the same state in the colonia, and this phenomenon is revealed through consideration of patterns of micro-level (colonia or barrio) network-mediated migration, as opposed to meso-level (city) and macro-level (state) network-mediated migration. Although some stage migration is apparent among women, Mexicali tended to be the first destination of at least half of the women (almost all of whom were of rural origin). (*Doña Consuelo's early migration history, as will be seen in the following chapter, from a variety of ranchos to a pueblo—now a small city—could be seen as stage migration, though her future migrations were network mediated.*) A comparison of female versus male rates of migration to Mexicali and Baja California shows that women and men from the same state of origin do not move in equal numbers to Mexicali or to Baja California as a whole. On the northern Mexican border, women generally outnumber men. In 1990, the ratio was 98 males per 100 females (Williams and Eastman 1994). This is in keeping with the finding that since the 1950s more women than men from rural areas have migrated to towns and cities (Chant and Craske 2003, 234), taking advantage of the larger labor market for women there, and because if they are abandoned or separated, they receive less social condemnation for being female heads of households than they do in the tradition-bound rural environment at origin (Chant and Craske 2003, 236).

Women migrants within Mexico tend to be disproportionately single and either separated, abandoned, or widowed, and single mothers tend to accompany parents. Young, single women seem to be attracted to the border by the possibilities of finding work in the maquiladoras (Carrillo and Hernández 1988; Iglesias 1985; Tanori Villa 1989), underscoring women's generally ignored status as labor migrants (Kofman et al. 2000). None of the women in Colonia Popular had migrated to Mexicali in order to work in the maquiladoras, but some of their teenage daughters were employed in these assembly plants.

Women's Networks and States of Origin

Most of the 114 in-migrant women I interviewed in Colonia, 59 (51.8 percent), came with or joined husbands who had preceded them there (table 1). Of these women, 50 (43.9 percent) accompanied their husbands, and 9 (7.9 percent) joined their husbands after they had established themselves in Mexicali. Another 21 percent (24) came with both parents or with mother to join father, and 2.6 percent (3) came with father and siblings only. The fathers were all widowers in these cases. These 27 cases are omitted from the analysis here in the interest of focusing on the contrast between "traditional" and "independent" female in-migrants.

Table 1. Who Accompanied Female Migrants
Resident in Colonia Popular (N=114)

"Traditional" female migrants

Came with or joined husband	51.8%
Came with mother and father or came with mother and joined father	21.0%
Came with father and siblings only and joined no mother	2.6%

"Independent" female migrants

Came with mother and mother and siblings only and joined no father	9.7%
Came without company or assistance of mother, father, or husband	14.9%
Total	**100.0%**

Source: Colonia Popular interviews, 1988–92

The remaining 24.6 percent (twenty-eight) can be considered as women migrating independently or single-female in-migrants—women who came with mothers, but without fathers—and will be included here. Of these twenty-eight women, eleven (9.6 percent) came with their mothers only or mothers and siblings only. Their mothers were widowed, separated, abandoned, or single parents. Seventeen (14.9 percent) came unaccompanied by mothers, fathers, or husbands, and eight of these were widowed, separated, abandoned, or single mothers who brought children with them to Mexicali.

Single mothers who were dependents of their parents or included within their mothers' female-headed household were not interviewed. Drawing on data from the Mexican Migration Project consisting of random samples from fifty Mexican communities, Cerrutti and Massey (2001, 190) found that "38.7% of all females with U.S. migrant experience were unmarried daughters who clearly followed a parent northward; another 36.9% were married women who followed their husbands in migration.

Thus three-quarters of all females with migrant experience left on their first U.S. trip only *after* a parent or husband had already gone." The figures are similar for internal migration to Colonia Popular: about a quarter of women migrants there came independently. Notably, Cerrutti and Massey did not specify under whose auspices independent female international migrants migrated, nor did they specify whether sons or daughters tapped mother's or father's networks in the migration process.

The fifty-nine women who came with or joined husbands correspond to what Gabaccia (1994) has labeled "nuclear family" and "family reunification" immigrants. Several of the women's husbands had been deported to Mexicali when the Immigration and INS picked them up for working in the United States without documents. Of the fifty-seven in-migrant men interviewed, approximately 25 percent had visited Mexicali with friends or relatives before marriage—some in a failed attempt to cross into the United States. Others had gone there to secure work or to confirm that relatives would extend aid in the form of housing before returning to their home state to accompany their wives and children to the border or both. The wives of these male migrants to Mexicali can be considered "traditional" female migrants, as they accompanied or joined husbands in that border city.

The story of Francisco and Victoria provides an example of nuclear-family in-migration. They migrated to the border with the aid of male cousins from Francisco's mother's side of the family, and Francisco joined his cousins, who had established themselves as independent brickmakers in Mexicali. After working with one of his cousins in the brickyards to learn the trade, he eventually rented his own brickyard, and with the help of his wife and children, he made bricks there for more than fifteen years.

Don José and doña Teresa provide an example of family-reunification migration. José initially migrated from a rancho in Jalisco to Mexico City, where he met and married Teresa. When the shop where he made shoes went bankrupt, he accompanied friends to Mexicali and crossed the border into the United States. Unable to find a stable job there, he returned to Mexicali and, having determined that the family could work together as cardboard and metal recyclers in the municipal dump, sent for Teresa and their five unmarried children (three were married and stayed in Mexico City). He then bought a residential lot in Colonia Popular with the savings from his work in California (lots in the colonia originally sold for about US$200).

Juana, Mari, and Consuelo can be considered independent migrants. Juana, who was an unmarried mother when she arrived in Mexicali from Veracruz, had accompanied a Mexican family who planned to take her to the United States, without documents, to work as a domestic servant. Fearing the crossing, Juana decided to stay in Mexicali with a female friend. She eventually was able to send for her daughter after she found work in a fish-meal factory where she met her present husband. Mari, a divorced mother from Sinaloa, joined a female friend who lived in Colonia Popular for a short time before renting her own house in the same colonia. Her friend Julia had migrated with her husband and children to join Julia's stepfather and the woman he had married after Julia's mother died. Notably, Julia and her husband were enabled to migrate because of her ties with her stepfather. Later, Mari was able to migrate through the auspices of Julia. Consuelo, Juana, and Mari can all be considered "independent" female migrants, though Consuelo's mother had preceded her.

(Doña Consuelo migrated to Mexicali with six of her children after the dissolution of her marriage. Her mother and stepfather had relocated to Mexicali from Jalisco in 1956, when doña Consuelo made her first trip to that border city. When she returned in the early 1970s, having opted out of an abusive marriage, she found work as a cook at a local country club and set up an independent household. In 1985 she acquired a lot in Colonia Popular, several kilometers from the colonia where she was living. She was able to work because her mother, living in a nearby colonia, could take care of the children. In the 1980s a married son migrated to Mexicali from Mexico City and eventually traded houses with a sister who had a lot in Colonia Popular. In the 1990s two unmarried daughters and a live-in niece helped to sustain her household by working in a maquiladora that manufactures paper supplies.)

In table 1, nuclear-family and family-reunification in-migrants have been combined under the label "traditional" (75 percent) and compared to the "independent" (25 percent) female in-migrants. The various states of origin appear to send different proportions of each type of in-migrant, but this sample is too small to reach any firm conclusions about these differences. Nonetheless, if Hondagneu-Sotelo's (1992, 1994) findings on female Mexican immigrants to a northern California barrio are generalizable, then these women may be either challenging patriarchal traditions or taking advantage of a weakened patriarchal order.

The distribution of machismo and patriarchal or neopatriarchal regimes in Mexico appears to be clinal, gradually changing over space (Wilson 2003, 2005). Caulkins (2001, 110) has argued that the contemporary rejection of a conception of culture as a bounded, stable entity should lead to "conceptualizing culture in terms of clines of continuous variation." I use the term patriarchal cline in order to envision the variation of patriarchal or neopatriarchal traits in different parts of Mexico.

Others have struggled with the fact that patriarchy and machismo are differentially distributed in Mexico. For example, González-Lopez (2005, 6) refers to "various regional patriarchies" in Mexico that "reproduce regional femininities and masculinities." She distinguishes between "rural patriarchies" and "urban patriarchies," the former being "the hardcore and more intense expressions of patriarchy and gender inequalities that appear in small provincial locations, or *pueblos*" and the latter as "the disguised or de-emphasized gender inequalities more commonly seen in larger urban metropolises, such as Mexico City" (González-López 2005, 92). Although this bipolar model is of some value—despite the fact that a large proportion of the populations of Mexican cities is composed of rural in-migrants—it is important to point out that patriarchal traits vary among rural communities as well. For example, they are apparently stronger in Zacatecas and Durango than in Jalisco.

All five women who migrated to Colonia Popular from Zacatecas (table 2) came to Baja California escorted by their husbands. While Durango shares the stern neopatriarchal values of Zacatecas, half the women from Durango migrated independently, suggesting that neopatriarchal traditions are being more successfully challenged there. A random sample of in-depth interviews conducted in the colonia supports this assertion. Petra, for example, a woman from Durango, was forced by her husband to move into a house with another woman with whom he was having sexual relations. He forbade Petra to raise her eyes when they were walking down the street together so that she would not see the women he flirted with. He also subjected her to physical and emotional abuse during his drinking bouts, including riding over her on a horse while she was pregnant. Eventually she left him (or perhaps he left her, having crossed into the United States without returning or sending remittances for several years). She took her seven children to Mexicali and several years later acquired a lot in Colonia Popular with a common-law husband she had met while living in a field with her children.

Table 2. Origin of Female In-Migrants to Mexicali Resident in Colonia Popular in 1992 by Immigration Experience

State of Origin	All Female In-Migrants to Colonia		Traditional In-Migrants to Colonia/All Fem. In-Migrants to Colonia		Independent Female Migrants/All Fem. In-Migrants to Colonia	
	No.	%	No.	%	No.	%
Sinaloa	19	16.7	16	84.2	3	15.8
Jalisco	18	15.8	16	88.9	2	11.1
Sonora	12	10.5	9	5.0	3	25.0
Durango	10	8.8	5	50.0	5	50.0
Michoacán	9	7.9	5	55.6	4	44.4
Nayarit	8	7.0	6	75.0	2	25.0
Mexico City	8	7.0	7	87.5	1	12.5
Guanajuato	6	5.3	5	83.3	1	16.7
Oaxaca	5	4.4	5	100.0	0	0
Zacatecas	5	4.4	5	100.0	0	0
Other States[*]	14	12.2	7[**]	50.0	7	50.0
Total	**114**	**100.0**	**86**	**75.4**	**28**	**24.6**

[*]The following were states of origin for one woman each: Aguascalientes, Baja California Sur, México, Nuevo León, Puebla, Querétaro, and Veracruz (N=7). Chihuahua sent 4 women and San Luís Potosí 3.

[**]One woman each from the following states came without parents or husband, representing 100 percent of women from each of these states: Aguascalientes, Baja California Sur, Querétaro, and Veracruz (N=4). No women from Chihuahua came without men, and all three women coming from San Luís Potosí were independent migrants.

Source: Colonia Popular interviews, 1988–92

Further evidence for differential rates of female migration according to state of origin comes from a comparison of women's and men's migration patterns from eight of the major sending states and Mexico City to Baja California and to Mexicali (table 3).

Table 3. Female to Male Ratios among In-Migrants to Mexicali and to Baja California from the Eight Major Sending States and Mexico City[*]

	Female/Male Ratios of In-Migrants to Baja California (1990)	Female/Male Ratios of In-Migrants to Mexicali (1990)
Total Population	99.6	100.2
In-Migrant Population	101.2	104.1
Source State		
Durango	105.3	112.7
Guanajuato	93.0	94.5
Jalisco	105.0	105.0
Michoacán	100.8	97.3
Nayarit	115.2	122.8
Sinaloa	112.4	116.2
Sonora	107.8	109.4
Zacatecas	98.0	93.7
Mexico City	87.7	88.1

[*]Female to male ratios rather than the more traditional (for demographers) male to female ratios are presented in order to underscore the overabundance of females from some states and their relative scarcity from others.

Source: INEGI 1991, 1993

According to the 1990 census, more women than men migrated to Mexicali from the states of Nayarit, Sinaloa, Durango, Sonora, and Jalisco (in that order) (INEGI 1993, 1991b). Males outnumbered females in migration from Zacatecas, Mexico City, and Guanajuato, while the sex distribution was roughly equal for migrants from Michoacán. The same pattern holds true, in general, at the state level, although Mexicali received a slightly larger proportion of female in-migrants from Sinaloa, Sonora, Nayarit, and Durango than the state as a whole and proportionately lower from Zacatecas and Michoacán. Almost equal proportions of female in-migrants to Mexicali and Baja California are found from Guanajuato and Mexico City, with these two origin points sending far fewer women than men. Perhaps this is partially because of distance and the fact that undocumented men from Mexico City to the United States who are deported to Mexicali have farther to travel in order to attempt to recross the border. Nonetheless, Jalisco, also far to the south (though not as far south as Mexico City), shows similar sex ratios. The differences in female in-migration and the resultant skewed sex ratios from state to state and region to region within Mexico also may reflect a cultural cline of neopatriarchy; that variable neopatriarchal practices in various regions of Mexico may affect women's migration possibilities is a topic for further research.

Women's Macro-, Meso-, and Micro-Network-Mediated Migration

By using the terms micro-, meso-, and macro-levels of migration I am focusing on the hierarchy of geographical locales that receive migrants. This is different from the methodological micro-, meso-, and macro-levels Brettell proposed (2003, 2–6), the micro- consisting of individual life histories; the meso- the consideration of households, networks, groups, and communities; and the macro- the analysis of the overarching politico-economic system that propels migration. It is also different from Faist's (1997, 195), who distinguishes between "(1) political-economic-cultural structures on the level of the international system, the country of origin and country of destination" (structural or macro-level); "(2) density, strength and content of social relations between stayers and movers within units in areas of origin and destination" (relational or meso-level); and "(3) the degree of freedom or autonomy of the potential movers" (individual or micro-level). These are useful ways of looking at migration; however, here I am using these terms in a geographical sense as pertains to internal migration. Although my micro-level data were gathered from interviews, the meso- and macro-level data were gleaned from government statistics. For purposes of this chapter micro-level refers to migration to a particular and distinguishable neighborhood or colonia, the meso-level to migration to the city in which that colonia is located, and the macro-level to migration to the state in which that city is located. Such analysis would be difficult to do on a transnational level, since the host society seldom keeps statistics on the state of origin of Mexican immigrants to a particular town or city.

At the macro- and meso-levels we can examine the percentages of female in-migrants to Baja California and to Mexicali from various states as recorded by the 1990 census (table 4.4). The 1990 census encompasses women of all ages, including dependent female children. The interviews from the colonia included only adult women who were married to a head of household or who were themselves heads of household.

For each census period from 1900 to 2000 Sinaloa, Sonora, and Jalisco have been among the top three states sending in-migrants to Baja California (Butler and Pick 1991, table 2; INEGI 1993, 2004b). Between 1950 and 1990 Jalisco sent higher percentages of in-migrants than any other state. Between 1900 and 1980, about one-half to two-thirds of the immigrants originated in Jalisco, Sinaloa, and Sonora (Butler and Pick 1991), and those three states also have sent the highest percentages of women to Mexicali and to Colonia Popular. There are differences in the proportions each of these three states sent, however, depending on whether the analysis is focused on the micro-, meso-, or macro-level.

There are slight differences in the proportion of female in-migrants from each of the major sending states in Baja California as compared with Mexicali and Colonia Popular (table 4). Jalisco sent proportionately more women to Baja California than are represented in the city of Mexicali or in Colonia Popular, and Sinaloa and Sonora sent proportionately more women to Mexicali and to Baja California than to the colonia.

Interviews conducted in Colonia Popular revealed a number of micro-level chain clusters. For example, among the eighteen women interviewed

Table 4. Origins of Female In-Migrants to Baja California and Mexicali as Compared to Origins of Female In-Migrants Resident in Colonia Popular in 1992 from Eight Major Sending States and Mexico City (in Percentages)*

State of Origin	Origins of Female In-Migrants		
	To Baja Calif. (1990)	*To Mexicali* (1990)	*To Colonia Popular* (1992)
Jalisco	17.0	14.7	15.8
Sinaloa	15.2	20.0	16.8
Sonora	9.7	16.2	10.5
Durango	4.8	4.3	8.8
Michoacán	9.7	9.3	7.9
Nayarit	5.7	5.6	7.0
Mexico City	7.2	4.1	7.0
Guanajuato	6.3	8.5	5.3
Zacatecas	4.0	4.4	4.4
Totals	**79.8**	**87.1**	**83.5**

*Aguascalientes, Baja California Sur, Mexico, Nuevo León, Puebla, Querétaro, and Veracruz sent less than 1 percent of the female population of Baja California and sent only one woman from each of these states to Colonia Popular. Chihuahua and San Luís Potosí sent less than 1 percent of female in-migrants to Baja California and less than 1 percent to Colonia Popular. Oaxaca sent less that 1.5 percent of female in-migrants to Baja California and less than 4.5 percent to Colonia Popular and to Mexicali.

Source: INEGI, 1991, 1993; Census of Colonia Popular, 1990

who were born in Jalisco, there was a mother, daughter, and daughter-in-law cluster occupying three lots, and one cluster including a man and his wife, his sister, and his nephew's wife occupying another three lots.

Among the nineteen women interviewed from Sinaloa, two were sisters and four were the wives of brothers from Sinaloa who had migrated to Mexicali in chainlike fashion during the 1970s. Similar clusters of relatives occurred throughout the sample of 114 women. The importance of women's networks is suggested by the fact that women residing in Colonia Popular have more relatives living on other lots in the colonia than men do (43 percent as compared to 40 percent)—though the difference is not statistically significant. Both women and men migrating to Mexicali tended to have relatives already living there (52.6 percent of women, 61 percent of men).

Women's Networks in Migration to Colonia Popular

The importance of women's networks on the micro-level is apparent from my interviews. Married couples were almost equally as likely to join the wife's relatives (23.7 percent) as to join the husband's relatives (28.8 percent). Women migrating independently were more than twice as likely to join their own female relatives (28.9 percent) as to join male relatives (10.7 percent). Furthermore, women migrating without the aid of a husband or father were just as likely to join friends (10.7 percent) as they were to join their own male relatives. If mothers (7.1 percent) and mother's relatives (21.4 percent) are added to the category of "own female relatives," the proportion of women joining female kin rises to 57.1 percent. Roughly similar percentages of nuclear-family female migrants (20.3 percent) and independent female migrants (17.8 percent) had no one to join. The figures strongly suggest that women's networks are equally important as men's networks in facilitating traditional nuclear-family migration to this border colonia, and they are of great significance in facilitating the migration of women who lack the aid of husbands or fathers, more than half of whom were aided by other women or at least joined other women.

The model of network-mediated migration, in which destinations of migrants are determined by the location of kin or friends, is often opposed to the stage-migration model, in which migratory movements take place in steps to overcome the friction of distance, an important intervening variable in migration decisions (E. Lee 1966; Butler and Pick 1991). Thus, stage-migration models predict that rural residents will first move to the city nearest them and then to a more distant location. The two models are not necessarily mutually exclusive, however, since networks are multilocal and network members—whether linked by strong or weak ties—may be scattered across a number of geographical sites (e.g., Ho 1993; Kearney 1986, 1995; Kearney and Nagengast 1989; Nutini and Bell 1980;

Uzzell 1976; Wilson 1994, 1998a). The strength of network ties may be a central variable in determining whether a stage pattern is found. If network ties are stronger between kin or friends at greater distances, there may be no intermediate stopping points between origin and destination. Alternatively, what looks like stage migration may well be a "foraging pattern"[1] (Wilson 1992; 1998a) in which migrants first search one place and then another for relatively stable employment, beginning this process at the point closest to home. This would be the pattern expected for those with no or weak network ties to people in other locales. Where transnational migrant networks are well developed, for example, members of rural communities go directly to work sites in the United States with little or no stage or foraging migration on the Mexican side of the border (Massey et al. 1987; Wilson 1992). Nevertheless, transnational migrants may try out a number of locales where they have network members once across the border (Wilson 1998a). The direct point-to-point migration internally may be found where networks channel people into specific places.

Data from Colonia Popular reveal both patterns: apparent stage migration to Mexicali as well as direct migration from the place of origin—whether it be rancho, small town, or city—to the border. The patterns differ in intensity for men and women, however. More than half (52.6 percent) of the 114 women interviewed, regardless of place of origin (rural or urban), came directly to Mexicali without prior residence elsewhere, while only 27 percent of the men from towns and 45.4 percent of men from ranchos did so (table 5). These differences may not be statistically significant given the small sample size. Nonetheless, 61.4 percent of the entire sample of male heads of household had migrated to another place within Mexico before arriving in Mexicali, while women who had migrated elsewhere before coming to Mexicali constituted only 47.4 percent of the sample.

It can tentatively be concluded that women involved in traditional patterns of family-reunification or nuclear-family migration are less likely than men to demonstrate stage migration or foraging behavior. According to traditional gender ideologies in Mexico, men were expected to be the primary wage earners; thus men often made migration decisions without consulting their wives (Hondagneu-Sotelo 1992, 1994; Wiest 1983). Men

Table 5. First Destination of Female (N=114) and Male (N=57) In-Migrants to Colonia Popular by Place of Origin

Place of Origin: Females

	Rancho/ejido		Pueblo		City		Total	
	No.	%	**No.**	%	**No.**	%	**No.**	%
First destination								
Rancho/ejido	2	6.5	1	2.0	1	3.0	4	3.5
Pueblo	4	12.9	5	10.0	1	3.0	10	8.8
City	9	29.0	19	38.0	12	36.4	40	35.5
Mexicali	16	51.6	25	50.0	19	57.6	60	52.6
United States	0	0	0	0	0	0	0	0
Total:	**31**	**100.0**	**50**	**100.0**	**33**	**100.0**	**114**	**100.0**

Place of Origin: Males

	Rancho/ejido		Pueblo		City		Total	
	No.	%	**No.**	%	**No.**	%	**No.**	%
First destination								
Rancho/ejido	1	9.1	4	10.8	0	0	5	8.8
Pueblo	2	18.2	5	13.5	1	11.1	8	14.0
City	2	18.2	16	43.3	4	44.5	22	38.6
Mexicali	5	45.4	10	27.0	3	33.3	18	31.6
United States	1	9.1	2	5.4	1	11.1	4	7.0
Total:	**11**	**100.0**	**37**	**100.0**	**9**	**100.0**	**57**	**100.0**

Source: Colonia Popular interviews, 1988–92

were typically the pioneer migrants (Balán, Browning, and Jelin 1973) and therefore could be expected to migrate from one place to another until they encountered a location where a relatively stable income or perhaps a preferred kind of work could be found. At this point they would send for or return for their families.

Greater network density over time might be expected to lead to more direct migration to Mexicali and an attenuated stage-migration pattern. To examine this possibility, I compared the number of migrants before

1965 and from 1965. The 1965 cutoff year was chosen because three important economic events affecting migration and employment occurred at that time. The Bracero Program (1942–64) had just ended, and men living in the interior of Mexico could no longer easily contract work in U.S. agriculture. Some had begun to look for other employment alternatives, while others had decided to cross the border illegally, many stopping in Mexicali on the way. The Border Industrialization Program had begun to open up new employment for young women. Finally, soil salinization had reached its destructive peak in the mid-1960s, and the valley of Mexicali had ceased to produce cotton for international markets. The seasonal cotton harvest had drawn many men, with and without their families, to Mexicali in earlier periods. After 1965, men had to seek other types of employment there, and the bulk of this employment was less seasonal and more stable.

Almost four times as many women from Colonia Popular came directly to Mexicali after 1965 than before that year. Almost equivalent proportions of Colonia Popular men came directly to that city before and after 1965. Proportionately fewer men (20 of a subsample of 57, 35.1 percent) than women (59 of 114, 51.8 percent), however, came directly to Mexicali both before and after 1965 without having first migrated elsewhere. These results suggest a number of possibilities.

First, as mentioned earlier, women's migration patterns may be more conservative than men's, at least during the period under consideration (before 1990), especially if the women are involved in family-reunification or nuclear-family migration. Their male companions or fathers may have been exploring a variety of places before settling permanently in Mexicali.

Second, what appears to be stage migration may be the result of opportunities (including network aid and labor-market conditions) in multiple locations. (*Doña Consuelo's apparent stage migration, for example, took her from rancho to rancho in Jalisco as a child and then to the small city of Tepatitlán, also in Jalisco. From there she came to Mexicali to visit her mother, who had joined an aunt of hers. There she met a man who had migrated first to Mexico City, then taken up a short-term work contract in Mexicali. She accompanied him back to Mexico City, but after their marriage dissolved, she came back to Mexicali. Although the first part of her migration history is apparently stage migration, in reality she went where network resources were at her disposal.)*

Third, women's migration networks leading directly to Mexicali appear to be stronger than men's. This may be partially explained by the preference for female workers in many maquiladoras located along the border (Carrillo and Hernández 1988; Fernández-Kelly 1983; Iglesias 1985; Tanori Villa 1989; Tiano 1987). Female factory workers and their families have marginally more economic resources to sponsor the migration of kin or friends than unemployed women who are dependent on the male head of household. Women also find jobs in the informal sector along the border (Anderson 1988) that provide a relatively independent income that can be used to sponsor kin.

Fourth, stage migration may be a pattern followed by pioneering migrants from a given community who, once established at a final destination, provide aid to friends and kin. It is possible that, after a stable family or emergent community of migrants is established, a network-mediated migration pattern begins to take shape. If this is the case, men and women showing a stage-migration or foraging pattern may be among the first migrants from their communities, whereas those who come directly to Mexicali may be part of a more mature migration stream.

Conclusions

A number of questions remain open for future research on both internal and transnational migration. One is how micro-level network-mediated migration constitutes meso- and macro-level network-mediated migration, in a geographical sense. A number of researchers have suggested the existence of nodal persons or families providing linkages to a variety of geographical sites. My research on the rancho Los Arboles in Jalisco showed that transnational migrants often crossed the border with or joined consanguineal or affinal relatives or friends from other ranchos or even other states (Wilson 1992, 1993, 1998a). Furthermore, in-migrants to Los Arboles from at least two other neighboring ranchos and from the state of Zacatecas often tapped their networks at origin to aid themselves and friends born in Los Arboles in finding housing and work in the United States. In one case, a man from the state of Guanajuato who had been deported with a number of men from Los Arboles, provided network assistance to some of these men during a subsequent crossing. This is one instance of many that show how weak ties can be converted to strong ties (Granovetter 1973; Wilson 1998a) as part of the migration experience.

Interrancho and interstate marriages, as well as other spatially situated experiences in Mexico or elsewhere, may form the basis for network expansion beyond a community incorrectly envisioned as closed (Roseberry 1995; Wilson 2009). Networks at origin thus continue expanding over the generations. The pattern described as stage migration (but in fact a kind of foraging pattern) does not preclude network-mediated migration, since network members may be living in a number of geographical locations. Furthermore, networks have the potential to expand and incorporate new members at every stopping point through offspring's marriages or compadrazgo relationships. Stage- or foraging-migration patterns, however, may be more typical of pioneering migrants than of later migrants to the border and beyond. Once pioneering migrants are established in Mexicali, they pull in friends and kin. This is suggested by the fact that a greater proportion of male and female residents of Colonia Popular migrated directly to Mexicali after 1965 as opposed to before that year: networks were maturing over time.

Analysis of data from Colonia Popular has shown that women migrated with their husbands (nuclear-family migration), following their husbands (family-reunification migration), and independently. Thus, female migration to this colonia exemplifies the three distinct patterns of female transnational immigration Gabaccia (1994) identified. Second, the data show the existence of women's networks—independent from men's networks—that facilitate female migration to the border and mirror Hondagneu-Sotelo's (1992, 1994) conclusions for female Mexican immigrants in a barrio in the San Francisco Bay area of northern California. Third, given the role of women's networks in facilitating internal migration from interior states to Mexicali and the subsequent and consequent clustering of women from the same state within the same colonia, it can be concluded that women's migration patterns can best be explained in terms of the network-mediated-migration model.

The data strongly suggest that the dynamics of internal migration to this Mexicali colonia can be understood and analyzed in terms of the concepts and theory developed in the study of transnational migration (Wilson 1993; see also Cohen 2004). Whereas internal migrants overcome the friction of distance with aid from network members, transnational migrants overcome by means of such aid both the friction of distance and the barriers legal-political borders pose. The latter can be envisioned as engaging in counterhegemonic activity (Wilson 2003). Women may migrate with or follow their husbands, but, both internally and transnationally, many women are migrating by means of their own kinship and friendship networks, whether to Colonia Popular, Mexicali, or across the border. Finally, the differing proportions show that network-mediated migration leads to a clustering of women and men from the same state (and actually the same community) of origin in specific cities and neighborhoods within those cities, a phenomenon recapitulated in transnational migration.

The stories of Consuelo and her daughters presented in the following chapters allow us a glimpse of the way these processes affect individual lives.

CHAPTER 5

Consuelo's Story

Consuelo came to San Diego to tell me the story of her life, arriving by Greyhound from Calexico on Sunday, August 10, 2003. She was accompanied by her daughter Lorena, who returned on the next bus back because she had promised her husband that she would do so. We drove down from La Jolla—my mother-in-law, brother-in-law, his wife, and I—to pick her up. Her visit was to last two weeks, one week before we went to visit her daughter Irma in Lake Tahoe Town and one week after, and during the visit she was going to tell me about her life. This was a project we had planned since about a year after I had gotten to know her in Colonia Popular in 1989. My mother-in-law and her offspring live or have lived there, and for about nine months each year from 1988 to 1994 I had lived there too.

Doña Consuelo had never read a book, though she knew I wanted to write one about her; she cannot read or write. She imagined scenes from her life as they might be seen in one of the many *telenovelas* (soap operas) she has watched since electricity came to Colonia Popular in 1984. These telenovelas were the template for her stories, of which she was the heroine. Although some of the anecdotes seemed fantastic, I had no reason to believe they were invented or exaggerated. Many were, in fact, understated. As she talked about her life, she often closed her eyes to reenvision the incidents of which she told me. Some of the stories she told me are recorded here.

From Rancho to Rancho

"I was born in 1937. Right now I am five years old [eyes closed, she counts the years on her fingers]. We are living in a very ugly house in Tepatitlán, Jalisco. Around me are my mama and my papa. I am a poor but happy child. I have a brother named Salvador, and he is sick. A bull tossed him with his horns in the patio and the *susto* (shock) caused his gall bladder to explode. And that was the reason he died at the age of four. And my mama used to give me warm tortillas, and they stuck in my throat, and I asked her why they did so. Well, without salt, without beans, they just stuck there."

(Corn tortillas are very dry when eaten alone. When other food is available they are used to wrap bite-sized pieces in. Only the very poor once ate tortillas with nothing else.)

"From there, we went to live with a señora called Petra, and her husband was named Marcelino. I did not like the señor Marcelino because I saw how he walked past my mama and said things to her. That he liked her. That she was pretty. After that my father said he didn't like it there, and from there we went to live in don Inez's house. There my brother Felipe was born. They made me and my brothers Mateo and El Güero and my papa go outside. And I put myself between my two brothers because I have always been afraid of cats, and I told them I was very fearful of the cats in the kitchen. And they told me, no, that it was the baby who had been born. [The two brothers were Mateo, the eldest sibling, and El Güero, younger than she. The baby Consuelo had mistaken for a cat, was Felipe. See genealogy 1.] I was mistaken. The baby was very little, very thin, but I loved him. I took care of him, tried to take care of him and protect him from everything."

Once she and Mateo buried Felipe up to his head and put flowers around him. When they returned home their mother asked where Felipe was. "He died, and we buried him" they said. Her mother went to look for Felipe, found him, dug him up, and hit them both for what they had done. Another time she and Mateo put Felipe on the kitchen table and folded his hands over his chest and told their mother he was dead. She hit them for that, too. . . .

"Then in don Inez's house they wanted to steal El Güero. A señor arrived one night, and we were alone, Mateo, El Güero, and I. My mama had taken Felipe with her. And the señor said El Güero was very beautiful. He asked if we would let him go to the store. And Mateo said no. And I, who was very much the fighter, said no. I told him to go and talk to my mama. When we saw my mama turn the corner we were very happy because the old man was not going to be able to take my brother away. And then my mama arrived. They began to argue, and we went inside. And we went inside, and my mama stayed to argue with him and said we were not orphans, and if we were alone it was because she had left to buy groceries.

"Then they told my mama that her stepmother had died. And she went to Yagualica, and when she returned she returned with my grandfather. They brought many hens and many burros, and we were thrown out of don Inez's house. Then we went to El Mesón. In El Mesón my sister Lupe was born. My mama was charged with giving water and feed to the burros and horses, and they [the owners] rented rooms. And there, while I was playing in the corral with my brother Mateo, we found some money. But a señor ran us off and took it away. After that a señor, who was called Benito, I believe, killed the owner, and we had to leave El Mesón. And we went to live with Babalaika—but in that house I began to grow, and by then I was ten years old [pause]. At that time I saw a very handsome boy in front of my house. He was called Rubén. And I liked to see him very, very, very much. But I was ashamed for the boy to see me because I was very fat, and my mama dressed me in an ugly way, and I was ashamed for the boy to see me. Then one day my mother *jalaba mis orejas* (lit. pulled my ears; fig. scolded me) in front of the boy, and I was very ashamed. And the boy told her 'Don't pull at her because she is my *novia* (sweetheart).' And I felt ashamed. [She sighs.] Those times. I was saddened because they [the boy and his family] left the town. Tamara, my life was a story. We roamed here and there like *sanjuaneros*."

(Sanjuaneros were followers of St. John, known for wandering up and down the countryside to preach. A similar sort of roaming from place to place was common among a number of the poorest who eventually arrived in Mexicali and helped found Colonia Popular. Don Ramón, the father-in-law of one of doña Consuelo's daughters, remembers traveling with his father from one rancho to another in Jalisco to look for work making bricks and, in the off season, to sell the sweetbreads his mother made. Another man's father and family wandered from one place to another in the bordering states of Colima, Jalisco, and Michoacán seeking land to rent or sharecrop. The very poorest in the city continued this wandering—helping to invade new colonias, leaving them when they found they did not have enough income to pay their share of electrical and water utilities, and going on to establish a new colonia once again. This occurred with regularity until in 1992 a governor from the Partido Acción Nacional (PAN) was elected. Among the first things he did was prohibit the establishment of new colonias by invasion of vacant land.)

"[My brother Samuel] was the son of a sweetheart of mine. You are going to know one of my secrets. My mama had relations with my sweetheart Gustavo. I being fifteen years old, my sweetheart exchanged me for my mama, and that is why I left home. [Consuelo's mother had gone to Mexicali six months after this brother was born, joining an aunt of hers there. She went there to get away from her husband. There she remet the man who became her last husband, who was a first cousin she had known as a child, and also a nephew of the aunt she stayed with.] I left with another sweetheart of mine called Moisés. I made him my sweetheart because I wanted to leave home and I could not go alone; I needed someone to pay for the bus. I stayed with him four or five months. He bought me furniture and rented a house for me, and in the evenings he would take me out. We lived together very happily, until one day a señora arrived with a boy child and said it was his, and because of my inexperience I did not want to take the child because he was blind—because she was going to give him to me and I didn't know how to take care of him. And I left him—my sweetheart—and went to work for a señora.

"At work I got to know Víctor Aguilar, the father of Edgar [Consuelo's first child], and we went around together for a while and during this time I got appendicitis, and I had very strong pain, and he came and found me with a traffic officer and didn't want to listen to me. We were talking when Víctor arrived, and he got jealous and spoke to me in a very ugly way. The next day the pain still hadn't gone away, and Víctor took me to the Red

Cross of Guadalajara. There they told him that if they did not operate immediately I was going to die. And since I was a minor they didn't want to operate because my parents weren't there to sign for permission. And I told them that I would be responsible for my own life. And so the operation took place.

"Then there in the Hotel Catalán where we were staying, I didn't know why some men were guarding me, *pistoleros* (lit. gunmen; bodyguards) of Víctor's, watching me. They were pistoleros because they didn't let me go alone anywhere. It turned out that they were people of much money and pride—I'm not sure what—and Víctor went out and always left me money in the bureau drawer and a pistol. Thus I passed my time. And I became pregnant with the boy.

"And for three days I did not leave the hotel room. After three days I went down to tell Víctor the news, and I found him with a woman. And I entered his room and smashed the vases and everything we had, and I returned to work for Señora Elena [where she had been working when she met Víctor]. And after that my brother Mateo and Lorenzo, who had been my sweetheart, came, and they took me from Guadalajara to Tepa [Tepatitlán]. Well, from there on my calvary began. I was two or three months gone when I returned to Tepa. My son was born on December 14 [some days after she turned sixteen, in 1953]. Then one of Víctor's pistoleros saw me in Tepa and came to look for me, but I hid.

"And after that my father returned us to the rancho Los Yugos [where he came from and where doña Consuelo had been born] because it was a shame that I had had a child without being married. Wait, Tamara, I am mistaken. From there we went to Villa Obregón, which was in Las Cañadas. We followed the horse races and the *peleas de gallo* (cockfights), and we rented a room in Las Cañadas, and we were Teresa [who died before reaching maturity], Felipe, Lupe, and Edgar, forty days after his birth, and we had not eaten all day when a señora and a señor passed by with burros, many burros. They had come to the fiesta of Las Cañadas. And the children were sitting outside in the street, and the señora said, 'Look what pretty children.' She asked me if they were mine, and I said no, they were my siblings. And she asked me who my parents were. And

I told her Lucía Arenas Sánchez and Marcos Rosacalba Hernández. And they told me that the señor was a first cousin of my papa, but I didn't know him. And they invited us to come to the rancho [Los Yugos], and we went, all of us, with them [pause].

"And there we stayed a while. In a month my papa joined us [pause]. Then he took us to a rancho called La Peña Colorada. And there, well, at times we had food to eat and at times not. And I worked as a peon, a bricklayer, with him. Well, there we began—here comes the good stuff, Tamara. Well, since I was not ugly, I had a very good body, *los viejos* (the old men; alternatively, a rather disrespectful term for men in general) were killing themselves over me. Ay, Tamara, the sustos they gave me! There were times that in the evenings I waited until the sun went down for us to go to my uncle Arcadio's because hunger made us leave my papa's house. And one day I met the mayordomo of the rancho, mayordomo of La Peña Colorada and of Los Yugos, and he asked me where I was going, and I told him I was going to my uncle's. And he asked me for what? And I told him we were going there just to visit, but the children spoke up. My brother Felipe told him that we were going to eat there because there was nothing to eat in our house. And from there on in, we were no longer hungry, because the mayordomo brought me everything. He brought me milk, beans, eggs, lard, sweets. Everything, but in exchange for my body.

"When I didn't want to anymore, he was going to kill me. And I was up on the roof to hide from him, and he found me and told me, 'Come down or I'll let loose a bullet.' And I told him, 'Well, kill me because I am not going to come down.' May he rest in peace, he's dead now. I found out when I went to the rancho last year, with La Muñeca [her sixth daughter], in September it will be a year. [It comes out that the mayordomo was married when Consuelo was his mistress.] 'Cuca' was his wife's name, but she never knew anything. He was very reserved.

"During that time I worked with the women of the rancho. I helped them carry water, to grind [corn for tortillas], to sweep. I helped them with everything. And then I returned again to Los Yugos, left my papa. And went to Los Yugos with the children [pause]."

Consuelo's mother had gone to Mexicali six months after Samuel, the half brother, was born, joining an aunt of hers there, and was living with a man who was a first cousin and nephew of the aunt she stayed with. Consuelo was left at fifteen to take care of her siblings.

"Then we returned again to La Peña—La Peña Colorada, and in the evenings Felipe and I weeded the furrows to sow. And he was so little, my poor little brother. And a young man named Pancho gave me a hen and twenty-five eggs that the hen had laid. With the good luck that God gave us we managed to get twenty-five chicks. And we harvested the corn we had planted in the furrows of the cornfield. Well, my father arrived from the rancho Gavilán and began to sell my chickens and give away my corn. We didn't have white corn; Felipe and I planted only black corn. And my neighbors got very angry that he sold my chicks, my hens, rather, and they helped me return to Tepa again. Felipe, Lupe, and Edgar came with me. Mateo was working in a butcher shop in Tepa. He was grown by now, and he had married Jerónima. Then a man began to like Jerónima, and Mateo had to leave Tepa because the man was going to kill him. They were married by law, but the viejo liked Jerónima—she was very beautiful—and he was going to kill Mateo, and Mateo had to leave and go on to Mexicali."

From Mexicali to Mexico City to Mexicali

From Tepa Consuelo went with her three siblings and her son to a rancho outside Tepa but in the same municipio. There, she had problems getting herself and her charges enough to eat. She went several times to look for her father in Tepititlán, but could not find him.

"The next day I talked to my comadre Amalia, and I told her I was going to Guadalajara to find work. And we went, María, Gilberto—a good friend—and I. María and Gilberto did not leave my side. My mama had sent me money to take the children to Mexicali, but my papa found out and took them away from me. Only Edgar, who was mine, stayed with me.

"Well, then, we were breakfasting in Señora Nena's restaurant when a first cousin of Víctor came by. And he came up to me and asked if the child was mine. And I told him yes, and he asked me who was his father. And since they did not know, I told him Víctor. And then he offered me money for the child. I said he wasn't an animal to sell or give away. Well, like a lightning flash the *judiciales* (police) were upon me. A girl had heard Víctor's mother say that I had been found with the child. The señora [Víctor's mother] wanted the child at any price. And then I went to the Hotel Gigante, where I was staying, and afterward I spoke to Alfonso, a friend. I hid in his car, but the police were on the corner, all around us, to take my child away. And Alfonso took me to the train station and left me there, and I hid myself so that no one would see me. And I went to Mexicali with Edgar.

"And there I got to know Juan Carlos. My mother cooked for him. She was boarding him. He was paying her to make food for him. And thus began my bad luck of *trancazos* (beatings). He was very jealous. He hit me often. In front of my mama. Once my mama invited me to go to the 16 of September [Mexico's independence day celebration] gathering, and he hit me upon my return. And sometimes I was talking to him, and he began to snore, and I spoke to him, and he told me my conversation bored him. At times I slept on the floor without covers, because he took them away from me. He threw me out of bed. And then I had my first miscarriage, after Manuel [Consuelo's second child]. It was my first miscarriage. She was a girl."

By this time Consuelo and Juan Carlos had moved back to Mexico City, where Juan Carlos had lived most of his life and where his parents and siblings lived. He worked as a baker there, as he had in Mexicali. "Juan Carlos registered Edgar as his own. He [Edgar] is also a Guzmán. [It comes out another day that Víctor never saw his son Edgar.]

"When I first got to know Juan Carlos I had a sweetheart who was named Evaristo, and my mama did not like him because he was poor. Then he said he was going to go to *el otro lado* (the other side, i.e., the United States) and would buy a car so that she would let him see her daughter—me. And he indeed did bring the car back. But he died— some barrels exploded, and he died—in Guadalajara. Then after Evaristo was Manuel García. He sang to me [she sings part of a song]. He is still living, in the United States, and is really rich, Tamara. All his siblings live in Palaco [a lower-middle-class and increasingly crime-ridden colonia in Mexicali].

When I asked Consuelo why she had stayed with Juan Carlos so long when he hit her often, she answered, "I don't know. There were times when he spoke to me kindly and calmed me down." Asked if he also hit the children, she said, "Once when we were carrying groceries back from the store I hit Edgar. And Juan Carlos hit me, and he left me with all the groceries and took Edgar and Manuel to the rancho. No. He was not mean with the children. After Ramón was born he hit me a lot. And it is Ramón who looks most like him."

[And you didn't do anything?] "Yes. Why not? Once I grabbed a knife and my mother-in-law said, 'You appear to be very brave,' and I said 'Yes I am and if not, I wouldn't have grabbed it.' And once my brother-in-law was going to hit me, and I told him, 'Come closer *tu hijo de tu . . .*' (a portion of a common but very serious insult, *hijo de tu pinche madre*, son of your damned mother). No, I wouldn't let any of them touch me. Once my mother-in-law and I began to argue, and I said, 'Hit me, I am all alone' [in life, i.e., there was no one to defend her]. Once Juan Carlos tried to hit me with his fist, and I ducked, and he hit the medicine cabinet on the wall and cut his hand.

"Juan Carlos didn't want to give me money for shoes, and one day I stole money from him. And my mother-in-law noted that I was carrying money in my socks, and she took all but six pesos away from me, and I went and bought my tennis shoes for three and a half pesos.

"One time he hit me because a comadre of mine said I was in the park. And I had gone there to treat Ramón and Irma for the bites that had come out from [the fleas on] the rats, and the *vieja* (old lady, a deprecating term for a woman, though often used by men to refer to their wives) came and said she had seen me in the park. Well, that's where the clinic was. And he was going to hit me. But I called over the señora who had accompanied me, and she told him that he was a fool for believing everything he heard.

"Oooh, [he hit me] a mountain of times. I went about with a black eye. For this reason the woman gave me money to go back to Mexicali. She told me that there my children could go naked because there was no cold to suffer through. No, he was mean to me.

"Once he arrived, and I always bathed him, I always had clean clothes for him. Drunk every day, and I would bathe him. 'Why,' my mother-in-law asked, 'do you bathe him?' And I gave him food in his mouth, placed it in his mouth; I bathed him. In every way I tried to get along with the family, because I was alone and I tried to be liked by them, but in any case I wasn't liked by any of them. . . .

"Juan Carlos had a vieja who was very tall, very big, from Zacatecas, and he was very short. And I followed him, and she asked me who I was. 'I am your mother [a way of indicating superiority],' I said. 'I am his wife.' I was nineteen when Manuel was born, twenty-two when Ángela was born. . . . . I had Ramón when I was twenty-five. And the vieja is asking me, 'Since when?' [Juan Carlos said] that he went with María because she was chasing him. She was much older, and she wouldn't leave him alone. And the children of the vieja came to my house, and he said that I was his sister and our children were his nieces and nephews. Well, the woman stood and stared. He was maintaining two homes. 'No,' I said to the vieja. 'I am his vieja.' I said to Juan Carlos's father, 'Look, this is the son of the vieja Juan Carlos has.' And his father said, '*No más ésta faltaba* [That's the last straw],' and threw him out of the house. Well, then he went to Zacatecas [with the other woman], and I followed behind him. I went and hauled him out of her house.

"We were there for a while—he worked in a bakery that was on Calle González Ortega, and it closed, and then we went to the rancho—to Los Yugos. There we stayed for some time with my papa. He [Juan Carlos] made bread to support us, and he sowed furrows as well, but then he went back to Mexico [City], and I had to follow him. He left the harvest and went to Mexico, and he started seeing this vieja once again. And that was when I came here, to Mexicali, you understand. And after that I did not return to him. . . .

"And then they took me to the train, my comadre Katya accompanied me. She paid for all the tickets for me, and the people on the train gave us food. They asked how many children there were, and I told them so many, and they said, '*¡Arriba la mujer* (Long live women!)*!*' I arrived in Mexicali all beaten up and dirty. And I went to work in El Campestre [a well-off residential area that includes a country club] as a servant." [She tells me the names of all the women she worked for—and told me of one woman from Sinaloa who liked to experiment with different recipes. If she didn't like the result she sent the food home with Consuelo.] "I was happy working for her," Consuelo said.

When Consuelo returned to Mexicali in 1972, she had eight children with her; Edgar had stayed in Mexico City with his stepfather. The man she met in Mexicali, Lorenzo Ruiz Romero, repaired cars and later managed boxers in Las Vegas.

"He was very good to me but he was a woman chaser. He had many viejas. He had forty-five children. He never hit me. Once he came and said he was going to kill Chano (her last—common law—husband) if he hit me again. He said he had stopped coming to see me so that I could find happiness, but if Chano hit me again he was going to come and kill him. [Chano also hit you?] Yes. But Lorenzo never hit me. No, Chano was very abusive. And as soon as Lorenzo went away he became very *valiente* (brave, often used sarcastically) once more. Lorenzo said it was better to leave a woman than to hit her because a man who hit a woman was not a man. When we lived together Lorenzo would go away for days, and I didn't know where he was, and when he came back, he came with truckloads of watermelons, of everything. He was good to me. He never hit me. But then there began to come viejas after viejas looking for him and . . . [she does not finish the sentence]. Well, Tamara, I tell you that was the way he was. He had his wife who was named Gloriana, but she left him for the same reason, because he was a womanizer."

Consuelo said she thought the worst thing that could happen to a woman was infidelity.

"Lorenzo brought his father-in-law to eat at the house and one of his wife's brothers. . . . But they never looked upon me badly. They said it was not my fault. Well, Lorenzo deceived me. But as soon as I knew he had a wife, I left him. Let's say, he did not live with her, but he had children with her and all. So I left him. But that's the way he was. As soon as he got tired of women he left them, but he never got tired of me because I never asked him for money or anything else. And he said he felt content in the house because no one was bothering him, asking for money or anything.

"I had many children, and I had to work in order to feed them. There were nine, but Edgar had stayed in Mexico [Mexico City]. I had eight with me. . . . But he was good because when I went to work he fed them, he brought them *carne asada* (grilled beef), he made food for them, and things like that. I respected him, and he respected me. He was happy when I became pregnant with Lorena. He congratulated me, he embraced me. Happier than Chano was [when she became pregnant with Chano's daughter Rosario]."

In the four years they spent together, Lorenzo fathered three of Consuelo's daughters, and when he was dying in Tecate in July 2005, one of his daughters with his legal wife contracted Consuelo's daughter Lorena (his first daughter with Consuelo). La Muñeca and Lorena went to see him several times before he died in November 2005. Their sister Anamaría, also one of his daughters, was unable to visit him, as she feared crossing the border back into the United States without papers.

Consuelo's third husband and father of her youngest daughter was Chano Solís, and she remained with him for twenty-one years.

"Well, with Chano I came and went with the little girl [Rosario] in my arms. I came and went to the Club Campestre [a country-club complex not far from Colonia Popular]. I put her in a bureau drawer while I made the food. There the governor arrived and said, 'When do you think you will embrace my little girl?' Do you know who the governor was? Milton Casteñedas. I stood staring at him. Well, he was joking with me. I said, 'Right now, señor, right now I will embrace her.' And he asked me why I was working, and I said to maintain my many children.

"Lorena [her sixth daughter] and I bought the house Chano lives in. But seeing as how we could not leave our work, he went to the offices with doña Chabela, the owner, and put it in his own name. We separated after he got involved with Cuca Sánchez [a married woman from the colonia with whom Consuelo believes Chano had an affair]. I left him. When I found him with Cuca Sánchez I didn't want to have relations with him anymore, but I prepared his food, washed his clothes, cleaned his house."

Chano and doña Consuelo lived two blocks apart. Years ago she had told me they lived separately because he was always arguing with her sons, who, unmarried, lived at home with her. During the years I lived in the colonia, he was often at her house to eat, and if he did not come she would send him food with two or three of her daughters—one of them always his daughter Rosario. "But then, when he stopped coming to the house, it was because he had this vieja [Ester, with whom he still lives]."

Consuelo tells me of the final breaking point with Chano. He had been drinking and driving (with Ester in the car, though Consuelo did not know it at the time), and the police told him that the next time they caught him drinking and driving they were going to take his car away. He did not believe it, it seems, and the next time they caught him they impounded the car. He came to Consuelo and asked to borrow fourteen hundred pesos to pay the fine and get back his car, and she lent him the money. Late that night she went to his house and found him laughing with Ester, "*riendo de mí* (laughing at me)," she said. She told him that he had to pay her back by Saturday. He protested but did so. She never had anything to do with him again.

Consuelo tells me, "I am glad to be here [in my apartment in La Jolla] because we are at peace, we are alone, and in the house we couldn't have said anything. Because my daughters are there, and they would have said, 'Ay mamá, how was this, and how was that?' And it's not a secret to have three husbands. My comadre Aurelia knew all of my three husbands. [Your daughters know of them, right?] Yes, but they don't like me to talk about it because it is shameful."

Deaths in the Family

"My sister Lucy [the only child of Consuelo's mother and stepfather and the person who took care of their mother while she was bedridden and comatose] hit my mama because she used to urinate in the bed—and I buying her diapers. My stepfather threw us out of the house, and I said that while I have this little piece of meat that is my Mama, I am going to return, but afterwards I am not. And since she died I have never returned."

Consuelo's mother lived with her husband and the one daughter in a colonia about two miles up the highway. When I met her in 1989 she was bedridden and could not talk.

"She got burned [had a bedsore on her calf; Consuelo points out where on her own calf] and smelled a lot, and I bought her Fabulosa for her clothing and Pinasol and chlorine and diapers, and once Teresa [a friend from the colonia who is very involved in the Roman Catholic Church] and I took a priest to the house, and the viejo [her stepfather] threw us out, together with the priest. For this reason, now that my mother is gone, I don't go to my stepfather's house. Then my father died, but my stepfather is still alive.

"My mama died March 10 of 1990. My papa died September 6 of 1991. He died a year later. . . ."

Consuelo was the one who took care of her father when he became ill and later bedridden. His wake was held at her house in Colonia Popular, her daughters serving coffee to those who came to pay respects over the nine-day period. He had come to Mexicali some years after Consuelo's second migration there.

"Just imagine it, Tamara, my mama made dinner, and then she went to bed and stayed there for three years. They said she had arthritis."

Relatives in the United States (8/15/03, Friday)

Consuelo remarked that she could have relatives in the United States:

"My grandfather Edgar [her father's father] went to San Francisco and then to San Jose and left my grandmother, Lorenza [his wife], with the whole family. It says on my birth certificate that my paternal grandfather was in the United States and because of this was not present. He left everyone. He left his wife with all their children [pause]. My papa believed that he had half siblings on the other side, but he never found out and didn't know when my grandfather Edgar died." [When I interviewed Consuelo's father in the colonia in 1990, he stressed this disappearance of his father somewhere in the United States. His father never returned nor sent money for the family. They believed him to be alive there, however, and did not suspect that, for example, he had died on crossing the border.]

Preparing for Lake Tahoe Town

(At the end of the week we are to go to Lake Tahoe Town for Consuelo's granddaughter's quinceañera party and for Irma and Raúl's wedding—both to be celebrated the same day. Raúl and Irma have lived together—with one period of stormy separation—for almost sixteen years. They had been married by civil law on February 14, [2003], and will marry in the church in August. Consuelo wonders what we should say in the airport if they ask where we are going. To visit your daughter, I suggest. "But if they ask names?" Consuelo inquires. "She doesn't have papers." I say we can say we are tourists.

This evening I call Irma. Raúl answers. I ask him what he thinks we should say, that Consuelo does not know what to say if the immigration officials should stop us and ask where we are going. That you are going to a quinceañera, he says. I suggested that we could just say we were tourists. Yes, say that, he said. That you are staying in the [Lake Tahoe Town] Hotel. I tell him Edgar [Consuelo's eldest son] had mentioned working in that hotel to me. Raúl also worked there, for six years, until he had the accident that incapacitated him. Raúl says that one of his padrinos-to-be will come for us. That he himself cannot enter the Reno airport because he does not have papers.

I then talked to Irma, mentioned that her mother was always trying to clean the house. "That's the way the señora is," she replied laughing. Consuelo and Irma then talked at length.)

Commentary

The list of Conseulo's children and their birthplaces (table 6) is an outline of her migration history.

She was with Juan Carlos sixteen years, with Lorenzo four years, and with Chano twenty-one years. Of Chano she says, "He brought up all my children," but this refers only to the ones who came north to Mexicali with her and did not include Edgar. It was partly because he insulted her adolescent sons that Consuelo had separated from him, and she continued

Table 6. Consuelo's Husbands and Children

Children	Year born	Where born	Father
Edgar	1953	Tepatitlán, Jalisco	Víctor Aguilar
Manuel	1956	rancho outside of Mexicali	Juan Carlos Guzmán
Ángela	1960	Col. Las Minas, Mexico, DF	" "
Carla	1962	rancho in Jalisco where Consuelo was born (Los Yugos)	" "
Minerva	1964	" "	" "
Ramón	1966	Col. Las Minas, Mexico, DF	" "
Carlos	1968	rancho near Mexico, DF	" "
Francisco	1969	Col. El Chapulín, Mexico, DF	" "
Irma	1971	" "	" "
Lorena	1974	Col. Petrolera, Mexicali	Lorenzo Ruiz Romo
La Muñeca	1975	" "	" "
Anamaría	1976	" "	" "
Rosario	1980	" "	Chano Solís

cooking for him and washing his clothes. She felt she had to do that so that he would provide money for Rosario's keep, especially her school supplies and school uniforms. The definitive separation—with no relationship whatsoever between them—came because of his infidelities, of which she first became aware almost five years after she went to live in her own house.

The men in doña Consuelo's life were part of her in situ adaptation networks as she migrated from rancho to rancho and from rancho to towns in Jalisco, to Mexicali, to Mexico City, to Zacatecas, and then once again to Mexicali. Weak ties became strong ties as acquaintances were converted to sweethearts and sweethearts became common-law or legal husbands or otherwise providers of goods. Expansion of networks at destination is also gendered in this way, with couple formation and mutual aid, including economic and emotional support, occurring in a live-in or live-out "marital" arrangement. These strong ties can be severed, and network ties diminished, in the case of separation. "As family composition [because of serial monogamy] changes, so do the people who constitute networks of assistance and the goods to which they have access" (Menjívar 2000, 183). It can be surmised from Consuelo's account of her life that her network members changed as her husbands changed, as did the goods and services and the emotional support to which she had access. Paralleling changes in husbands, however, were changes in location, which also led to the loss of old and acquisition of new network members.

Translating Consuelo

Consuelo's story is atypical in many ways, yet she shares commonalities with other Mexican women. Comparing her life with Esperanza's as developed in Ruth Behar's *Translated Woman: Crossing the Border with Esperanza's Story* (2003), reveals the following similarities and differences. In contrast to Esperanza, who had told her story to others, doña Consuelo told her story only to me, but both women knew that their stories would be presented to a large public, and both envisioned their stories in filmic terms.

Esperanza was an Indian who generated income as an ambulant vendor in a nearby town most of her life; though Consuelo was also poor and of rural origin, she had no Indian identity and engaged in a variety of income-generating activities over her lifetime as she moved from rancho to town and then to city.

Esperanza came from a damaged home marked by her father's violence and lack of employment, which had led her mother to abandon him and temporarily abandon their children. Consuelo also came from a broken home, where her father's intermittent absences and infidelities had led her mother to abandon the family and migrate from Jalisco to Mexicali to join an aunt. In contrast to Esperanza, Consuelo did not talk much about her parents: it was with an interview with her father in Colonia Popular—where Consuelo had taken him in to care for him during the last weeks before his death—that he told me that his wife had left him because he, as an occasional bartender, had met and gone with many women.

Esperanza had children with only two men, Consuelo with four. Their last partners were in both cases younger than they were. Esperanza had a number of children who died shortly after birth; none of Consuelo's children died, though she thinks that she once miscarried triplets. Esperanza had only three children who lived until adulthood; one has the impression from her story that they did not help her economically. Consuelo had thirteen children, all of whom provided some kind of resources (food, money).

Both Esperanza and Consuelo married men who beat them and were unfaithful to them. Consuelo's husband Juan Carlos even put her in a casa chica situation, living sporadically with a woman from Zacatecas who bore him children at the same time Consuelo did. After Consuelo abandoned him, he moved in permanently with this "other woman," and Consuelo's daughter Irma [Irma tells me] even went to live with them for two years. Later, with her third husband, Lorenzo, she herself lived in a casa chica situation as the "other woman," though she was not aware of this until after all three of their daughters had been born.

Esperanza attacked a woman with whom her husband was having an affair, and Consuelo beat up a woman whom her last common-law husband, Chano, brought to his house, even though he and Consuelo lived in separate houses. For her their relationship was kept alive by his occasional visits (which often included conjugal visits), her daily sending of meals to him, and his monetary contributions for the daughter they had together. Although this incident is not recounted in her story here, she told me about it in the colonia a few days after it happened, saying she had pulled the woman (who was married to another man in the colonia), out of the bed (and house) by the roots of her hair. Notably, given her paucity of resources, including network resources truncated by her coming from a broken home and her geographical mobility, doña Consuelo used her sexuality—her relationships with men—as a resource (see Hirsch 2003, 272).

Despite the fact that, as Gutmann (1996) has underscored, there may be multiple ways of being macho, some even positive (see also Mirandé 1997), doña Consuelo's children's fathers were all unfaithful, which can

Genealogy 1. Consuelo's family

HAS NEVER LIVED/WORKED IN THE U.S.

HAS LIVED/WORKED IN U.S.

BORN IN MEXICO, LIVES IN U.S.

BORN IN U.S.

be interpreted as emotional and psychological violence. Three were emotionally disparaging, physically violent toward her, or both, including Víctor, Juan Carlos, and Chano. Whereas Juan Carlos did not display violence toward the children, Chano was mean to her sons—one of the reasons she moved into a separate house. In sum, doña Consuelo's life, like Esperanza's, was negatively impacted in one way or another by machismo. At the same time, neither woman could depend on a man to support her and her children. Consuelo's pursuit of a living for herself and her children has been lifelong.

CHAPTER 6

Doña Consuelo at Work

The emergence and survival of female-headed households has been
linked with the possibilities for female employment, the compatibility of
income-generating activities with child care, the level of compensation
for women's work absolutely and relative to that of men in their class, and
the availability of other sources of income, such as child labor or welfare
(Blumberg 1993, 16). As we have seen, women in Latin America in general
and in Mexico in particular work in both the informal and formal sectors
of the economy, though they commonly earn less than men (Berger and
Buvinic 1988; Ypeij 2000). Whether certain income-generating activities
are compatible with child care is heavily dependent on the household's
stage in its life cycle—whether there are children old enough to be sent
to work or help the female head in her economic activities or replace
her in her child-care responsibilities (e.g., González de la Rocha 1994).
Doña Consuelo, though only intermittently a head of household until
her sixties, engaged in a number of income-generating activities, and so
did, successively, each of her children. When she left her husband Juan
Carlos in 1972, her second-eldest son, then sixteen, accompanied her
and was the first to contribute resources to Consuelo's household. (Her
firstborn, Edgar, stayed behind in Mexico City.) Her daughter Carla,
then twelve, could replace her in caring for the younger children. As the
children grew they helped doña Consuelo in her informal-sector work,
and the three youngest daughters eventually sought employment in the
maquiladoras. Her children made economic contributions to the household even when she was living intermittently with Lorenzo and then
continually with Chano.

In general, the economic well-being or even survival of the poor in Mexico depends on diversification of their economic activities. Doña Consuelo has both worked for wages and been involved in the informal sector as a domestic servant, a garbage picker, an ambulant vendor of ceramics, and a seller of drinking water and sodas from her house. Like rural women elsewhere in Latin America who supplement their income by raising small livestock and poultry (Hecht 1985; see also Hart 1973; Peattie 1975), she has raised a variety of what she calls *mis animales*, including, sometimes consecutively and sometimes simultaneously, a cow, chickens, ducks, rabbits, goats, or pigs in the corners of her thirty-by-fifteen-meter house lot in Colonia Popular. For years she has sold from her house Coca-Colas supplied directly to her by the factory. Having secured a living space for herself by invading a lot in Colonia Popular, in 1990 she took part in another land invasion to secure a lot for one of her sons. By acquiring another house lot, doña Consuelo increased the family "wealth" and reinforced the obligation of at least one of her sons to help support her. In the pages that follow, I will present some anecdotes about doña Consuelo's work and a description of the invasion of lands in which she and other mothers resident in Colonia Popular took part in order to secure house lots for their offspring. These snapshots are representative of how many poor Mexican women make do, while often not appearing as "employed" or "economically active" on census lists.

Work Anecdotes

Consuelo worked on and off in a shrimp-packaging plant in Mexicali for a number of years from the late 1970s to the mid-1980s. The manager first put her to work sorting, but she could not do it, she said, "because I couldn't distinguish between the small, medium, and large ones." (It was almost a decade later that Manuel, her second-eldest son, took her for an eye exam and bought her the eyeglasses she had needed all her life. She was so thrilled with her new glasses that for some years she slept with them on, and this has become a family story.) Unable to sort shrimp, Consuelo was moved to shelling them. She remembers how cold her hands would get (the shrimp were packed in ice) and how her fingers would turn red and swell up. There was a union in the packaging plant, but because she only worked seasonally she was unable to join and was often treated as a scab by the other workers.

For two or three years, with the help of Anamaría and her niece Mónica, she sold ceramic ashtrays and statues that she bought downtown door-to-door in Colonia Popular and in nearby colonias. She always took a daughter or niece (one of her brother Felipe's daughters, when they were living with her) with her so they could write out the receipts or mark down what customers were paying if paying on an installment plan. Although able to make change and do simple sums, doña Consuelo had never been to school or learned to read or write. When she finally got a telephone in the mid-1990s, she would usually ask a daughter or granddaughter to place a call for her. She had telephone numbers written down on a sheet of paper hung above the shelf where the phone rested and claimed she knew whose number was whose, and in an emergency just pressed the corresponding numbers on the dial. If help was available, however, she avoided doing this.

She had done laundering and household chores for a family in Tepititlán, Jalisco, before moving on to Mexico City. In Mexico City she was initially employed as a live-in domestic servant; after marrying Juan Carlos, she worked alongside him in his bakery business. In the 1980s she was a servant in a wealthy colonia several kilometers from Colonia Popular and then worked for some years as a cook in a local country club. Several times I accompanied her to the nearby dump (now closed) where, with the aid of one or more of her four youngest daughters and occasionally a niece, she gathered cast-off clothing. Some of these discarded clothes went into the family wardrobe, but most were washed in the manually operated machine in front of her house, which was filled with water from a garden hose attached to the one faucet on the lot. Then Consuelo would iron them, fold them, box them, and have one of her sons drive the boxes over to the bus station to be sent to her daughter Carla, then living in Mexico City. Carla would sell them in the vast, infamous Tepito street market and return half the earnings to her mother on her occasional visits back to Mexicali.

Obtaining Property

A few families in the colonia have augmented the family's property by invading lands in order to acquire a lot for a son or a daughter, and Consuelo is among them. This was especially the case when Colonia Nueva Oportunidad was established, although efforts to acquire lots sometimes reached as far afield as San Quentín. Usually it was the woman of the household, with some help from her husband, if she had one, who undertook this effort (see Massolo 1992). Since it was illegal to own more than one property in a squatter settlement, the new property was solicited in the name of (and for the benefit of) one of the household's offspring. Married couples, including those married by common law, were given preference in acquiring lots in a squatter settlement and so were sons or daughters supporting a parent. This means of accumulation was cut off when Ernesto Ruffo of the PAN assumed the governorship of Baja California in 1992 and made illegal any future land invasions. Instead, preplanned housing tracts with services—known in Mexico as *fraccionamientos*—were set up. Since a certain minimum income is required to obtain a lot in a fraccionamiento, the very poorest no longer have the hope of obtaining one.

In 1990 doña Consuelo took part in the land invasions that led to the eventual establishment of Colonia Nueva Oportunidad and thereby acquired a lot that came to be titled in the name of Francisco, one of her married sons. Don Nato, a brickmaker living in Colonia Popular, also acquired a lot for his daughter there. Two other women from Colonia Popular, Teresa and Socorro, a comadre of doña Consuelo, also took part in the invasion. The process required much endurance: a daily presence on the invaded lot was required, and each invader, or *colono*, had to take a turn standing watch in case the police came to dislodge them. Teresa and Socorro were unable to fulfill the constant-presence requirement because of competing economic responsibilities and lack of the aid of offspring, and when the colonos were transferred from the site they had originally invaded to another site, they were not considered qualified to receive a lot. One of the criteria for assigning lots was that the recipient be either a couple or woman with offspring, none of whom had other properties in their names. Of the women from Colonia Popular who took part in the invasion, only doña Consuelo had a married son who qualified at that time.

The original area invaded I will call Colonia Primer Paso. I accompanied Socorro, Teresa, and Consuelo there many times and stayed overnight with one or another of them on several occasions. Below are entries from my field notes that give some idea of the work they had to do to acquire a lot there.

Tuesday, February 13, 1990
"Yesterday Doña Consuelo, carrying her granddaughter, son Manuel's youngest child, with her, and I went to Colonia Primer Paso, about 3 kilometers from Colonia Popular. First we took the bus a kilometer or so down the highway. We got off at some green buildings and entered the fields beside them, crossing through a barbed-wire fence, to begin our approximately 1 and 1/2-kilometer walk to the new colonia. You can see the cardboard shacks from the highway.

"There are 1,500 lots in the new colonia, I learned. The lots are about 150 square meters, about half the size of those in Colonia Popular which are about 300 square meters.

"Doña Consuelo and I walked past Teresa's lot, next to Socorro's. Teresa's eldest son in Mexicali was there. He and three other young men were cooking over a fire in the yard when we arrived about 12:30 p.m. We went to the next street and turned down it, passing two cardboard huts before arriving at Doña Consuelo's. Next to Doña Consuelo's house, to the north, Don Nato has his little abode, build of scrap-wood, as is hers. He has no property but hopes to acquire a lot for his only child, a daughter.

"Doña Consuelo has a small sofa, a full sized bed, and two small tables in her about 3 x 3-meter room, constructed mainly of cargo pallets and roofed with a plastic tarpaulin. There is a picture of the Virgin of Guadalupe on the west wall above a small table. Before we leave Colonia Primer Paso, Doña Consuelo lights a candle to the Virgin, crossing herself and her granddaughter.

"Doña Consuelo always left a candle burning in front of the picture before returning to Colonia Popular. Once she asked me if I thought a fire would start. I suggested putting the candle, contained in a glass container, into another, larger glass container so that if it fell it would burn out. Doña Consuelo did so but said "*La Virgen cuida*," (i.e., the Virgin would not let a fire get started).

"We had come because Consuelo's *manzana* (a square block) had guard duty today. Consuelo thought she had to be there from 1 to 3 p.m.; actually the watches are for 3 hours and this one was from 12 to 3. At about 1 we walked down her street and continued on to the next block, passing two little makeshift stores on the way. Then we turned left and walked two blocks east to the rudimentary guardhouse. Six other women were there, as well as two adult men and two young men and seven children, all under 6 years of age, including Doña Consuelo's granddaughter, still in arms. One of the young men placed himself by the gateway where he lowered the plastic ribbon attached to a post to permit the cars given permission to enter to pass into the colonia.

"Only one car was not permitted entry. The young man challenged two others, but the older men recognized them and told him to let them pass. A woman driving a truck passed by the guardhouse and said a lawyer would be coming, would say he was the *abogado* (lawyer), and to let him pass.

"More than 20 cars, pickup trucks, and vans were permitted into the new colonia in the hour and a half I was there. These included two vans bringing children back from schools in other colonias, a pickup truck which came to pick up garbage, and a truck selling 5-gallon plastic bottles of drinking water. A *pipa* (water truck) also circulates in the new colonia, leaving washing water in the barrels each colono has set up right outside her/his lot. . . .

"Ramón, Doña Consuelo's son, is now working in the carrot-packaging factory, which has reopened. Donã Consuelo is earning 10 thousand pesos [about $4.50 at that time] a day for preparing food for the administrators of the carrot-packaging plant. A señora brings her the food, and Doña Consuela prepares it at her house in Colonia Popular, then carries it to the plant. Doña Consuelo usually stays overnight on her new lot, as someone must be there to claim possession. Fridays she takes her daughter Anamaría, and Anamaría's cousin Caro or Monica (daughters of Consuelo's brother Felipe) to stay with her. During the week they stay in Colonia Popular, since it is closer to their school.

"Doña Consuelo comes back to Colonia Popular in the morning to make the five lunches for her sons (usually tacos, wrapped in aluminum foil), she tells the women while we are on guard duty. She must make food for her son Manuel as well, she explains to me, since his wife has hurt her arm. Then she makes lunch for the carrot-packaging plant people. She also makes meals for her ex-husband Chano (who pays her for doing this, she sometimes says). Sometimes Anamaría and La Muñeca do this."

Thursday, February 15, 1990

"Teresa and I go to Colonia Primer Paso together and stop by to visit Doña Consuelo. While Doña Consuelo heats water for the coffee over the stove made of an empty metal barrel—the same one she had cooked on when first arriving in Colonia Popular, she told me—Teresa tells me about the leader of the invasion. He is the organizer for the Union of Colonias Populares (UCP). She names four or five of the colonias that he had helped establish previous to Colonia Primer Paso. 'He gives the orders. If he tells people they must be on their lots, they stay on their lots, or their lots can be taken away,' Teresa says, Doña Consuelo agreeing. 'And no excuses are accepted.'

"Tomorrow, Doña Consuelo tells us, she will walk to the colonia where her mother lives (about 2 kilometers from Colonia Popular) to make lunch for her mother in the morning. She will make her son's lunches tonight and the girls will put it in burritos in the morning. Then Doña Consuelo will return to Colonia Popular—she hopes to spend two hours in the dump from 9:30 or 10 a.m. Then she will do some ironing, and then carry some clothes to wash back to Primer Paso. She will wash them by hand, to have a presence on her new lot. This she tells us about her schedule for tomorrow. She invites us to come to her lot (in Colonia Primer Paso) about 3 p.m. day after tomorrow to have *tripas* (cow intestines, fried and usually served in corn tortillas, as a taco)."

Saturday, February 17, 1990

"Last night I stayed in Colonia Primer Paso with Doña Consuelo. Doña Consuelo, Anamaría, Monica [a daughter of Consuelo's brother Felipe, who lives with Doña Consuelo], and I walked to the colonia about 2:30 p.m., carrying the salsa Doña Consuelo had made, a bowl of cut cabbage, a bag of clothes Doña Consuelo planned to wash, and other things, first walking down the highway, then entering through the barbed wire fence to walk across the fields.

"It was very cold and windy; Doña Consuelo was afraid that if we cooked outside there might be a fire. This week someone's house had caught fire and the man who had been in it was in the hospital badly burned, Doña Consuelo relates. She expressed her worry to Don Nato, who invited us inside his house next door where he has a stove made of a barrel with a chimney made of a pipe to carry the smoke outside. Doña Consuelo, at his invitation, put the beans on to cook, and a pot of water for coffee. . . .

"Doña Consuelo, Anamaría and Monica and I slept (except me, unused to sleeping with so many people at once, though I napped) in the one bed in the one-room house, crosswise on the blankets covering it, as the girls sleep at home in Colonia Popular: Anamaría, her two cousins, La Muñeca, and Rosario all on one mattress on the floor. The bed was rather uncomfortable, since it was made of cargo pallets with the pieces of wood constantly hitting some bone in one's body!

"They got up at 6:30 a.m., and Doña Consuelo began to wash the clothes she had brought. She had collected these clothes in the dump. Presently I am at her house in Colonia Popular writing up these notes, while she irons these clothes. She plans to sell them door-to-door in Colonia Primer Paso tomorrow.

"Doña Consuelo's sons did not help her bring the building materials for the house and furniture to Colonia Primer Paso. She paid a neighbor in Colonia Popular to do this, giving him 10 thousand pesos per trip. Nor did they help her build the cargo-pallet house; she and her daughter Lorena did this. She defended her sons when I pointed out that her daughters were always at work in the house while her sons were lying around watching television. She said that this was because they supported the household (i.e., contributed money from their work). One of them did work full-time, and another sporadically, and another hardly at all. When Consuelo's two daughters (Anamaría and La Muñeca) and the two nieces who lived with her (Caro and Monica) began to work in the maquiladoras they were still expected to do the clothes washing, food preparation, dishes, etc. From examples like these, also observable in other houses in Colonia Popular, I am tempted to conclude that daughters are 'over-socialized' into a nurturing role while men are 'undersocialized,' learning to expect service from women and full liberty to behave as they wish as long as they are providing (some) economic resources—and this despite the fact that women may be providing economic resources as well.

"About 5:30 p.m. Socorro, Doña Consuelo and I returned from Primer Paso, walking to Colonia Popular. Doña Consuelo carried a bundle of clothes I could hardly lift, balanced on her head. She is 52, about 5' 2" though squarely built, probably weighs about 150 pounds. She has had 13 children and one miscarriage. (I do not know where she gets the strength!) Later Socorro helped her, carrying the bundle on her head for the last kilometer. Socorro said she once carried piles of newspapers on her head, to deliver to houses. She has had 8 children, is also about 5' 2", and very thin, probably weighing less than 100 pounds."

Sunday, February 18, 1990
"The weekly meeting had begun about 3 p.m. The leader and another man spoke from the back of the truck to an audience of about 200 people. He read two articles concerning the colonia and his role in it which had come out in the newspaper. Later Teresa told me they had paid 700 thousand pesos so the newspaper would publish these articles.

"Afterwards the other man read a list of rules for the guards. Then the leader read them again, asking people to vote on each point by raising their hands. All points were accepted with no discussion: that each lot would send a member to stand watch; that any member of the family could be sent to comply with guard duty; that the watch would last three hours; that men would stand watch during the night and women during the day; that there was to be no drinking in the colonia until it was regularized and if anyone was caught drinking on watch the bottle would be taken away and the person would be punished (what the punishment would be was not mentioned).

"The leader added that it was better if the women left the children at home while on watch. (There was some murmuring.) But, he said, if they had no one to care for their children, then they could bring them along.

"The leader pointed to a small white structure behind the audience which had printed on it in blue hand-written letters: Consultorio (Clinic) and Cuidado Médico (Medical Care). He told the assembled people that doctors from the university would be arriving to give care on Mondays, Wednesdays, and Fridays from 9 a.m. to 12.

"Then he pointed to an office, to one side of where he was speaking, also a small, temporary structure. People should begin to bring their documents (he did not explain what these were, but people seemed to understand their birth certificates) and two photographs there any day beginning Monday, from 2 to 5 p.m. They would be given a credential permitting them to enter the colonia. It would cost 15 thousand pesos.

"People began protesting at this: that the cost was great if they had many family members. It was decided on the spot with little discussion that only the person in whose name the lot would be would be required to get this credential.

"The leader expressed his opinion that after reading the newspaper articles he did not believe the people would be removed to another site— a rumor that had been circulating for the past couple of weeks. He also mentioned that Monday and Tuesday a census was going to be taken of who was living on what lot.

"The meeting lasted only about half an hour."

About two months later Colonia Primer Paso was closed down, and the colonos were removed to a nearby stretch of land, parts of which the brickmakers had used. Doña Consuelo was assigned a lot and had to transport the water barrels, tables, and wooden pallets to the new colonia, Nueva Oportunidad. She had originally wanted to put the lot in the name of her son Carlos, explaining that it was he who provided the most support to the household (he was the only full-time worker), but Carlos had no birth certificate and was unmarried. Her son Francisco therefore went to live there with his wife and their two children, and the lot was registered in his name. In 1999 he sold it and bought one in Colonia Popular, about a block from his mother's house. For doña Consuelo, acquiring the lot in Colonia Nueva Oportunidad had meant walking back and fourth, about a six-kilometer round trip, for some months, usually carrying bundles of clothing, often weighing fifty pounds or more, to wash by hand in Primer Paso. Then she took them back to Colonia Popular to iron (there was, of course, no electricity in the new colonia), then once again back to Primer Paso to sell them to fellow colonos. She also arranged to make lunches for her sons and earn a bit by making food for the administrators of the carrot-packaging plant. Sometimes her son Felipe stayed at the house in Colonia Primer Paso, but she did not want to burden him with such a long walk (about three and a half kilometers) to work.

Conclusions

I am aware of only one work (Massolo 1992) that underscores the predominant role of women in the invasion of lands for the establishment of squatter settlements—this in Mexico City. Nonetheless, women's activities in organizations pressing for the acquisition of services such as electricity, sewerage, and potable water, and in helping in the construction of self-built housing in the squatter settlements has been documented both for Mexico and elsewhere in Latin America (see, for example, Chant 1987; Craske 1993; Díaz 1988; Moser 1987a, 1987b; Vélez-Ibáñez 1983).

From the above anecdotes it is apparent that doña Consuelo's economic portfolio was diverse and often spontaneously generated, including anything that could provide income or tie offspring to her to ensure their support in her old age. As a poor woman, she is not alone. Many women in Colonia Popular raised chickens to supplement the family diet, and some raised rabbits. Many went to the dump to collect articles for family use, including discarded clothing, magazines (worth about a third of the daily wage back then), household utensils, mattresses, furniture, and other items, including canned foods discarded from the supermarkets because of damage to the cans. Several women invaded Colonia Primer Paso in order to secure lots for their offspring. The invasion of lots in squatter settlements is no longer an option for the poor, and the planned communities designed to replace them are beyond their reach. Transnational migration thus becomes more appealing as a way of generating income.

CHAPTER 7

Anamaría's Story

The story of the migration of Anamaría, Consuelo's daughter, begins with her mother-in-law Miriam's and her husband Roberto's stories. I first heard them from Joana, one of Miriam's brothers' wives (see genealogy 2), who had migrated to Waters, Arizona, with her husband, Jaime. Joana had worked since 1999 for a company that laundered sheets and towels for hotels throughout Arizona and Nevada. When I first interviewed her on one of her weekly return trips to Colonia Popular in 2002, she was interested in getting a union into the plant, and this had been achieved by the time I first visited Waters in 2003. Joana's husband had been the first to go to Arizona, where he played with a band he had organized in a town on an Indian reservation. Attending one of his group's concerts were friends of his and Miriam's from Mexicali who lived in Waters. Miriam was the first to go on a permanent basis, having been invited by these friends through her brother. She no longer socializes with these friends, however. Jaime, Joana, and their five sons—the latter intermittently—then followed.

Miriam's Story
Miriam was born in 1955 in her father's hometown of Hermosillo, Sonora, but brought up on an ejido (a collectively owned farm, sometimes individually tenured, sometimes worked in common) near Mexicali. She first came to Waters in 1996. After working for six months in a restaurant, first as a dishwasher then as a preparer, dishing out the food on plates, she had moved to her present job in the local hospital's kitchen and cafeteria. She began as a dishwasher and now works as a "runner," taking the food trays to patients. (By 2009 she had worked there twelve years.) In 2003 there

were only three other Spanish-speakers in the hospital, all women—a Mexican-American from Texas, a Guatemalan, and a Peruvian. In 2004 a woman from Michoacán was hired.

Miriam had never worked anywhere else in the United States, although she has half siblings born in the United States and living in California (see genealogy 2). She knew the family that networked her into Waters from the ejido outside Mexicali to which her mother, separated from her father, had moved when Miriam was a child. The family with whom Miriam had contacts had first lived in Poston, Arizona. (The father of the family was a field hand, working in agriculture in the Poston area. After receiving Special Agricultural Workers' amnesty under the provisions of IRCA, he arranged papers for his wife and offspring. They then moved elsewhere in Arizona.)

All three of Miriam's two sons and one daughter had worked in Waters, though only Roberto, the eldest, had chosen to settle there—at least semipermanently. Her daughter Gloria had come, accompanied by her husband, shortly after Miriam arrived and had stayed for two years. Gloria had worked as a housekeeper in a local hotel and her husband as a cook in the same restaurant where Miriam was then employed. The couple had eventually returned to Mexicali. Miriam's youngest son, Jonathan, had come later and worked in construction. He too had returned to Mexicali, where he later married. In 2007 Gloria and her husband again joined Miriam to work in Waters. In that year Miriam moved out of Roberto's and Anamaría's household and with Gloria and her husband put a down payment on another house. (Because Miriam had a Social Security card, she could negotiate the buying of a house. She had done so in 2001 for, and with the help of, Anamaría and Roberto.)

Miriam's work in Mexicali was more white-collar than her work in Arizona. She was trained as a nurse's aide and worked for a while nursing private patients. Immediately before establishing herself in Waters, she had held two jobs: in the morning she worked in an import office, and in the afternoon she was a receptionist in a doctor's office. She told me that if she had had a chance for further education she would like to be a nurse. She was studying English with a tutor who came twice a week. Her loss of status through migration was not unusual. The homogenization of class status in terms of jobs taken in the United States as compared to those held in Mexico, and the overall tendency of workers with higher status in Mexico to take lower-status jobs in the United States, has been noted in the migration literature (e.g., Wilson 2004). Immigrants from underdeveloped countries tend to take unskilled and semiskilled jobs in the Western industrialized countries to which they migrate (Castles and Kosack 1973), and the undocumented from Mexico in the United States have generally been concentrated in low-skilled jobs considered "unattractive, demeaning, dangerous, dirty or comparatively poorly paid" (Gómez-Quiñones 1981, 21).

Miriam's mother and father, long separated and remarried, both lived in the United States. Her mother, married to a Mexican-American, lived in El Centro, California. Her father, a legal resident, lived in San Ysidro, California. Of Miriam's thirteen living siblings and half siblings, the five who were the children of her stepfather were born and lived in the United States. Besides her brother, Joana's husband, who also lived in Waters, she had two sisters in El Centro, a sister in Heber, a brother in Brawley, and a brother in San Diego, all in California. She has visited all these U.S.-based siblings, and they have all come to visit her in Waters. Her mother has also come to visit.

Miriam and her offspring had lived in the same colonia as doña Consuelo, across the street and two houses up, from the establishment of the colonia in 1983 until 1995. Then Miriam had sold her lot there and bought a cheaper one in Colonia Nueva Oportunidad, where doña Consuelo had acquired a lot for her son Francisco. Miriam had sold the much larger lot in Colonia Popular in part to help pay off debts, but she also preferred Colonia Nueva Oportunidad because it had more stores, a pharmacy, a medical clinic, and *tortillerías*—things missing in Colonia Popular. She felt that since Nueva Oportunidad was at least ten times larger than Colonia Popular, she could live with less intrusion into her private life than in Colonia Popular, where all the neighbors knew one another and gossiped about what everyone was doing. She planned to sell the house and lot in Colonia Nueva Oportunidad as well, though, as soon as her daughter received her government-sponsored housing. Miriam reasoned that she does not plan to live permanently in Mexicali again, and if she went for a visit she could stay with her daughter.

Miriam had had a border-crossing card for many years. The first time she came to Waters she had a residence permit acquired through her second husband, who had received SAW amnesty and was living in Calexico. During this time she also acquired a valid U.S. Social Security card. The residence permit carried the proviso that she could not return to Mexico until her green card was issued. She did go back to Mexicali, however, and when she tried to cross the border to return to Waters, her residence permit was taken away. She then bought a fake green card from an INS officer for seven hundred dollars. When she tried to cross into the United States with it, it too was taken away, and she was fingerprinted and photographed. After this experience, she remained in Mexicali, in her house in Colonia Nueva Oportunidad, for two years. Meanwhile, Anamaría and Roberto continued living in Waters.

When next she tried to cross the border, this with a coyote in San Luís Río Colorado, Sonora, she was caught and deported. She tells me the immigration officer in charge of her deportation bought her a hamburger—for which she remembers him fondly—and entered into the computer only five years of "punishment," during which she could not apply for papers to cross into or reside in the United States. This was added to five years of previous "punishment" for attempting to use false papers to cross. When his shift was over, a woman immigration officer replaced him, and this officer changed the "punishment" period from five to twenty years, making a total of twenty-five years that Miriam could not legally apply for any kind of papers to enter the United States. The kindness of the first officer and the meanness of the second have become part of the family's migration lore.

Some weeks later Miriam successfully crossed the border from Mexicali, navigating two canals in small boats, to arrive in Calexico. She spoke of her terror at getting into the small boats, both loaded with so many people that she feared they would sink—all this in the middle of a dark night. In Calexico she stayed in a safe house for several days and narrowly escaped being deported again by *la migra* (the immigration authorities) by pretending to be a nurse taking care of an elder person living in the house. From Calexico the same coyote took her to her sister's house in Heber. From Heber, her sister—a U.S. citizen—helped her to return to Waters, driving the car in front of the one Miriam was in while in cell-phone contact to make sure that the immigration checkpoints were not open.

When Miriam returned to Waters, she moved back in with Anamaría, Roberto, and their three children, who were living in a rented apartment. Soon afterward, they bought a four-bedroom house together, a house badly in need of renovations that Roberto, with the help of his friends, has successfully carried out. Miriam once considered building her own house in the large backyard: she complained that she had no privacy in her wing of the house. Her grandchildren constantly arrived to see her. Eventually, as we have seen, when Gloria and her husband returned to Waters, she put a down payment on another house nearby and moved there with them.

When I first interviewed Miriam in Colonia Popular in 1990, Roberto was only fifteen years old and attending secondary school. Miriam told me then that her mother and father had separated when she was two years old, and her mother had brought her and three of her siblings from Hermosillo, Sonora, to Mexicali in 1958. She had begun working at the age of twelve, cleaning houses. She finished secondary school, however, and had taken both a secretarial course and a course to become a nurse's aide. She nursed in private houses. She had been working for three years for a company that bought and sold industrial equipment.

Miriam had remarried by then, and her second husband worked as a welder, constructing wrought-iron fences and other wrought-iron structures under private contract. In 1981 she had received a border-crossing card and crossed to Calexico once a week to do shopping. She had recently lost this card and was applying for a replacement at the time I interviewed her almost fifteen years ago. Her first husband had gone to the United States with a green card (his parents also had green cards). Miriam did not know where he was. Her father, who also had a green card, was living, along with two of his sisters and one of his brothers, in the San Diego area.

When I asked her at that time where she would most like to live, Miriam replied, "San Diego." She has never lived there, however, despite the presence of her father, aunts, uncles, and cousins there. Now in Waters, she said that she would prefer to live in El Centro, where her mother lives, or if she could support herself there, even more in Ensenada, where her mother came from.

Roberto's Story

When I interviewed Miriam's son Roberto about his migration history in September 2003, he answered in a combination of Spanish and very good English. The following is an account of his and his family's arrival in his words:

"I arrived in Waters April 2, 1997. My mom was here and my sister and my brother-in-law. They got here in February, and they got an apartment, and I came to visit and stayed. I still wasn't together with Anamaría.

"I had worked in Coachella, near Indio, California. I was working with a guy in construction from February to March 15, 1997. Then I went back to Mexicali, and then I came here. I was living in Mecca and went to work two or three miles away in Indio. We were building an apartment, a house—a great big house. I was helper of everything. He [the man for whom he worked] did everything—electricity, plumbing, drywall, windows, doors, he did everything. I met him in Mexicali, and he told me he needed a helper. I was working in Price Club in Mexicali when he told me to come.

"I worked about one year in Price Club. I was supervisor of the cash registers. Before that in an electronics factory in Mexicali—another year. Before that I was working at—I don't remember because I had so many jobs—in a car wash in Mexicali. In a factory making spoilers for cars.

"[In Waters] I began in Taco Taco [a fast-food, quasi-Mexican restaurant whose name, along with the names of respondents' workplaces, I have changed]—cooking—until about September, October 1997. And I was working in a car wash at the same time: 8 to 4 in the car wash, 6 to 1 or 2 a.m. in Taco Taco—so I could buy my first car here. A friend of mine who was in jail sold me his car.

"Then I went to Mexicali and got to know Anamaría about September. I stayed for two months and came back here and started working at Morgan's [a working- and middle-class restaurant selling American food] in January 1998. [Didn't you work in a factory?] [I know this from Anamaría.] Started June or July of 1998 until September of the same year because the factory closed, closed down. I quit Morgan's in August because I thought Wilkinson's [the factory] was better because of the health insurance. Then I went to Yahoo Boats—and I began buffering boats, and I was working at the same time in Taco Taco for two months. I was working in both places. Then in November '99—it was in February '99 that I went to the auto body shop—they paid me better, getting the cars ready to paint them. My work ended there. Instead of forty hours they gave me twenty, twenty-five, so I decided to quit. Then I returned to Morgan's in July '99, and Rogelio was born in August. August 8. Then I went to work in a bar [he names it] also cooking, for five months. Then they cut my hours. I was working in Morgan's 7 a.m. to 2 p.m. and in the bar 3 p.m. to 9 or 9:30 p.m. when they closed. Since June '99 I have stayed with Morgan's."

When I returned to visit in July 2004, Roberto had quit his job in Morgan's and gone to work on the vast sewerage system being constructed in Waters, among other things installing manholes. He had gotten this job on the recommendation of the husband of one of Anamaría's friends—a friend she had made at Taco Taco, where they both worked. This friend and her husband, her sister and her sister's husband, were also from Mexicali, though Anamaría had met her and her sister for the first time at work. Roberto was still working on the sewerage system in 2008, and his employer had offered to sponsor him for a green card.

"[My brother Jonathan] was single. He came twice, first in '97, and then he went to Mexicali and returned here in 2000. He worked in Morgan's, the same time as I did. He worked making block walls, he worked in the hospital, doing construction. He worked in the factory along with me. It was he who got me the job in Morgan's. They took him on fifteen, twenty days before me—I started in December or January. He hasn't worked anywhere else in the United States. I haven't seen him in eighteen months. He is living with a woman and has a child with her—in his house in INFONAVIT [he names the neighborhood the housing complex is in]. An aunt gave him the INFONAVIT house. He works in a factory right now, in Mexicali.

"[My sister Gloria] was living here and invited me to come and stay to help pay the rent. I was their [Gloria and her husband's] roommate for eleven months until they decided to move back to Mexicali. They live in [Colonia] Orizaba right now, but they have a house in Xochimilco as well. They got here because of my mom. She moved here with a friend of hers in December '96. [I know] because she and I were living together in Mexicali. She invited my sister first. My mom, my sister, my brother-in-law, and Ricardo [his mother's brother's son], and I lived together, and my other cousins and my aunt and I. People were always coming and going. My mom went to Mexicali for almost a year and a half as well. Only I stayed here, except for one and a half months in '97. I married in May of '98. Fifteen days after we got married Anamaría and I crossed—we got married so we could get a passport for [Román], this little guy [a son Anamaría had before beginning her relationship with Roberto, who treats him as his own]. I have had a local passport [a border-crossing card] since I was five years old. We fixed everything, and they [Anamaría and Román] got a Mexican passport and visas to cross, in Tijuana.

"Where would I like to live? In Ensenada. It isn't big, nor is it small. It has a beach. Nice climate. I have always liked Ensenada. Then, it is close to the border, to Tijuana, to San Diego. I am accustomed to the border. Because of the work here, I do not go."

Earlier Roberto had complained that there was little to do in Waters, less than in Mexicali—fewer movie theaters, fewer places to go. His maternal grandmother was originally from Ensenada, and, as we have seen, his mother also would like to live there.

Both Anamaría and Roberto have crossed to Waters with border-crossing cards and a permit to go farther north. Several times they have had someone going to Mexicali turn in their permits so that they appeared to have returned to Mexico. They did not do this the last time and therefore cannot return to Mexico because they will not be allowed back in the United States.

Anamaría's Migration and Work

Anamaría was born in 1976 in Mexicali, the child of doña Consuelo's second husband, Lorenzo. Anamaría has three children: the eldest, Román, born in Mexicali in 1997, Luís, born in Waters in 1999, and Lizbet, born in Waters in 2001. She gave me the following account of her migration history in September 2003:

"I crossed the first time May 27, 1998. I crossed with my husband and my mother-in-law, all of us with local passports. We married May 15, 1998, and I crossed May 27 of the same year. We have been married five years now. We will have been together six years in November. I began working in a factory where they cleaned pieces of iron—I don't know what they were for. I worked only two months, only a little while, because they closed down the factory. Roberto was working there too. And then I didn't work because I became pregnant with Luís. For about two years I didn't work. Then I worked in housekeeping at [a tourist hotel] for about a year.

"After that I started to work in Taco Taco—now for almost four years—but I asked for a leave of about five months to go to Mexicali. I went in 2001—Lizbet had already been born. I had the three children with me. I went in July and returned the day after Christmas. Román and I had local passports, and we came with my brother-in-law—Rosario's husband. He worked in a car wash here for some months—I'm not sure how long. He had a local passport too. He lived with Roberto, left to live with some other muchachos (boys, young men) when I returned. [Notably, Rosario's husband is not from Colonia Popular. The network ties that facilitated his temporary migration to Waters were the result of his being married to Anamaría's sister, thus becoming friends with Anamaría's husband.] "The other two children—Luís and Lizbet—crossed back with an American friend who said they were her sister-in-law's children."

Anamaría told me that she would like to stay in Waters "because it is very difficult in Mexicali—economically. And apart from that I like it better here. It is more peaceful (*tranquilo*) here. There, it seems to me, there are more drugs. It is very ugly there." Drug use has increasingly become a problem in Mexicali in general and in Colonia Popular in particular.

In the 1980s the drug of choice was marijuana, and most men in their twenties had tried it. By 2000 harder drugs, including crack and amphetamines, were being used by young people, and glue sniffing was common among boys as young as eleven or twelve. As far as I know, drug use was mainly a male pastime and a burden to both mothers and wives. Some young women now seem to be engaging in marijuana use.

Anamaría had found her work at Taco Taco through a bilingual Jehovah's Witness woman she met in Waters who helped her fill out an application form. When I asked her how she was treated at work, she replied: "The manager is really nice. He is American. He lived in Tijuana, [but] he doesn't speak Spanish. He helps us a lot. For example, he shows us what is misspelled in English, he gives us the chance to learn more. For example if we cannot go to work, he lets us off. Things like that." Anamaría tells me that all the kitchen help is Mexican, but the cashiers are American. When Anamaría invited doña Consuelo and me to meet her at Taco Taco for lunch, this division of labor was obvious. Anamaría earns $6.75 an hour. Her hours are highly erratic, and she never knows more than a few days ahead of time when she will be called in to work from four to ten hours a day.

Anamaría's friends included a Mexican-American woman born in California and María and her sister Paula, both from Mexicali but met in Waters. Two of these women were her co-workers at Taco Taco. The other close friend, Lisa, became the wife of a young man from Colonia Popular, a man who had been one of Roberto's friends in Mexicali. Lisa had worked with Anamaría and Roberto in the iron factory. By 2004 Paula's husband's brother had arrived with his wife Jeanette, and Anamaría was becoming friends with her as well.

Before coming to Waters, Anamaría had worked in a maquiladora in Mexicali for five years. "We did all kinds of work, packaging cosmetics, putting together books, packing stationery-store things—whatever came our way. La Muñeca [her sister] and Mónica [her cousin] also worked there, La Muñeca for seven or eight years, Mónica for about six. I was fifteen years old when I started, and I left when I was about twenty-one. I became pregnant when I was twenty, and Luís was born when I was twenty-one. I worked while I was pregnant until they gave me disability [pregnancy leave] when I was eight months pregnant."

When Anamaría was fifteen and Mónica was living in doña Consuelo's house, the two girls were trying to finish a bilingual secretarial course after both had finished secondary school in a nearby colonia (there is no secondary school in Colonia Popular). I gave doña Consuelo money so that they could go to school without working, but that arrangement lasted only a few months. Doña Consuelo sent them to work—there was never enough money in the household. When I returned to visit the colonia, where I often took my meals in doña Consuelo's house, I observed their routine. They would go to school, then to work in the maquiladora during the afternoon shift, then come home to wash their clothes (most often by hand) and sometimes serve their unmarried brothers dinner, and wash the dishes afterward. When I told Anamaría of this, she wanted me to tell Roberto, because he thought she had had it so easy as a child.

When I returned to Waters in March 2004, Roberto had stopped working as a cook and gotten a new job. The husbands of Anamaría's friends María and Paula have been working on the sewerage system almost since its initiation, with María's husband finding work there first, and María's husband recommended him for the job, according to Roberto. According to Anamaría, it was Paula's husband Juan who got Roberto the job, however. Paula's husband's brother, a recent arrival, also got work on the sewerage system through Juan, Anamaría points out. Roberto is ambivalent about his new job. He earns fifteen dollars an hour but only works five days a week. At Morgan's he was paid thirteen dollars an hour but earned more a week because he worked more hours. I asked him if he liked his work on the sewerage system better than cooking. "Both," he said, remarking, "I was a cook six years"—as though somewhat tired of it now.

Anamaría, who said she liked to cook, did all the cooking at home: Roberto had never cooked a meal in the house, she said.[1] She usually served him on a tray-table in the living room, as he watched television or a DVD. Their part of the house—three bedrooms, a large kitchen, and a living room—has three televisions: one in the boys' room, one in their bedroom, and one in the living room. They had a car, which Roberto drove, and a van, which Anamaría drove. (Roberto taught her to drive shortly after her arrival in Waters.) They live a number of miles from the business district in which they worked and went shopping, too far to walk, and there was little public transportation in Waters. Miriam had her own car, as well as a television in her bedroom and another in her small living room. None of these consumer goods were available to any of them as children in Mexicali, though by Roberto's and Anamaría's teen-age years they did have television in their parents' houses.

Anamaría's two youngest children are U.S. citizens by birth, while their mother, father, paternal grandmother, and eldest brother live in Waters without documents (see table 7 and genealogy 2). This mix of legal and undocumented children as members of the same family is quite common. Undocumented women often have children born in Mexico as well as children born in the United States (e.g., see Hirsch 2003, 251). Children born in Mexico and brought to the United States at an early age are often known to immigration scholars as the "1.5 generation" as opposed to children born in the United States, the second generation. Rumbaut (2007, 349) suggests that age at migration is an important influence in adaptation processes and distinguishes between the 1.75 generation (aged from birth to five); the 1.5 generation (aged six to twelve) and the 1.25 generation (aged thirteen to seventeen). Each generation will adapt to the destination society in different social and familial contexts.

Table 7. Anamaría's Children

Child	Year born	Where born
Román	1997	Mexicali (Colonia Popular)
Luís	1999	Waters, Arizona
Lizbet	2001	Waters, Arizona

One Thursday in March 2004

Miriam and I talked about an hour—out on the porch—last night. She often came home from work exhausted. The hospital needed more workers, she explained. The dishwasher was no longer there, so the food-service people now had to wash the dishes and do all the cleaning. There is a Mexican woman—the first other than Miriam—also in food services who has been working there about four months. She is from Michoacán, Miriam thinks. She believed that you had to have a Social Security card to get a job in the hospital. She had one that she got in Las Vegas once when she applied to immigrate and was given temporary status. This program is no longer in effect, she tells me. It lasted only two or three years, she thinks. She paid a lawyer at the time to file papers for her.

Miriam tells me about her boyfriends, met in Waters—one from El Salvador, who is now in Los Angeles, one from San Luís Río Colorado, Sonora, who is now in jail for killing a man and injuring his wife while driving while he was on drugs. Miriam sends him money occasionally. He is thirty-five, she forty-eight. She has dated many young men, she says, but there is no future in it. She can no longer get pregnant, and after a bit *"el hombre quiere ver su sangre"* (men want to see their blood). She would like to marry again, though. It would be her third marriage.

Reflections

Doña Consuelo spent her days and evenings during March 2004 in Waters embroidering her tortilla covers while sitting in front of the television in the living room, watching Mexican movies, in black and white, from the 1940s and 1950s, and an occasional color one from the 1960s. She knows the songs sung in them and sometimes sings along. Anamaría has a movie station in Spanish from their cable company. In the evenings, Consuelo sometimes watches novelas.

Just nine months ago she was on foot most of the day, cleaning and recleaning the kitchen, washing floors, vacuuming carpets, washing dishes, washing her clothes by hand because she does not know how to operate the automatic washing machine. Now she has pains in her back and high cholesterol, and the doctor has prohibited her from drinking coffee or soda or eating fats or eggs. She walks painfully slowly through Wal-Mart, where we go at least once a week, and through Home Depot, where Anamaría and Roberto went to buy paint for the boys' bedroom. I remember her as she walked daily the three kilometers to Colonia Primer Paso and back, carrying on her head at least forty pounds of clothing to be hand washed with water from barrels, so she that could have a presence during the invasion and acquire a lot for one of her offspring. One day she breaks down crying, saying that as much as she would like to help out, she no longer had the energy. That she felt completely useless, of value to nobody. By the end of 2007 she was dependent on her daughter-in-law and three Mexicali-based daughters to take care of her; at first she went to their houses to stay on a rotating basis, but because she missed her house, they agreed that each would stay with her there, a night at a time. Otherwise she would have been alone; after being beaten up by her ex-husband early in 2007, La Muñeca had moved to another colonia.

During a phone call in April 2005, Anamaría told me she had quit her job at Taco Taco when it began to get cold, in November of the previous year. She said Lizbet, her youngest, often got colds in the winter, and she wanted to stay home and take care of her. Roberto also wanted her to stay home to take care of the children instead of working. Initially, Anamaría took care of other people's children in her home. She earned two dollars an hour for each child and estimates she made almost two hundred dollars a week, more than her wages at Taco Taco. She did not feel she could charge more, given that the mothers were making the minimum wage. Anamaría is used to caring for children. Her nieces and nephews filled her mother's house in Colonia Popular at all hours of the day and sometimes overnight. She had always cared for babies and young children. I had never heard her yell at a child or seen her spank a child; she reprimanded them in a low voice, though she seldom hugged or kissed even her own children. That she and Roberto had a large back yard, filled with swings and more recently a trampoline, helped her in caring for the children. By March 2005, the number of children she cared for had dwindled, however, and she was back at work in Taco Taco; by late 2006 she had been made general manager of the kitchen in the local branch. She had shown herself submissive to Roberto's demand that she resume the role of mother, but their need for income had given her a reason to return. In both cases, she showed that she put family first, echoing the account of a Chicana cannery worker who, "by evoking the "traditional" family ideology—'my family comes first'—. . . could rationalize what to her seemed the nontraditional act of continuing to work. . . . " (Zavella 1991, 323). Nonetheless, it must be kept in mind that Anamaría had had a nontraditional upbringing in the sense that her mother doña Consuelo had worked through all her alliances with men. What may be traditional for the middle class is often not so for poor women.

Anamaría proudly told me that Román had been named student of the month in February 2005. I had bought the children some books while I was staying at their house, and Anamaría said that Roberto was now buying them books as well and that the school has also given books to Román, who had just finished first grade. His teacher had told her that he translates for other students who spoke only Spanish. He helped her learn English, Anamaría said. She would read to him out of one of his books and ask him to tell her when she mispronounced a word, and he would correct her: "No, this is the way to say it."

Conclusions

Miriam's account of her crossings without documents show the danger she faced both physically and emotionally. Her situation keeps her in the United States, and it also keeps Anamaría and Roberto there. All hope for a new amnesty that will permit them to travel back and forth to Mexico. As we have seen the increased costs of crossing the border are leading more and more of the undocumented to settle permanently in the United States. These costs are caused by increasing surveillance of the border through rising numbers in border patrol and use of military technology, the consequent higher prices of coyotes (human smugglers), and augmented border deaths as immigrants were diverted from traditional crossings to more inhospitable terrain. As a result more and more of the undocumented are settling permanently in the United States with fewer, if any, trips back home (Cornelius 2007; Inda 2006; Massey, Durand, and Malone 2003).

Miriam's brother Jaime—Roberto's uncle—and his wife and sons have kept their border-crossing permits current and typically return to Colonia Popular for weekends.

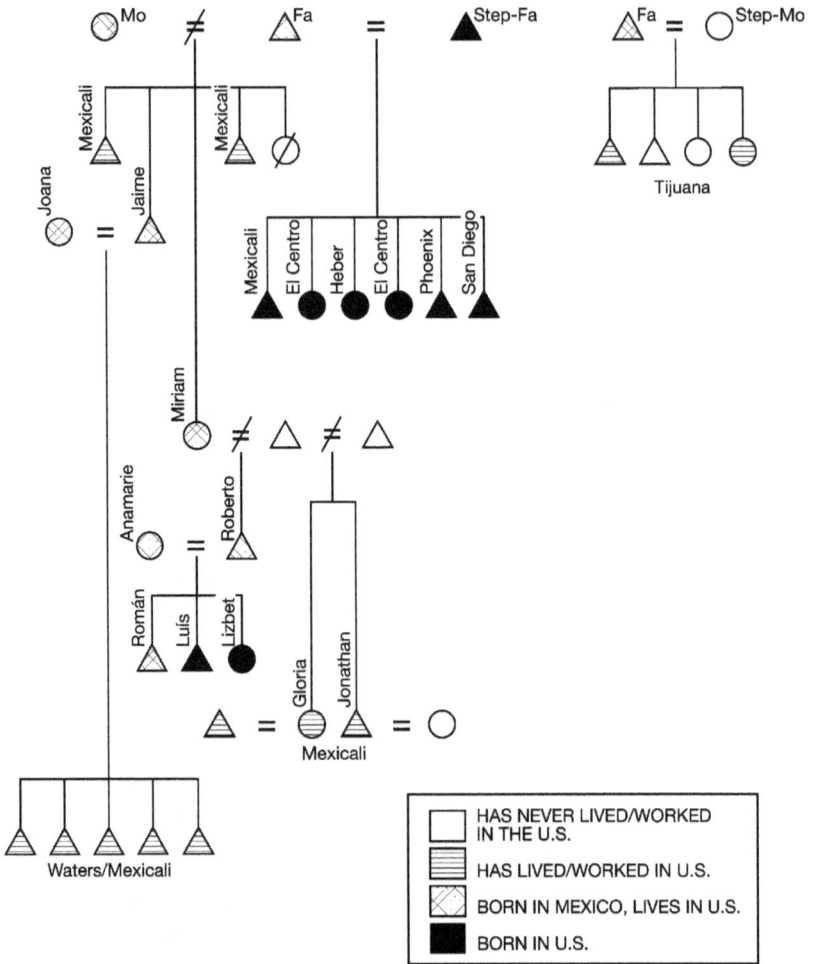

Genealogy 2. Roberto's family

Anamaría and Roberto, unable to cross back and forth to Mexico, remain in close contact with happenings in Colonia Popular because of doña Consuelo's visits and Jaime and Joana's weekend returns there. Consuelo, Joana, and Jaime thus function as transnational links between place of origin and place of settlement, though, as she has aged, Consuelo has found it increasingly difficult to play this role. Nonetheless, in the summer of 2006, when La Muñeca still lived in Colonia Popular with her mother, Anamaría and Roberto sent their two U.S.-born children to stay with Consuelo, thus strengthening transnational ties as the children got to know their aunts, uncles, and cousins. Joana and Jaime took them there and brought them back.

Most of Anamaría's and Roberto's friends and acquaintances in Waters are from Mexicali, and almost all, with the exception of Roberto's cousins and two friends from the colonia, were met at their work sites in Waters. This common origin in Mexicali has provided the basis for initiating conversation and establishing commonalities of experience and milieu.

CHAPTER 8

Anamaría's and Roberto's Networks

Of the fourteen in-depth interviews I retrieved in Waters—in September 2003 and March 2004—four involved Anamaría, her husband, her mother-in-law, and her husband's aunt by marriage, and eight were with people or their relatives connected to Anamaría and Roberto though their work sites, principally Anamaría's. Some of the women who worked at Taco Taco with Anamaría became her best friends in Waters, and their husbands became friends of Roberto: this was their local adaptation network, and in it initially weak ties became stronger. Anamaría's and Roberto's networks are somewhat segregated, though they occasionally see their friends as couples (table 8). Anamaría sees most of her female friends without their husbands or Roberto being present, and Roberto sees many of his friends without their wives being present. As will be seen, this social adaptation is very different from that of Irma and Raúl, who see their friends almost exclusively as couples and socialize with them more often than Anamaría or Roberto do at home with their friends. Three of the couples with whom Anamaría and Roberto socialize most are from Mexicali, though they met for the first time in Waters.

Julio, the husband of one of Anamaría's friends and the father of another, became an interview subject when I went to their apartment to interview the women and he made it known that he, as head of household, would be the spokesperson for his family. Graciela, his wife, and Soriana, his daughter, were present during the interview, however, and Soriana especially often added information. After the interview was over, Soriana talked at length about her recent marriage and hopes for the future in the United States. Interviewing Julio about his migration history was valuable

Table 8. Members of Anamaría's and Roberto's Networks at Destination

Anamaría's Network		Roberto's Network
At least one member of the couple known in Mexicali		
Lisa (Arizona)	=	RIGO (Colonia Popular)
JOANA (Colonia Popular)	=	Jaime (maternal uncle) (Colonia Popular)
		JOANA AND JAIME'S FIVE SONS
Met in Waters		
MARÍA (Mexicali)	=	María's husband (Mexicali)
PAULA (María's sister)	=	Paula's husband (Mexicali)
	Lucas (Paula's and María's father)	
ELENA (Sonora, then Mexicali)	=	Elena's husband (Mexicali)
Graciela and daughter Soriana (DF)		

Note: Places of origin of network members are in parentheses. The strongest links are in capital letters. Notably, Anamaría's links with wives of the couples are usually stronger than Roberto's links with their husbands. If the link is roughly equal the names are placed in the middle.

because he had been one of the first Mexicans to arrive in Waters, a little more than twenty-five years after the town was established.

Oldtimers

I interviewed Julio at the kitchen table in the two-bedroom apartment where he lives with his wife, his baby son, his daughter Soriana and her husband, and their newborn. Graciela and Soriana sat on a nearby couch; Soriana eventually came to sit at the table with us. Julio, forty years old in 2003, told me that he had arrived in the United States for the first time in 1988:

"I arrived October 29—to California. I arrived in Anaheim, Orange County. Everything is for—for a better future for my family. All my family is from the DF [Distrito Federal, or Federal District, often used in place of Mexico City]. My father is not alive. My mother is in the DF with siblings of mine. I stayed for three years in Anaheim. I worked in [a fast-food hamburger chain that he names] for two years and then in a hospital. In the hospital I worked in the kitchen. There are various jobs there—I took food to the patients, besides cleaning the kitchen.

"From Anaheim I came here with my family in 1992. When I arrived here eleven years ago it was sparsely populated. It has changed a lot since then. Now it is considered a city. I knew about Waters from a friend who arrived here first. My brothers came here before me, then I arrived. He [the friend] told us there was much work here and the wages were the best—better paid than in California.

"I began work here in [The Lavandería, where Joana works, though Julio does not know her]. I worked there four years, from '92 through '95. From there I went to work in the plastics factory here in Waters. I was there almost four years as well, from '95 to '98—no, '99—and then I went to work with Mitsubishi—the car dealer—and I worked there a year, cleaning all the autos, waxing them, et cetera, and then I went to work with my brother, who owns a car-painting workshop. I was there two years. After that I began working with the Chevrolet dealership, doing the same thing, cleaning autos. I have been working there since."

One of Julio's sisters and three of his brothers (of a total of three sisters and four brothers) currently live in Waters or its environs. Of the brothers, one owns a car-painting shop, one works in the Chevrolet dealership with Julio, and one lays tiles.

Graciela, shy and reserved, seldom speaking, upon my questioning told me that she had worked for three years in Taco Taco, quitting only when she was well along in her pregnancy. Before working at Taco Taco, she had worked for four years in a local tourist hotel as a chambermaid.

Soriana, born in 1980 in Mexico City, recently gave birth to a baby boy. She had previously worked with her mother and Anamaría at Taco Taco. Soriana tells me she was ten years old when she arrived in the United States. She graduated from high school in Waters. Her husband, who works as a tire technician in Waters, had come to the United States from the Distrito Federal because of the lack of money to continue his education as an accountant.

When I remarked that it seemed to me that here in the United States people from Mexicali tended to group with others from that city, from the state of Jalisco with others from that state, and from the Distrito Federal with others from the Distrito Federal even if they had not known each other before, she said, "Yes, because there are different customs. For example, in Sinaloa men are more *machista*. And also, if you are from the same place there is more to talk about." In other words, origin in the same place can be a way of establishing commonalities among erstwhile strangers. It can be a basis for how networks are established or extended at destination.

Soriana told me that when the family arrived in Waters none of the social-service personnel spoke Spanish and there were no Latino children in the schools. She was the only Latina [the word she used] in primary school, ten or eleven years ago. She had graduated from high school in 1998, and by that time there were many Mexicanos in the classes, she observes. In secondary school there were only two or three, but in high school there were enough so that an ESL (English as a Second Language) class was established. Now there is such help in primary school, and social services seek employees who speak both Spanish and English. Julio mentions that he had permanent-residence status, but he could not arrange papers for his wife because they were not legally married. Soriana had petitioned for legal residence on the basis of her father's status. She was eager to receive her papers so that she could work as a telephone operator for the local violence against women association, where she felt bilingual personnel were needed. Soriana once thought of returning to Mexico to study in a university there, but now that she has a child born in the United States, she does not think she will do so.

Best Friends

Anamaría's best friends, sisters who work at Taco Taco, are from Mexicali as she is, and so are both their husbands. Anamaría, Paula, and María help each other out with child care; one night while I was staying with Anamaría, Paula brought her eleven-month-old baby to leave with Anamaría while she and her husband went out to a dance. They also cover for each other at work: if one of them needs to take a day off, one of the others will volunteer—with the permission of the manager—to fill in on that shift. I interviewed María on the evening of September 23, 2003, at the kitchen table in Paula's apartment. Anamaría and Paula were present at the table, and María's husband wandered in and out of the room. I never got a chance to interview María's husband or Paula, but María gave me information about both—with their knowledge, since they were present at the time. María remembered the exact date of her arrival in Waters: December 8, 1996:

"My husband had already come to work—he was unable to find a job in Mexicali. He crossed illegally. A señor who had a jewelry store—my husband is a jeweler—came to Mexicali and asked him to come to Waters." The man was an American brought to Mexicali on vacation by a friend of theirs, who was working in Waters.

"My husband currently works in construction—constructing the sewerage system. I waited about a month after my husband crossed to come here, crossing with my sister Paula [all had border-crossing cards]. At the beginning he worked as a jeweler—but the señor didn't pay him, or he didn't pay him for the hours he worked. He gave nothing that he had offered." Both María's father and sister Paula's husband had also worked on the sewerage system.

"All my work has been in fast-food restaurants. And also cleaning floors at nights in [she names a well-known supermarket chain]. I worked for three years in [a fast-food hamburger chain—the same one Julio had worked for in Anaheim]—my first job. I don't remember, two or three years. I lasted almost a year in [the supermarket]. Right now I have three years in Taco Taco. I am in charge of the kitchen there. I cook, wash dishes, help the others in everything, even sweep. They were going to open a restaurant, and we [she and her sister Paula] went and put in an application. I have worked there since the first day it opened."

When I asked her where she would like to live, María responds, "Here in [Waters], but I would like to be able to return to visit. Two years ago I was in Mexicali. I had to cross back with a coyote." She had originally crossed the border with a local passport, or border-crossing card, but her card had been revoked when she failed to return within the time allowed.

She had chosen Waters "because here there is no vandalism, no gangs. Here it is peaceful." She told me that when she stayed in Long Beach, California, for a couple of months with her husband's aunt, she was constantly frightened by the sound of ambulances. She had gone there because she was pregnant, and the aunt knew where she could get medical care, but she had refused to stay long enough to have the baby there. Her husband had returned to Waters and had no car to come and get her in California, so, she explained, she found a ride back to Waters with an acquaintance. María and her husband have three children; a daughter was born in Mexicali in 1995, a son was born in Waters in 1997, and a daughter was born in Waters in 1999.

Paula was pregnant at the time I interviewed her sister María and continued working at Taco Taco until September 2003, when she was seven months gone. Her husband's brother had arrived in 1999 and his wife Jeanette in 2001. María's husband had placed first Paula's husband and then Paula's husband's brother in work on the sewerage construction project. It was Anamaría who first got to know Jeanette (rather than Roberto, who worked on the same project with Jeanette's husband, though on another crew), through Paula, Jeanette's husband's brother's wife.

María's father, Lucas, comes and goes to Mexicali, where his wife and younger offspring live, on weekends with a border-crossing card. I interviewed him on September 26, 2003, while he was giving doña Consuelo and me a ride from Waters back to that city. Lucas was born in Mexicali, the youngest of eleven children, in 1958. His mother and father had migrated to Mexicali together from a rancho near Fresnillo, Zacatecas.

"More than six years ago I came to Waters—to visit my daughters—both of them were here. I worked for a year in Waters but without Social Security or anything, in construction, building houses. I returned five years ago—in 1998, about then. That was when I returned and worked for two years with a señor, doing the same." After that he worked for a while with a landscaping company based in Las Vegas. "Then I stayed a year in Mexicali. Then I returned here a month ago, to visit my daughters and my sons-in-law. My son-in-law, María's husband, said I could work with him [on the sewerage construction project]. And so I stayed.

"I always entered with a local passport, since 1972. Before that, because I had a local passport since I was a child. When I was thirteen years old, I worked in a factory in Lake Harbor City, near Wilmington, California, in a factory that made car parts and then in one that made carpets. I have also worked in the melon fields in the Imperial Valley and also in Fresno [where his eldest sister once lived]. I also worked six months in Phoenix, in construction, building warehouses."

When the amnesty came, Lucas was working in the state of Colima, building schools, and did not hear about the program. This was true despite the fact that some of his siblings had obtained amnesty. Three of his four sisters and two of his five brothers have legal residence and live in the Wilmington-Long Beach area. Lucas does have a Social Security card, which he acquired in the 1970s when it was still easy to get one.

Lucas has six daughters and two sons. His eldest daughter, aged twenty-eight, lives in Long Beach with her husband. María (aged twenty-six) and Paula (aged twenty-four) live in Waters. The other five, all aged eighteen or younger, live in Mexicali with his wife. He has six grandchildren, three born in the United States, and Paula will soon give birth to his seventh. This family cluster thus is a transnational family cluster with parents born and brought up in Mexicali, offspring in undocumented status in the United States, and grandchildren born American citizens. It is an example as well of male kin accessing female networks and also an instance of network expansion though affinal ties, with daughters mediating their father's migration to and adaptation in Waters with the help of their husbands.

Newcomers

Elena is a new friend of Anamaría; her husband works on the same sewerage construction site as Roberto. In this instance it was Roberto's work site that became the locale where weak ties were converted into stronger ties, despite the fact that Elena's husband later moved on to other employment.

When I asked her to tell me about her migration to Waters, she replied:

"I came with my husband and son—he is now eleven months old. We didn't know anyone upon arrival, but then we got to know people from Mexicali. They told us [about Waters]—a [female] friend who has family here—and we came to visit, and we liked it, and so we stayed. My sister came afterward. She has been here a little less time than us. She is single. Anamaría got her a job at Taco Taco.

"My husband is in charge of a gasoline station during the night shift. Before we came, my husband came first and stayed with a brother of our friend. He came in November of 2003. He began work at the same place as Roberto—on the construction project—through the recommendation of the friend's brother who was also working there. He didn't like the work and looked for something else. He has been working about a month and a half at the gasoline station."

Elena's parents are from Hermosillo, Sonora, and it was there that Elena and her two siblings were born. (This is also where Roberto's mother Miriam and his uncle Jaime were born.) Her parents have lived for many years in San Luís Río Colorado, a drive of about an hour and a half from Mexicali. Her father owns a trucking company there. His trucks "carry wheat, sorghum, corn—mostly wheat—from the Mexicali Valley to Hermosillo, Obregón—everywhere in Sonora and Sinaloa." Elena's brother has a degree in international business from the Universidad Autónoma de Baja California, Mexicali, and her sister studied the first semester of communications there, then decided to drop out. Elena has a degree from UABC in accounting. She met her husband at the university while he was acquiring a degree in business management. Elena names the colonia in Mexicali where her husband's parents live—one of the better off in that city. After marrying they rented an apartment in a middle-class colonia and eventually bought a house. She, her husband, and their son crossed the border with local passports, as did her sister, who later joined them. "We are planning to stay if my husband can find work related to his education, but if not, we plan to return.

"The friend who told us about Waters worked with my husband. He

[Elena's husband] was material manager in a maquiladora. He worked about five years there. Right now he earns no more than he did then, but on the construction project he earned more [than he did in Mexicali]. I worked in a customs agency before. I was head of the personnel department. The company helped with the importation of merchandise, cars, everything. I worked for five years there. Since my husband and I graduated from the university we have held the same jobs in Mexicali."

Elena has visited San Diego, where she has an aunt and cousins who are legal residents. She has also visited Los Angeles. When I asked her if she liked it in Waters, she said yes. "I miss Mexicali, but I like living here. Because my husband worked on the construction project, we have friends from Mexicali here, friends we didn't know before arriving." Women's importance in mediating migration networks is shown in this story as in Miriam's: a female friend gives news about a place and says that work is available, and others follow.

Roberto also developed friends at work sites. He became good friends with a man from Zacatecas with whom he worked for a short time at a car wash. This man and his wife—who have since left Waters—invited Roberto and Anamaría to visit their rancho with them. Because at that time Anamaría and Roberto still had valid border-crossing cards, they did so, staying there with their friends for several days. This is an instance of ties at destination leading back into the origin country but to a different point from the one previously experienced—a widening of network contacts in the origin country because of network expansion at destination.

Colonia Ties

Rigo, a friend of Roberto from Colonia Popular, had moved to a nearby town in Arizona in the late 1990s. Rigo, Roberto, Anamaría, and Rigo's future wife worked in the same factory for some months after Anamaría first came to Waters. Anamaría became friends with Lisa, a Mexican-American born in California, and when Rigo expressed his interest in Lisa to Roberto, Anamaría started matchmaking. Rigo stopped by the house for several hours every week. Anamaría said he seldom brought Lisa (whom he eventually married) because she was working full-time as a manager of a fast-food restaurant in the other town, where she and Rigo now live. Nonetheless, Anamaría counts Lisa as one of her good friends. Rigo works in a metals factory in that town. Before coming to Arizona, he had worked in maquiladoras in Mexicali—more factories than he can remember, he says. He had once worked in a factory in Mexicali with Jorge, a son of doña Consuelo's comadre Socorro. Rigo visits the colonia occasionally and almost always sees Socorro's sons, who live across the street from doña Consuelo's house in Colonia Popular. Roberto is also friends with his cousins, the five sons of Jaime, his mother's brother. These cousins come and go between Mexicali and Waters, often staying to work in the latter city for months at a time.

Conclusions

Most notable about Anamaría's and Roberto's peer networks is that in all but a few cases they were forged in Waters. (The exceptions are those of Rigo and Roberto's five cousins.) They were thus adaptive networks that were created at destination, rather than being facilitating networks anchored in origin. This is probably more common in urban-based emigration than rural-community-based emigration. For migrants from rural communities, facilitating and adaptation networks are often the same, but for urban-based migrants they may not overlap to the same extent. In urban areas, families from a variety of states and communities within those states live side-by-side, and their origin networks, some of which may have nodal members in the United States, do not overlap. Rather an urban family's network comes to overlap with another family's through intermarriage of their offspring, and either family's migration network can be tapped in the migration process. Thus, Anamaría would probably never have ended up in Waters if first her husband's mother and then her husband had not pulled her there.

Second, Anamaría's and Roberto's networks, though overlapping in most cases, are relatively segregated: Anamaría may have strong ties with wives while Roberto has weaker ties with their husbands. Roberto has more face-to-face contacts with his cousins and his friend Rigo than Anamaría does. Anamaría, by contrast, has almost exclusive contact with his mother's brother's wife, Joana, whom she has known since both lived in Colonia Popular.

Third, both Anamaría's and Robert's networks at destination were forged though friends made at work sites. Anamaría's friends became her friends because they were co-workers, friends of co-workers, or relatives of co-workers. Weak ties were converted into stronger ties. Roberto came to know their husbands, and one of them helped him find a better-paying job. Now he works with Anamaría's friends' husbands and has brought Elena into Anamaría's network, through having been employed at the same work site as her husband, however temporary Elena's husband's employment was there.

What distinguishes many of Anamaría's and Roberto's friends is their common origin or residence in Mexicali. When they converse they often mention landmarks in that city such as the Plaza Cachanilla or independence day celebrations at the Civic Center. They share a number of experiences of that city, though Anamaría and Roberto lived mainly in poor colonias and Elena and her husband in well-off ones. (María and Paula lived in a colonia not far from Colonia Popular, also known for its poverty.) The different class experiences of Mexicali seem to be blurred in the new setting in the United States: Elena's husband, with a BA degree, works beside those who have much less education and much less experience of affluence. The homogenization of class status in the United States is similar to that among transnational migrants from a rancho in Jalisco to California and Wisconsin (Wilson 2004). The better off on the rancho worked side-by-side with the landless in the same job categories, if not the same work sites.

Massey et al. (1987, 142) have pointed to the regional basis of friendship making at destination: "Common origin from a particular region, such as southern Jalisco or the Zamora Valley, usually implies a series of common experiences, customs, and traditions that permit easy communication and friendship formation. Migrants from the same part of Mexico may even share common relatives or acquaintances or have attended the same fiestas and fairs."

Anamaría arranged interviews among her strong-tie network members

(Paula and María) and newcomer Elena, as well as with weakening-tie network members (Graciela's family)—weakening because Graciela and her daughter no longer worked at Taco Taco, and they seldom saw one another anymore. In the case of almost all the people I interviewed, with Anamaría facilitating all interviews but the one with Lucas, there was a link to the person either through Anamaría's work site or, in the case of Elena and Lucas, though Roberto's most recent work site. Anamaría and Roberto seldom see their friends as couples, though occasionally one couple in the group decides to have a carne asada party, and people from all over Mexicali, even people they do not know, come to take part. Rather Anamaría visited her friends' homes while Roberto was working or resting and entertained them without their husbands in her house. As will be seen in chapter 10, this pattern differs from that of Irma and Raúl, who spent most of their time with other couples with whom they had already established a compadrazgo relationship, with whom they planned to do so, or with whom their compadres had established a compadrazgo relationship. This difference is in great part because Miriam and Roberto belong to a Protestant church, and Anamaría is a nonpracticing Roman Catholic.

Although doña Consuelo and I visited Irma and Raúl before we went together to Anamaría's and Roberto's the first time, I have presented the two couples' histories of migration in reverse order. Irma's and Raúl's adaptation was more complicated, as it was mediated through compadrazgo ties; their network members did not so often share a common work site. Except for the cousins they converted into ritual kin, they met their future compadres casually and were incorporated into compadres' networks as a couple.

CHAPTER 9

Irma's Story

I interviewed Irma, Raúl, and their network members in August-September 2003. Doña Consuelo and I went from San Diego, where she visited me to tell me her story, by plane to Reno. There Raúl and a compadre of his picked us up. Raúl's compadre has legal documents for being in the United States, but Raúl does not. Thus, Raúl feared entering the airport, where there are sometimes immigration officials, or so he thought. He thus sent his compadre inside the airport for us.

The story of Irma's migration first to Los Angeles and then to Lake Tahoe Town begins with the migration of her husband. Raúl's parents have a house built of bricks made by the family four houses up from doña Consuelo's in Colonia Popular. When Raúl and Irma first got together, they lived with his parents in this house. Unlike Anamaría, who has worked in only one town in the United States, Irma and Raúl had lived elsewhere in the United States before arriving in the Lake Tahoe Town. Raúl had had polio when a child, and his parents considered his crossing the border clandestinely an impossibility. His strong will prevailed.

Some months before my interviews with him, Raúl had suffered a bad accident. While repairing the roof of the hotel where he worked as head of maintenance, he fell off, injuring his spine and pelvis. He was operated on to put a steel plate in his pelvis, and some months after we left he had an operation on his spine. In April 2005 he still had terrible back pain. He had undergone a second operation in February that had done nothing to alleviate the pain but induced a heart attack (he was thirty-seven at the time). Since the accident, he has taken care of the house and chores and his and Irma's five children while Irma works, earning $10 an hour, cleaning tourist cottages. Her hours are variable; while I was visiting she worked fifteen hours one day and two another. An American woman who runs a property-management service employs her. One week the employer took $120 from Irma's salary "for taxes." When I asked Irma how her employer could take out money for taxes if Irma did not have a tax-identification number—which she has been trying, unsuccessfully, to acquire—she shrugged. I asked if she wanted me to call her employer. "No," Raúl said. "We cannot complain, or they will take the work away from us. One feels impotent here without papers. And we need for Irma to work." They knew that Irma's employer was simply keeping the money, but because Raúl cannot work right now, they must protect her employment status even if she is cheated out of the salary for twelve hours of work a week.

Raúl's Story

On August 18, 2003, sitting at their kitchen table, I asked Raúl to tell me how he came to the United States and eventually to Lake Tahoe Town. I interviewed him again on August 26, and he told me much the same story, with elaborations. Kandel and Masssey (2002, 982), writing about the culture of Mexican migration to the United States, report that "as migratory behavior extends throughout a community, it increasingly enters the calculus of conscious choice and eventually becomes normative. Young people who grow up and come of age increasingly expect to migrate internationally in the course of their lives." Pessar (2003, 96) points out that this "imagining, planning, and strategizing" is a component of living "in a transnational cognitive space." I would argue that this culture of migration also exists at destination, where especially those who have crossed the border without documents discuss the travails of their crossings with friends and kin to the point of creating their own legend of migration. Thus, Raúl told me twice about his crossings in almost the same words. Miriam also told me twice about her worst crossing and about the good and the evil immigration officers. Below is a composite of these two interviews with Raúl.

"The first time was in '89. I crossed from Tijuana. It was bad because I walked for about twelve hours in the hills and it rained and rained—I could hardly walk. It was ugly. This time I crossed, and we walked from seven at night until six in the morning, walking to cross into San Ysidro from Tijuana. I went to Los Angeles to a cousin's—my mother's nephew—in El Monte. A lot of us crossed together, but I had not even a brother or a friend with me. This time I came because long before I wanted to come, but my parents would not let me; they said I wouldn't be able to. I came because my wife and I separated. I drank a lot in the colonia." [Irma told me another day that he would come home drunk, overturn tables, throw things around, sometimes hit her. She mentioned this twice to me, once in front of Raúl, and he rather shamefacedly admitted it was true.] From El Monte Raúl went to work in Morgan Hill, California.

"I spent three months in Morgan Hill picking tomatoes, strawberries, and, how is it called, 'blueberry.' I worked in the fields for three months. From there I returned to Los Angeles to stay with a cousin [mother's brother's son] and began to work painting. My cousin was from Tepititlán [the nexus of commonality between doña Consuelo's family and Raúl's family]. He is a first cousin of mine. He was a painter. He had worked about twenty years as a painter. We painted all the fire departments in Los Angeles, Orange County, Long Beach, Glendale, Hollywood, Beverly Hills, Bellflower—me along with my cousin. I did this about seven years. Then I went to Corona, California, and worked in a calf stable, just little calves, giving them feed. My cousin is here now, in Carson City. He is painting a large house for our *patrón* (boss). The house is going to cost $40 million. The one that we painted five or six years ago he sold for $22 million."

From there he went back to Mexicali, he thinks it was in 1994, and returned to Los Angeles the same year.

"The second time I crossed also from Tijuana, in the trunk of a car. We were five people. Four men and a pregnant woman—in the trunk." He commented that the coyotes had no respect for people and did not treat them well. "And I continued on as a painter. I went to live in La Puente, California. There we lived for about six months, renting a garage. We lived in a garage. I lived with friends."

He returned to Mexicali for a year from 1996 to 1997, "and Tomás was born in that year [1996]. Because of the rain seventeen thousand bricks were destroyed, and this was the reason for returning to the United States. Our family patrimony was lost. I owed twenty thousand pesos. I had debts up to my ears. Tomás's birth [by Cesarean] cost six thousand pesos. I crossed to Los Angeles and stayed a week with my cousin [his mother's brother's daughter], my mother's niece [Liliana], and then I came to Lake Tahoe Town. And here I stayed.

"I stayed six years in Los Angeles, without returning to Mexico. I went there [to Calexico, California, across the border from Mexicali], and we crossed my wife and Erlinda [the eldest of their offspring], and they were in Los Angeles five years, one year less than me. Then she [Irma] left, and three months later I went back to Mexicali, about 1996. We stayed a year, and then I came back to the United States again because we couldn't live on what I earned on the brickyard."

Raúl's father, don Rafael, has worked as a brickmaker most of his life. All his children know how to make bricks and have helped him in his brickyard, acquired after he moved to Mexicali from Jalisco in 1984 (see Wilson 2005). When Raúl matured he bought his own small brickyard.

"I had my own brickyard, my truck to transport bricks. Irma sold the truck so she would be able to cross her second time. What we have is a house in Palo Verde, where my sister-in-law Minerva lives."

Minerva, doña Consuelo's third daughter, upon separating from her drunken, verbally abusive husband after eighteen years of marriage, moved into Irma and Raúl's house in Palo Verde—a few kilometers from Colonia Popular and near the brickyards—in 1999. Raúl and Irma were by then absent in the United States.

"I returned to Los Angeles for another—how many?—another three years. Three years and then I returned to Mexicali."

He and Irma were separated for three years, Raúl said. When I asked Irma about this later in the week, she said they were only separated for a year. Rumors had reached her that Raúl was having an affair with a woman in Los Angeles, and when she asked doña Consuelo what she should do, her mother encouraged her to go after him.

"I worked painting. I have always worked painting, except for the first three months in the fields. There in Los Angeles Bernardito and Ariel [two of their sons] were born during the five years Irma lived with me." (See table 9 and genealogy 3.)

Table 9. Irma's Children

Child	Birth year of child	Where born
Erlinda	1988	Mexicali (Colonia Popular)
Bernardito	1991	Los Angeles (El Monte)
Ariel	1993	Los Angeles (El Monte)
Tomás	1996	Mexicali (Colonia Popular)
Alicia	1999	Lake Tahoe

"After I went to Mexicali for that year (1996–97), I came here. My cousin [Liliana's brother] called me, and he was in Lake Tahoe Town, and I asked him if there was work for me. My cousin said it was far away, but yes, there was work. He paid the coyote for me, and I repaid him afterward. On that crossing I also left from Mexicali. I started out crossing on Monday, and they caught me about midnight and threw me out. And this same night we tried again. And then they grabbed us about four in the morning, and I went back to sleep at my house in Mexicali. And in the evening I went back again, and we tried again at eleven at night, and we crossed a field in Calexico, and they caught us again. Because of a señora. She lost her shoes when we were running, and I waited for her—she couldn't walk very well without shoes. I waited for the señora—she was forty-three, forty-five years old. And they grabbed four of us, we who were the farthest behind, and two got away.

"And when I finally got across it was on Sunday, and we crossed a field that was full of mud, and we got down on our bellies because just a little farther on was an immigration checkpoint. And that night we crossed to—what is it called?—Palm Springs, and from there they took us to Los Angeles the next day. They took me to a house and called my cousin and told him what street, what corner.

"This time it took me a week. From there they sent me by airplane to Reno—the husband of my cousin [Liliana] and her brother came to pick me up. And that is how I arrived here, and until today here I am. [All the cousins mentioned above and the one below are siblings. Notably, they are his mother's relatives rather than his father's, showing the importance of female links in the transnational migration process.]

"My cousin was working for the owner of Hotel Lake Tahoe, painting houses for the owner in Los Angeles. . . .[1] He is a millionaire like those you find written about in books. And he said to my cousin would he like to come and paint houses in Lake Tahoe.

"And I stayed a year alone here, living with my cousins. And then my wife came. She is almost five years here. Alicia [his youngest] was born here, in a hospital in Reno.

"My cousins came again two months ago to paint another house, and one of them has been here eight months this time. They come and go, sometimes to Los Angeles, sometimes to Tepititlán. My father is from a rancho near Tepatitlán, Jalisco. My mother is from a nearby rancho.

"I have been working for six years in Hotel Lake Tahoe. I was the first [of his immediate family] to come here. Then my brother Rafaelito came and worked two or three years here. Then my brother Adrián came— he stayed two years and then went back to Mexicali. Two months later he returned here. He went in December and returned in February, but he brought his family with him. [Adrián's wife is don Nato's daughter. Don Nato settled on the lot beside doña Consuelo's in Colonia Primer Paso (see chap. 6).] It cost him seven thousand dollars for him, his wife, and their daughter. He is still paying it off. They arrived at my house and stayed about fifteen days, and then he looked for a place to rent. And then my father came [as did his mother, both with residence permits arranged by their daughter in Fresno, whose husband acquired amnesty and later became an American citizen, as did she]. He will be here two years in November. I told him to come. For all of them, my brothers and my papa, I have found work at Hotel Lake Tahoe [Adrián and Raúl's father, don Rafael, work in grounds maintenance and gardening there]. I also found work there for an uncle [his father's brother]."

He had also found work for Edgar, his wife Irma's brother, painting at the Hotel Lake Tahoe when he came to stay for six months in 2002. In 2002 his youngest sister Rosalina also arrived, and Raúl got her a job at the Hotel Lake Tahoe as a chambermaid. In 2003, Raúl's father and mother, brother Adrián, his wife and baby, and Rosalinda were living together in a rented house about three miles from where Raúl and Irma live.

Asked if he planned to stay, Raúl said yes. "My children are here. They are studying well. My daughter is going to enter high school. I just hope my sister arranges my papers soon so I can come and go to Mexico and visit my other siblings, my other relations. My wife never worked, I never let her, until I had the accident. I worked here and there. I painted houses. My wife is working very hard. At times she works ten hours, once fifteen. She has only been working a month, a month and a half. When we arrived we lived in just this one room [the present kitchen-dining room]. We washed the dishes in the bathtub. I was the dishwasher.

"In Los Angeles I studied English only three months, and I am not ashamed to speak it. My brothers—it makes them embarrassed to speak English." Our interviews and conversations took place in Spanish, but Raúl often corrected his children's behavior in English—a language in which they, with the exception of Erlinda, who is bilingual—are more fluent than in Spanish. At one time he was working two jobs in Lake Tahoe: as a painter in Hotel Lake Tahoe in the daytime and in a pizzeria at night. Raúl is still friends with the pizzeria owner, who now runs a small grocery store.

One of the things Raúl likes here is that it is peaceful. There are no robberies or assaults, as there were when they lived in Los Angeles. Here they can leave things outside—the children's bicycles, the grill—and no one takes them. He said that in Los Angeles, if someone left a bicycle outside a store and went in for only a few minutes to buy something, the bicycle would be gone by the time he came out. His father, don Rafael, prefers Mexicali, and Irma told me she would rather live in Los Angeles where there were more stores, movie theaters, and things to do. Raúl would like to have papers so they could go back and forth to Mexico. Two of his children are undocumented. Erlinda was born in Mexicali a few months before Raúl crossed the first time. Tomás was born in Mexicali after Irma returned there from Los Angeles. Erlinda was almost a year old when Irma crossed the first time to join Raúl in Los Angeles.

Raúl is receiving disability checks because of the accident, almost as much as his previous salary, he says, but they have many medical bills. He mentions that he was being paid only eight dollars an hour, when someone with documents would have been earning fifteen dollars as supervisor of the painting and building-maintenance crew.

Raúl has five sisters and three brothers: a sister, now an American citizen, living in Fresno; his brother Rafaelito, without documents in Modesto, California; and a sister with a residence permit who sometimes lives in Waters (but has no contact with Anamaría) and sometimes in Mexicali. His youngest sister, twenty-one years old in 2003, works in housekeeping at the Hotel Lake Tahoe. She and her brother Adrián and his wife and child—all without documents—live with their legally resident parents about five miles away from Raúl. Adrián works in grounds maintenance with their father at the same hotel. One of Raúl's sisters has a lot in Colonia Nueva Oportunidad but is currently living in and caring for their parents' house in Colonia Popular; another brother, meanwhile, lives on her lot in Nueva Oportunidad. (See table 10 and genealogy 3.)[2]

Table 10. Raúl's Sibling Group

Sibling	Where living in 2005
Marisela	Fresno, California
Raúl	Lake Tahoe, Nevada
Yovanna	Waters, Arizona (has a house in Col. Popular)
Alma	Colonia Popular in parents' house: she has her own house in Colonia Nueva Oportunidad
Jazmín	Another colonia, Mexicali
Rafaelito	Modesto, California
Sergio	Lives in Alma's house in Col. Nueva Oportunidad
El Chiques	Died in an accident at the age of eleven
Adrián	Lake Tahoe, with their parents
Rosalinda	Lake Tahoe, with their parents

On August 26, Raúl took doña Consuelo, daughter Alicia, son Tomás, and me to the Hotel Lake Tahoe. He showed us the walls he had painted, the tile he had laid, the stones he had put on the exterior walls, and where he fell from the roof. We went to the casino and to the dance hall, which he would have liked to rent for Erlinda's quinceañera party, but it cost twenty-eight hundred dollars for three hours, and he did not have the money. He is proud of his work, especially his painting. He has developed a technique with an overlay of different colored paint applied with a cloth that makes it look like wallpaper.

Irma's Migration

Irma was not only working full-time, six days a week but also arranging for her daughter Erlinda's quinceañera party and for her own and Raúl's church wedding. Both were to take place at the same time on August 30. Preparing for the wedding and quinceañera involved sending invitations, making decorations, and attending meetings in the park where both parties were to be held. Meanwhile Erlinda was learning a number of dances—among others, a tango—with her four *chambelanes* (male dance companions), whom Irma had to go from house to house to fetch. Also, a few days before the parties, guests began arriving from San Jose and Los Angeles whom she had to entertain. In the hours when she could talk and do chores at the same time, we spent much time listing the padrinos for the wedding and the quinceañera party, and consequently I did not receive much information about migration history. The bits of it that she managed to tell me are as follows:

"The first time I crossed from Tijuana. . . . [She pauses and asks her mother when Anamaría's quinceañera party had been. July 20, doña Consuelo replies. I had attended it and remember seeing Irma there and her telling me that she would be leaving soon for the United States.] Well I crossed July 21, 1990. I crossed three times because twice la migra caught me. The migra caught us on the freeway the first time, and they threw us back into Tijuana at three in the morning. But we were lucky to meet a very nice migra—they gave Erlinda sweets. The second time they grabbed me in the middle of the hills because Erlinda cried when we were hiding. The second time the migra threw us back at five in the morning. After that we went rapidly up into the hills but in another place where there were trailer trucks. There, there was a *gabacho* (slang for a North American) who helped us hide on his land. We went walking on one side of the highway until we reached an airport, and from there we flew to Los Angeles."

The second time she crossed—this time to come to Lake Tahoe Town—was in 1999. She crossed from Mexicali. It was her easiest crossing. She just jumped the fence and walked over to McDonalds, where a couple who were her compadres picked her up. She went to their house in Los Angeles—the city where they had become compadres on the occasion of Bernardito's baptism. Raúl came for her in a car he had borrowed from a cousin's son. The car broke down in a small town on the way back, and they did not have any money or anywhere to sleep. A Jehovah's Witness from Mexico stopped by, took them to a motel in the next town, and paid for them for one night. A housekeeper at the motel took them to the county offices, which paid for two nights more in the motel and gave them coupons for food. The housekeeper who, like Irma's mother and Raúl's parents, was from the Tepititlán area, offered to let them stay in her house after their motel nights ran out. Eventually a cousin of Raúl arrived with money to fix the car and take them on to Lake Tahoe Town. Now, when they go to Los Angeles, they stop by to visit this woman. Thus can networks "accidentally" expand, given certain commonalities. These commonalities can include being born in or having lived in the same place or having parents who were born in or lived in the same place.

Irma and Raúl often drive to Los Angeles to buy clothing, linens, quilts, curtains, and other textiles in downtown Los Angeles that Irma sells door-to-door among the Mexican residents of the towns in the area where they live. This work is "invisible" to both of them, however, as both say Irma did not work until after Raúl's accident. Since then she has worked cleaning tourist cottages. On her day off and some evenings she cooks, though Raúl was often responsible for the children's breakfasts and an occasional evening meal. While we were there doña Consuelo thoroughly cleaned the house and often helped with meals, though Raúl felt it was his responsibility to prepare most of them. Raúl, cane in hand, also insisted on vacuuming the bedroom carpets, a daily chore.

The following selections from my field notes will give something of the flavor of their lives:

"Sunday, August 21, 2003. On the 30th of August Irma and Raúl are to be married in church and Erlinda is to have her quinceañera party at the same time as their wedding reception. Yesterday we (Raúl, Irma, the five children, Doña Consuelo, and I) went to Reno. We stopped at Wal-Mart to buy white shirts for the three boys for the wedding, but Irma found none. I suggested Mervyn's—where they had never been (though there were a lot of Latinos there). At Mervyn's they found shirts, complete with ties. Right after Wal-Mart we went to Payless for Raúl's wedding shoes— but we found none—because his feet are crippled by polio he can wear only loafers or tennis shoes. He found a pair of loafers at Mervyn's. From there he took us to a pizza place with long wooden tables big enough for the whole family and ordered the three-pizza-and-chicken-wing special for $50. He said that he and Irma and their children had been to every family restaurant in Reno over the past six years. From there we went to WinCo, where they go every two weeks for groceries. Irma estimates that they spend about $200 each time they go there. She buys things like milk locally when they run out. Prices are sky-high in the Lake Tahoe area markets. They bought bagfuls of tomatoes, *chiles de arbol* (small red and very hot dried chiles to add taste to salsas), *ajo* (garlic), *chiles California* (long dried maroon chiles used in making salsas for meat or poultry), potatoes, bananas, many vegetables: string beans, lettuce, spinach.

"Yesterday we ate pancakes, eggs, and hot dogs for breakfast; pizza, chicken wings, and fried potatoes in Reno for lunch; corn on the cob for dinner. The family eats three big meals a day, though often dinner for the children is a sandwich or corn flakes or animal cookies in milk. They made the pancakes and eggs especially for me, knowing it was one of my favorite breakfasts from the time Raúl took the children, Doña Consuelo, and me out to a casino restaurant for brunch while Irma was at work.

"In the evenings Irma and Raúl make decorations for their wedding/ quinceañera party. Thirty place settings with candles and imitation white flowers: 15 with a small photo of Erlinda and 15 with a small photo of Irma and Raúl attached. Raúl fashioned the 30 napkin holders, decorating them with a green leaf, a piece of gauze, and a photo, after Irma made him a model. Then Irma—enlisting my aid, as well as Erlinda's and sometimes Doña Consuelo's—strings the paper flowers she had cut out of 8 x 10-inch paper on long lines of thread, each flower separated by a straw. These many strings of flowers are to decorate the *palapa* in the state park where the reception will be held. Everyone in the house works. I sometimes wash dishes, and did about four loads of laundry for the family on Friday, and cleaned the tops of cabinets in the kitchen so Consuelo would not climb up on a chair to do so. Doña Consuelo washes dishes, the kitchen floor, the kitchen cabinets, the windows, and sweeps the patio daily. When she has nothing else do, she cleans jewelry or brass statues owned by the family—a few picked up at a garage sale we stopped for on the way to Reno—with baking soda, lemon and a toothbrush. Raúl cooks, vacuums the rooms, picks up the mail at the post office, goes to the bank, pays the electricity bill, and engages in other chores when he is not making the wedding/quinceañera favors. He does so cheerfully, feeling that it is his duty since Irma has taken on the role of the household breadwinner. . . .

"As you enter the kitchen door of first floor of the two-story wood frame house where Irma and Raúl live (the upper level rented to an American family), the first thing that strikes your eye is a make-shift altar. A statue of the Virgin of Guadalupe, surrounded by plants and photographs is placed on a shelf high up on the kitchen's wall. Among the photographs are one of Irma's father Juan Carlos with her when she was about 9 or 10 years old and another little girl. Irma tells me she lived for two years with her father and stepmother after Doña Consuelo moved to Mexicali and took up with Chano. I ask who the little girl is. 'A daughter he had with my stepmother at the same time he had us,' Irma replies. He had two daughters with the woman from Zacatecas. Doña Consuelo never told me about these children with his casa chica 'mistress.' Perhaps it was too painful for her to admit."

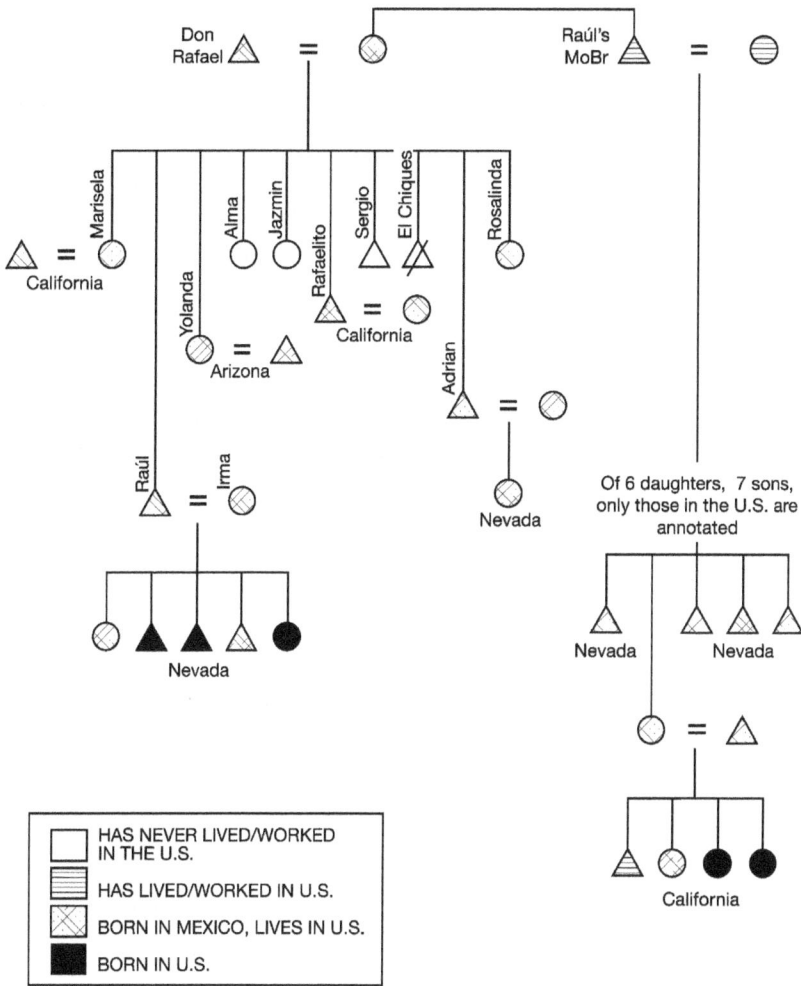

Genealogy 3. Raúl's family

November 2007

In October 2006 Irma, Raúl, and the children moved on to Carson City
to join his three cousins—the same cluster of brothers he had originally
joined in Los Angeles and then later on in Lake Tahoe Town. Raúl began
working with them installing electrical wiring, putting down floors, and
painting walls in new apartment complexes. By November 2007 he had
done this finishing work on projects in Carson City, Reno, and, temporarily, San Francisco. He continued in this employment through 2008.
Sometimes Irma and Raúl returned to Lake Tahoe Town to visit their
compadres, and sometimes their compadres came to where Raúl and
Irma live in Carson City to visit them, but daily interaction no longer
occurred. The following chapter explores their adaptation network while
they lived in Lake Tahoe Town.

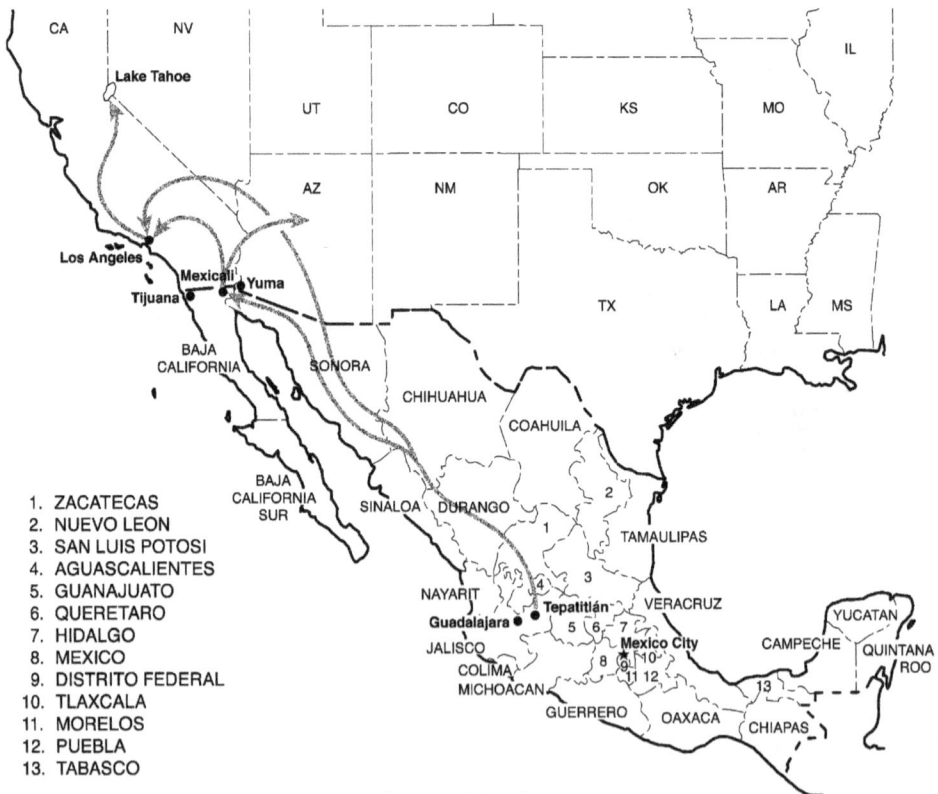

Map 1. Migration routes

CHAPTER 10

Irma and Raúl's Network

Irma and Raúl's network at destination contrasts with Anamaría's and Roberto's work-site-based networks. Irma and Raúl tie couples to themselves through establishing Mexican Roman-Catholic-based ritual kinship relationships with them. Though neither they nor their compadres (coparents, ritual kin on a horizontal axis, tied to one another through the blessing of a child or object) or padrinos (godparents, tied to their godchildren on a vertical axis of mutual responsibility) attend church on a regular basis, they regularly do so for masses given during life-cycle events. These include baptisms, confirmations, and first communions for their children; quinceañeras for their daughters (an optional, nonsacramental celebration); and marriages for themselves or offspring. It is not church attendance that is central to their interactions but the extension and strengthening of reciprocity networks that aid them in their adaptation to their destination. These reciprocity networks constitute their in situ social capital. They facilitate psychic adaptation to the new locale; Irma and Raúl visit and dine with other couples in their network, invite these couples for dinners and parties, extend and receive loans within the group, and help each other out in times of crisis or celebration. Because of their compadres in the Lake Tahoe region, Irma and Raúl have a buffer against loneliness and to some extent against economic insecurity.

With one or two exceptions (e.g., Ebaugh and Curry 2000), little attention has been given to the role of compadrazgo in facilitating transnational network-mediated migration or adaptation. Most scholars look only at kinship, friendship, and paisano (fellow community members)[1] ties, while some (e.g., Hirschman 2004; Levitt 2003; Mahler and Hansing 2005) focus on the church as the central organizing institution in immigrants' religious life, without considering ritual kinship that, while sanctioned by the Roman Catholic Church, does not necessarily involve regular church attendance. There is, however, some work on the role of compadrazgo in migration and adaptation in rural-to-urban migration within Mexico (e.g., Kemper 1977; Lomnitz 1977; Nutini and Bell 1980). Nutini and Bell have shown how adaptation to new destinations was facilitated for internal migrants from a small town in Tlaxcala to nearby, larger towns and then to Puebla and Mexico City through the establishment of ritual kinship ties. They identify thirty-one types of compadrazgo relationships practiced in the town of Belén, Tlaxcala, classifying them broadly as sacramental and required (baptism, confirmation, and marriage) and nonsacramental (e.g., the quinceañera celebration for fifteen-year-old girls).

Two events of central importance for Raúl and Irma took place while I was staying with them in 2003. The first was their wedding, and the second was the celebration of their daughter Erlinda's fifteenth-birthday party. Both involved the extension of compadrazgo relationships to incorporate new couples, the strengthening of existing compadrazgo ties, and a renewed recognition of the value of kinship ties with cousins located in the area and as far away as Los Angeles and San Jose, California, and in the case of doña Consuelo, mother of the bride, as far as Mexicali. At the same time some kinship and compadrazgo ties were actually weakened by these celebrations in terms of their value for giving or receiving emotional or economic support.

One would intuitively expect that during life-cycle events accompanied by labor-intensive and extensive celebration, strong ties would be reinforced and some weak ties strengthened, and in some cases this is what happened. Raúl's cousin Liliana came with her husband and children from Los Angeles to be padrinos of the wedding and of the quinceañera. They were accompanied by Liliana's father [Raúl's mother's brother] and mother and a sister of Liliana, all three of whom had come to visit from Tepatitlán, Jalisco. Liliana and her parents had scheduled their visit to the Lake Tahoe region to coincide with the celebrations. They also planned to visit with Liliana's three brothers, who had moved from Lake Tahoe Town to Carson City several years before. Two of these brothers—the cousins Raúl had joined first in Los Angeles and then in a town nearby where he now lives—came to the wedding and the quinceañera; the other was unable to take time off from work.

César and Manuela, who lived nearby, had become Irma and Raúl's compadres on the occasion of the baptism of their youngest child Alicia; these ties were strengthened when they became padrinos of coins (*arras*) for Irma and Raúl's wedding. Manuela's mother was from Tepatitlán, Jalisco, though Manuela had been brought up in Guadalajara. She had visited relatives of her mother's in Tepatitlán, however. Doña Consuelo had also lived in Tepatitlán, and several of her siblings were born there. This led to a number of conversations between them about the region. Irma had also lived near Tepatitlán when her father Juan Carlos and mother Consuelo, based in Mexico City, intermittently went to farm in a nearby rancho where Consuelo had lived as a child. Raúl, who was born on a rancho near Tepatitlán (as were his mother and father) and did not migrate with his family to Mexicali until he was fifteen, is considered by his friends and compadres to be from that region in Jalisco, not Mexicali. The commonalities established between Irma and Raúl's network members at destination are often based on one's own or one's parents' common residence—however temporary—or origin in the Tepatitlán region. These network members became acquainted only at destination, however. This Jalisco connection is not emphasized in Anamaría's and Roberto's networks, which are embedded in commonalities centered around origin in Mexicali where both were born. Thus even sisters can emphasize one or more "origins" in building and reinforcing ties: that of their own previous places of residence or of parents' previous or present places of residence.

Jonathan, who is Manuela's first cousin and also came from the Tepatitlán region, and his wife Carolina are compadres of César and Manuela. Compadres of compadres, they became Irma and Raúl's padrinos of the mass, the most important of the six ritual possibilities that the couple actualized for their wedding. (There were also padrinos of the coins, the ring, the souvenirs, the invitations, and the *lazo*, signifying union.) César and Manuela had introduced Irma and Raúl to their compadres, Hortensia and Gilberto, who came from a rancho in the state of Durango. Hortensia and Gilberto are also César and Manuela's compadres. Hortensia and Gilberto had become Irma and Raúl's compadres on the occasion of Erlinda's first communion, and these ties were to be strengthened by their becoming godparents of the nuptial benedictions for Erlinda during the portion of her quinceañera celebration held in the nearby Roman Catholic church. These are the most important of the padrinos in a quinceañera rite of passage; Erlinda would also have godparents who presented her with a Bible and a rosary, a bouquet, and a photograph album; bought the cake; paid for the music; paid for the dress (these latter were Irma's sisters Minerva and Carla, who, having no border-crossing cards, could not attend, though Minerva made the dress and Carla paid for the materials); paid for the photographs; paid for the video that was made; paid for the alcohol to be consumed; and a *madrina* (godmother) who placed the crown on her head during the ceremonial dances.

Weak ties were also strengthened between Irma and Raúl and Irma's cousin (her mother's sister's son) Salvador and his family. Salvador is a son of doña Consuelo's sister Lupe, who lives in Guadalajara, and was invited at doña Consuelo's urging. Irma had never met him. He had come to visit his aunt, doña Consuelo, in Colonia Popular, but Irma was by then absent in the United States. The strengthening of ties is predictable during life-cycle events, but because networks are fluid, expanding and contracting for individual, family, and community over a lifetime (see chap. 11), it is impossible to know in advance which strong-tied or weak-tied members will be chosen to take part in life-cycle rites of passage and which will accept the invitation to do so.

Somewhat counterintuitively, some strong ties may not be actualized or reinforced during important rites of passage. Thus Jorge and Julia, who had become godparents of Irma's sons Ariel and Rigo when Irma and Raúl still lived in Los Angeles, were scheduled to be padrinos of the cake for Erlinda's quinceañera party but were unable to make the trip from Ontario, California. Even strong kin ties do not guarantee a presence. Thus, Raúl's mother and father, though living less than five miles away, did not come to the celebrations or to the mass because Irma and Raúl had had a tiff with his mother some weeks previously. Strong ties that should have been reinforced were not. Parents' absence could lead to a greater feeling of rift, though Raúl excused it as the result of his mother's bad humor. Raúl's brother Adrián and his wife, though sharing a house with his parents, did indeed take part. Irma was disappointed that her brothers Edgar and Manuel, who had border-crossing cards, did not come to the party. Doña Consuelo, trying to placate her, explained that it was a long drive and they had to work. Irma pointed out, however, that Manuel had gone to Mexico City for weddings for his wife's relatives. She felt slighted and returned to the issue several times while I was there. Doña Consuelo may have conveyed Irma's disappointment to Manuel on her return to Colonia Popular. In any case, on the occasion of Irma and Raúl's son Ariel's confirmation in May 2006, Manuel and his wife drove up from Mexicali to serve as padrinos and brought doña Consuelo along.

Compadres

Except for Manuela and Jonathan, who were first cousins as well as compadres, the most important padrinos of the wedding and the quinceañera forged their ties at destination. Manuela was one of the first people Irma came to know after moving to Lake Tahoe Town; she and her husband had become Irma and Raúl's compadres when they baptized Alicia, their youngest child. They had met when Raúl and Manuela's husband César worked at the same pizzeria at night. After they became friends, César had asked Raúl if he and Manuela could be Alicia's padrinos. Once accepted, Manuela and César invited Raúl and Irma over for dinner, and the shared social life of the couples began. Thus there was a work-site connection here as in Anamaría's and Roberto's networks, though this type of meeting place was less common for Raúl and Irma.

Manuela and her cousin Jonathan's migration network is quite strong and extensive: they have many cousins in the area and are related to Héctor Rodríguez, one of the first Mexican men to have migrated to the Lake Tahoe region where they live. I never met Héctor, though Manuela twice scheduled me to interview him at her house. (Both times he had to work late.) His story is part of local lore, known by members of Manuela's and

Jonathan's kinship, friendship, and compadrazgo networks. I heard portions of his story from a number of people.

One night in August 2003 when Manuela, César, and their children came to visit Irma and Raúl (a routine occurrence), I interviewed Manuela about her migration history. As we sat at the table on the patio, with her husband, Irma, and Raúl occasionally present and the children playing in the nearby woods, Manuela told me about Héctor:

"A first cousin of mine [her mother's sister's son] arrived here twenty-two years ago, about 1980, '81, and there were only two Hispanos [the local term for Spanish-speakers, according to Raúl] here—one from Frías, Guanajuato, and one from Michoacán." Frías is a major sending community to a nearby town. Different towns around Lake Tahoe have different histories of Mexican migration, and some were settled earlier than others. Thus, Martínez Curiel (2004) gives examples of Mexican migrants who were present in the Lake Tahoe area as early as the beginning of the 1970s.

"He [Héctor] studied to be an architect, but he left this to come here to earn money to marry [a girl he very much loved, Manuela stressed]. He married and brought his wife here. She got sick and died. Not long ago he married a twenty-two-year-old, he being forty-three. His mother was from Tepatitlán."

Manuela tells me (and later her cousin Jonathan tells me) that Héctor and a cousin who came with him initially slept on a bench at the public bus stop until they were able to find work at a casino restaurant. (Raúl showed me the bench—a wooden one, barely long enough for a grown person to stretch out—a marker for the migration streams.) Beginning as a dishwasher, Héctor worked his way up to chief cook in the course of his career. "We all started that way," said Jonathan, who is now a kitchen manager at a luxurious Mexican restaurant chain.

"Héctor brought his brothers and then his mother and then a brother of mine." After her brother arrived, she and her mother came to visit with tourist visas. "I came about '86, and since the first time I arrived, I have stayed. I put in my application for agricultural workers' amnesty. My husband became a citizen." Her husband, César, added, "I put in for amnesty as well. In '97 they gave me citizenship. I was seventeen when I crossed."

Manuela had been working for the same Mexican restaurant—the same chain but in a different locale from the one where her cousin Jonathan was employed—for ten years and now earned $12.50 an hour. She had received a raise every year except that one. The restaurant manager had explained to her that they were not doing well enough to raise wages, but she thinks he was trying to irritate her so that she would quit, since she had been there so many years and therefore received high pay. "Beginners would be paid less," she pointed out. On another day she told me this story again, reflecting that the manager's actions might be an instance of racism. I think, however, that she was using the word "racism" as a gloss for "exploitation." Manuela said that she worked hard, sometimes making seventy *chiles rellenos* (a labor-intensive job) a day.

Before Manuela's arrival in the Lake Tahoe region, one of her two brothers—her mother had only three children before she was widowed at the age of twenty-two—had preceded her and worked in the same restaurant where Manuela came to be employed. "Now he is going to open his own restaurant in [a nearby town]. He has already rented a locale. For fifteen years he has worked two jobs, one in the restaurant and one in a pizzeria. Now he is working at [she names a well-known supermarket chain]."

Manuela can be compared to a *patrona* (female patrón) in a patron-client network (e.g., see Adler 2002) with the qualification that, rather than facilitating access to work, she facilitates social support. Manuela, through her cooking and inviting friends to her house, friends who are potential compadres or compadres of compadres, is an initiator or facilitator who adopts people into her and her husband's network, introducing them to other members. She thus facilitates their adaptation to the destination locale. In other words, instead of being a patrona of economic opportunities, she is a patrona of social opportunities, dealing not only with material goods but also with psychic well-being (see fig. 1).

Hortensia and Gilberto, compadres of Manuela and César, met Irma and Raúl at a Christmas party in the former's home. They became Erlinda's padrinos on the occasion of her first communion and then again for her quinceañera, thus compadres of Irma and Raúl. Compadres are thus becoming compadres of compadres and an "exocentric network," in Lomnitz's (1977, 133–34) (see chap. 3 above) terminology, is coming to be formed, within which all members have reciprocity relationships with all other members.

Sitting at Irma's kitchen table, I asked Hortensia about her migration history. She had come to Irma's partially because I was to interview her, but she and her husband and children often dropped in. Hortensia told me she had crossed the border in 1992, through a tunnel from Tijuana, accompanied by her three children, a brother-in-law [her husband's brother], and three of her husband's nephews. Before this successful crossing they had been captured three times by the Border Patrol and returned to Mexico. They made their way to her brother's place in Los Angeles, and there her husband and a cousin of his picked them up and took them on to Lake Tahoe. Gilberto had come to the United States in 1989 and was crossing back to see her and the children every year, having to recross with a coyote each time. Finally she had decided to join him in the United States.

Gilberto works as a food server in a casino restaurant, and Hortensia works in the laundry. She has previously worked in similar laundries— washing linens for hotels and casinos—the first one for three years. She hurt her hand while working in the first laundry and remained unemployed for a year. The eldest of their children, born in 1980, is married and living in the Lake Tahoe region. A seventeen-year-old son and a fifteen-year-old daughter live at home. All three were born in Durango.

Hortensia's mother and two brothers live in Chicago. Neither Hortensia nor Gilberto has ever been to Chicago, but she hopes to go fairly soon. Hortensia is expecting her mother to come for the quinceañera.

Carolina and Jonathan had also met Irma and Raúl through Manuela and César. They were padrinos of Irma and Raúl's wedding mass. There was a postwedding party at Irma and Raúl's house the day we had arranged for the interview, with much music and drinking, so we go, with Carolina's five children, to the children's arcade in a not-too-distant hotel for the interview. Born on a rancho near León, Guanajuato, Carolina had crossed the border from Tijuana to San Ysidro. From there she went to the San Diego airport and took a plane to Reno to join a younger brother in the Lake Tahoe region. (Apparently her first attempt at crossing went smoothly; she had no other comments about it.) Her brother worked in a large tourist hotel and got her a job as a chambermaid there. In 1989 she married Jonathan. The couple's children were all born in the Lake Tahoe region. Of Carolina's four brothers and four sisters, two brothers now live near her, and one brother lives in Chicago. Since her arrival Carolina has worked in housekeeping in a number of hotels.

In 1998 Carolina, Jonathan, and their then three children returned to Mexico to visit Carolina's mother, who was still living on the rancho of Carolina's birth in Guanajuato. Carolina had insisted on the trip, since she had not seen her mother in eleven years. Jonathan had residence papers, and their children were American citizens by birth. When they returned to Lake Tahoe, all but Carolina had crossed the border with documents; Carolina crossed with a coyote. The family had reassembled in Phoenix, where the coyote took her, then continued on together to Lake Tahoe. Jonathan has since become an American citizen, and Carolina has had a residence permit (a green card) since May 2003.

The children race around the children's arcade, come over to the table where we are sitting to ask for more quarters for the machines, to ask for a Coke; they swarm around us and we decide to give up the interview.

Walking back to Irma's from the hotel, Carolina told me, "We were very poor." She went to work at her daughter Berta's age, she says, [thirteen], "throwing manure on the cornfields" beside her mother. She went to school for only two years. Carolina said that she would have liked to study nursing but needed to have completed secondary school to do so. If she had been able to study, she would have become a doctor or at least a nurse. Carolina told me that Berta would like to become a veterinarian, for small animals. Berta, who was walking beside us, confirmed this desire. Carolina encourages her; she hoped that all her children would go on to college.

Both Irma and Raúl are also enthusiastic about their children's studying, but they are not familiar with the necessary routines: both finished only primary school in Mexico, while surrounded in their one- or two-room houses with a number of younger siblings. Irma tells Erlinda to study and then constantly sends her on errands. Raúl shouts at the children to study but leaves them to do their homework on the floor, belly down. The adults co-opt the only table in the house for their own conversations and almost constant visitors. The children seem to perceive studying as a punishment, involving shouts and threats, rather than a joy, though all the children are eager to learn. Raúl shouts in desperation: he wants his children to do better than he did. For several nights I helped the three boys with their homework, finding that one of their mathematics teachers has not explained an assignment very clearly. I told Irma and Raúl that the children needed a quiet place with a table to study and that it was better to encourage them without shouting. Raúl responded that he knew he should not lose his temper—but that sometimes they just did not listen. Both Irma and Raúl showed much respect for my advice—as though I were an expert after so many years of schooling. They felt helpless because they themselves had not had enough education or enough English to help their children with their assignments.

Cousins

Liliana, Raúl's cousin, and I talked on a bench on the patio of Irma and Raúl's house while she held her six-year-old daughter Erica, who has Down's syndrome, in her arms. Liliana told me that the doctors did not know why her daughter had been born with Down's syndrome, but that she [Liliana] had been working in a plant where they washed newly made cloth with heavy bleaches and other chemicals while she was pregnant. Liliana and her husband have three daughters and a son. The eldest, a son who was sixteen in 2003, and his fifteen-year-old sister were born in Tepatitlán. Erica and her three-year-old sister were born in Downey, California.

Liliana came accompanied by her parents and a sister, all of whom live in Tepatitlán, as well as her husband and children. They drove from Los Angeles so that Liliana could be one of the madrinas and to visit Liliana's brothers, who now live in Carson City, Nevada. It was this cluster of cousins that Raúl had joined in Los Angeles the first time he came to the United States and then followed to Lake Tahoe Town. Liliana told me that her father first came to the United States with los braceros (as a field hand under the Bracero Program of 1942–64):

"When I was little, in '63, I believe, he went for the last time. He told us how they suffered, how they came in a group and lived in a room together."

Our interview was abbreviated because Erica, a charming child, needs much attention. Liliana no longer works, she explains, as she must care for her full time. Notably, Liliana and her husband's and parents' appearance for the dual celebrations is an instance of strong ties being ratified and strengthened further.

Salvador's presence at the celebrations is an instance of weak ties being strengthened. He arrived with his wife and three children from San Jose. (His mother Lupe often came from where she lives in Guadalajara to visit her sister doña Consuelo in Colonia Popular. When I interviewed doña Lupe in Colonia Popular in 1991, her son Salvador had already crossed into the United States.) He told me that most of the time he worked as a roofer in San Diego, then moved on to San Jose to do the same.

"I crossed the first time in 1986, through Tijuana to San Jose, California. My papa was there. [Salvador's mother and father have been separated since he was a child; he has half-brothers and half-sisters on both sides.] He came to Guadalajara, and I crossed back with him. But the crossing was really ugly. We were in the hills for three days, and it was raining heavily. We went directly to San Jose. I began working in a cannery. Then I made some friends, and they got me a job in roofing, three months later. I stayed from '86 to '89 in San Jose. In '89 I went to San Diego and then in '95—no '96 [he asks doña Consuelo the year—she knows because he came to visit her in Mexicali that year before moving]—in '96 we came back to San Jose again." He had met his wife the first time he was in San Jose, and they went together to San Diego.

"I got my amnesty permit for having worked in the cannery—it was in agriculture, you know. Then they gave me a residence permit for five years. All my children were born here. We have gone many times to Mexicali, to Tijuana; the farthest we went was La Paz [Baja California Sur]. I was very angry with my relatives because when I came here I sent money to construct a house, and my uncle [his father's brother] sold it without my permission. That uncle had raised me as if he had been my father. But I am no longer angry."

Doña Consuelo, who was present during the interview, later contested this account. She said that his mother had given the house to one of her sons, Salvador's half-brother. When I asked Consuelo why Salvador had not told me the true story, she said that she thought it was because it hurt him too much.

"We are planning to sell my house in San Jose and return again to San Diego so we can see my *jefa* (lit. boss; mother) more often. You know, she goes to Mexicali quite often. But I am also thinking of arranging for papers for my mama so she can come here. I'm going to arrange for my mama and my papa. [In late 2006 his mother and stepfather moved permanently to Colonia Popular, Mexicali, and acquired a lot there. Salvador, according to doña Consuelo, went to visit them some months thereafter, after years of not having seen them.]

"I like money. I like to work hard. Always, wherever I go, I come to be the leader, the foreman, the supervisor. I have gotten the book of California laws. In order to get a license so I could work on my own. I took the exam at the back of the book twice, and I failed. I took my driver's license exam in English. . . . Everything I have tried to do I have achieved—when I sent in my papers for amnesty; when I wanted my house, I bought a house; when I wanted a new car, I bought one. The only thing I have not achieved is to go to Guadalajara or to Mexico City to meet my father-in-law, most likely because I have not wanted to—for something inside of me. I still feel bad about what happened [about the house]."

Salvador told me he had crossed the border clandestinely two times: the first time he came to the United States and once after he had his residence permit. The second time it was because he did not want his wife to recross after a visit to her parents in Mexico City alone. "A woman alone, they take advantage of her. They do things." The Border Patrol stopped them on this crossing, but Salvador simply said he had no documents and was deported along with his wife. They successfully crossed the next time.

Manuela
&
Cesar

Irma
&
Raúl

Jonathan
&
Carolina

Hortensia
&
Gilberto

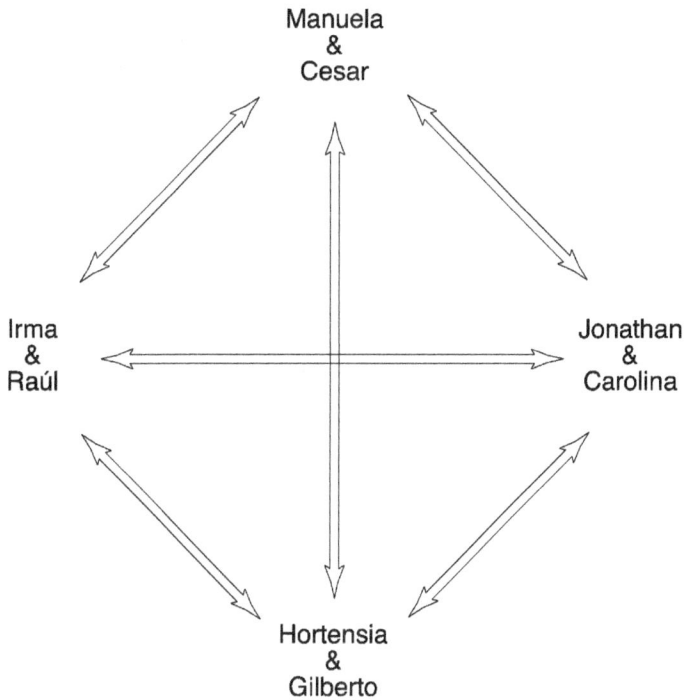

Figure 1. Irma and Raúl's Compadrazgo Network in Lake Tahoe Town

Conclusions

Irma and Raúl's wedding and their daughter Erlinda's quinceañera party served to strengthen strong ties among some kin and some compadres, to strengthen weak kin ties and create new compadrazgo ties, and to reveal which supposedly strong-tied kin or compadres they could count on and which perhaps they could not. The rift that began with an argument with Raúl's mother was widened by his parents' failure to attend. Since Irma and Raúl had extended aid to her brother Edgar when he joined them in Lake Tahoe Town 1999, Irma was especially hurt by his absence. Weak ties became stronger with Irma's cousin Salvador; in 2004 they went to visit him and his family in San Jose, and he returned one weekend to visit them. Others present at the events reinforced their preexisting strong ties with Raúl, Irma, or both. When in late 2006 Irma and Raúl moved on to Carson City, Raúl's cousins, who had established themselves there several years earlier, networked him into a hotel construction site they were working on and later, as mentioned above, into apartment finishing. Irma and Raúl continued to visit their Lake Tahoe compadres on weekends, but daily interaction was now foreclosed.

These migration network stories provide an opportunity for theorizing how sisters can become nodal points in male migration; how social capital, embedded in networks, can expand and contract over time—for individuals, households, and communities; and on the question of whether Anamaría and Roberto and Irma and Raúl can be considered transnational migrants.

CHAPTER II

The Urban Woman

and Male Transnational Migration

Although 51.4 percent of the males and 12.7 percent of the females I interviewed in Colonia Popular in 1988–92 had worked in the United States at some time, almost all had worked only for a short time in unstable jobs.[1] Most had crossed only once and stayed from two weeks to a year. Only 15 of the 157 families had members who had qualified for amnesty under the 1986 IRCA, all of them as Special Agricultural Workers. Many of those who had crossed the border and failed to establish themselves in the United States had done so from their ranchos or pueblos of origin and later returned to move their families to Mexicali. The accounts of the people I interviewed suggested that most male heads of household chose to return to Mexicali from the United States or not to attempt to cross at all because of the lack of adequate network resources in the United States, a desire to keep the family together in Mexico, or for both reasons. Most had come to the border because of lack of employment at origin or higher salaries in Mexicali. In the late 1990s it became easier for men to acquire border-crossing cards, largely because the Mexican government no longer required men to demonstrate completion of the required military service in order to acquire the Mexican passport that was prerequisite for receiving a card. Even though this document did not allow its bearer to work in the United States, it made entry into the United States less difficult than crossing with a coyote.

Upon my return to the colonia in 2003, many families who formerly had no or only unsuccessful migratory experiences in the United States now had offspring, both sons and daughters, living and working across the border. In contrast to a rancho, where dense and overlapping networks at origin funnel the population into a limited number of destinations in the United States (but see Wilson 1998a), the colonia scattered its children over many destinations. The migration stories of the children of the original migrants to the colonia illuminate three principles of migration: that migration networks may be tapped not in the place of permanent residence, long-term residence, or last residence but in places of prior residence of self, parents, spouse, or spouse's family;[2] that women may have the primary role in drawing both female and male relatives into the transnational migration stream; and that in urban centers, network extension is facilitated through sisters' marrying men who migrate to different places in the United States. Their brothers can then pick and chose what places they want to try out. Transnational migration networks at origin may be developing to such an extent that people who once had few if any network ties in the United States now have such ties.

That a migrant may join a migration stream from a spouse's place of origin and that men may tap the networks of women is illustrated in the case of Castulo, a brickmaker from Zacatecas, who arrived with his parents and wife in Mexicali several years before the establishment of Colonia Popular in 1983. Before acquiring lots in the colonia the extended family lived on the brickyards. In 1996, after having lived in that border city for approximately fifteen years, Castulo's wife insisted they return to her rancho, also in Zacatecas, for a prolonged visit. From there Castulo joined a migration stream to a small town in Texas, where he has lived and worked for six years in a cement plant. None of his brothers and sisters, or his parents' siblings, has ever worked in the United States. Notably, it was Raúl's *mother's* brother's children who facilitated his migration first to Los Angeles, then to Lake Tahoe Town, and then to Carson City.

In a second case, Manuela, born in Mexico City to a woman from Chihuahua (Consuelo's comadre Socorro) and a man from Quintana Roo, came to Mexicali with her parents when she was a child in 1984. Having finished secondary school, she entered a normal school for teachers in Chihuahua. After marrying and separating from a fellow student there, she returned to live with her parents in Colonia Popular. A few years later, in 1994, she returned to Chihuahua to visit some school friends and began to communicate once again with her husband, who was now in Phoenix, Arizona. Eventually he sent her money to pay a coyote and join him. She crossed with a younger brother, Miguel. Although Manuela returned after a year and a half, Miguel continued working in a factory there for seven years, returning to Mexico to attend the funeral of a nephew in late 2001. This account again shows that one can join a migration stream from a place other than one's place of residence and that women can provide men with the option of migration.

In both of the above accounts it was ties to women that enabled men to migrate. For Castulo, a return to his wife's rancho enabled him to enter a transnational migration stream, and for Miguel, his sister Manuela's opportunity to migrate to Phoenix made his migration possible.

The role of women is also significant in augmenting network expansion for men when their sisters marry into families with nonoverlapping but continually developing, transnational migration networks that lead them to different destinations in the United States, giving them multiple choices of places to live and work. This principle is illustrated by the experience of three interlinked families, one in which the daughters of one married into the two others.

Endogamous marriages are common in a given rancho or in any given cluster of nearby ranchos and in any given colonia or cluster of colonias in Mexicali. The difference between the rancho and the colonia in this regard is that in the rancho virtually all the parental generation were born there or nearby, whereas in the colonia the parental generation may come from a number of states and geographically dispersed locales within any given state. When the children of two families originating in different locales marry, each gains access to the other's constantly developing transnational migration networks, and members of the parental generation may have access to migration networks anchored in their places of origin, networks that continue to mature and develop over time (including the time after which they left their community of origin to live elsewhere in Mexico).

Doña Consuelo had thirteen children, including eight daughters. Four of her younger daughters married into families also resident in Colonia Popular. In three cases these families developed ties with later-migrating friends or relatives in the United States from their ranchos or towns of origin. Irma's husband's family had migrated to Mexicali from a rancho in Jalisco geographically distant from Consuelo's rancho of origin in the same state. The father of that family was a brickmaker who had crossed five times in the 1960s to work in the agricultural fields near Bakersfield, California, each time leaving from his rancho of origin, but had been unable to establish a permanent presence in the United States. In the 1980s, he and his wife and children had relocated to Mexicali and Colonia Popular (see Wilson 2005 for a first-person account of don Ramón's life). His son Raúl, married to Consuelo's daughter Irma, crossed the border to join cousins from his rancho of birth in Jalisco who had had migrated to Los Angeles. On a later crossing he joined some of these same cousins in Lake Tahoe Town. Irma followed him first to Los Angeles and later to Lake Tahoe Town. In Lake Tahoe Town he was joined by his father, two of his brothers, and a sister.

Anamaría's husband's family was originally from Hermosillo, Sonora. They moved from there first to an ejido in the Valle de Mexicali and then to the city of Mexicali in the early 1980s. Jaime and his wife eventually occupied a lot in Colonia Popular and his sister Miriam (Anamaría's mother-in-law) the one beside it. Neither Jaime nor his wife had any relatives who had worked in the United States. In the mid-1990s, Jaime, a musician, crossed the border to play at an event in Arizona and met a woman who had been a childhood friend of his and of his sister Miriam; she invited Jaime and his wife and sister to visit her in Waters. Miriam was the first to do so, and her son Roberto, whom Anamaría later married, soon followed. Anamaría later joined her husband, crossing in 1999 with a border-crossing card as he had. Jaime and his wife also became part of this migration stream, but they retained a foot in Colonia Popular, where they sometimes return on weekends and where some of their offspring remain.

Consuelo's daughters Irma and Anamaría were thus living and working in the United States by 1999 and their independent, nonoverlapping migration networks provided more than one migration option for their brothers. The eldest, Edgar, after receiving his border-crossing card in 1999, immediately crossed to work in Lake Tahoe Town, finding work in maintenance in the same hotel as Irma's father-in-law and husband. For several months in 2001, 2002, and early 2003, he went to install drywall in Arizona, where his sister Anamaría lived. The first time he crossed he stayed with his sister La Muñeca's husband's sister, but after La Muñeca and her husband separated, the families no longer kept in contact. Thus, it is seen that former network members can be lost because of life-cycle events—in this case a breakup of a sibling's marriage, which affected relationships with both families' members.

On later crossings Edgar stayed with Jaime and his wife and sons, since their rented house was bigger than the small apartment where Anamaría and Roberto lived at the time. He was initially employed in a large automobile repair workshop where his sister Anamaría's mother-in-law's brother Jaime worked. Later he worked putting drywall in houses under construction. Edgar's migration to diverse destinations was facilitated by his sisters' marriages into families with different migration options. Edgar plans to return to both Nevada and Arizona to seek more work in the future, as does his brother Manuel, also a drywaller and also in possession of a border-crossing card. One of Anamaría's brothers-in-law, Rosario's husband, who has network members in San Jose, California, where he has worked, also came to join Anamaría and Roberto to work in Arizona for a few months. The dispersion of sisters to different geographical locations as part of their husbands' families thus multiplies migration options for their brothers (and perhaps their brothers-in-law). Neither of the destination towns is a traditional receiving areas for Mexican migration, though a Mexican presence is increasing in both.

The dispersion of migrating sisters to various parts of the United States appears to be an essentially urban phenomenon. In cities the opportunity for women to marry into families who have immigrated from different states and widely different locations within the same state is heightened. Thus brothers in urban-based families find their migration options multiplied to a greater extent than brothers in rancho-based families, where

migration streams to certain destination points have been established sometimes over generations. This is because endogamy on a rancho or cluster of
ranchos provides less diversity in migration networks than endogamy in a
colonia containing residents from numerous points of origin.

It is clear that women's networks often facilitate male migration.
Furthermore, in cities, where sisters may marry men from families originating in several different geographical locations, a multiplicity of migration
options may be created for their brothers. The migration networks tapped
may be grounded in the place of permanent, long-term, or more recent
residence but also in the place of origin of the in-migrants to the city—
in-migrants who may be members of the parental generation. Cumulative
causation continues in their ranchos of origin after they migrate internally.
Not all potential network ties are activated, however. Thus Anamaría has
had no contact with her sister La Muñeca's former husband, who has lived
in Waters since 1995, or with Irma's husband Raúl's sister, who also lives
there, and neither Miriam or Jaime presently has any contact with the
friend who originally invited them to Waters. Further, in some cases, such
as divorce or separation of one of their members, network ties may be dissolved completely.

The Expansion and Contraction of Social Capital

Social capital can expand or contract for any given person, family, or
community over time, depending on local and household dynamics. In
other words, it is not a given for all times and all places. The migration
histories recorded above illustrate this process.

When Colonia Popular was established in 1983, Mateo Rosacalba,
originally from the state of Jalisco but then renting a house on the out-
skirts of Mexicali, quickly acquired a lot with his wife and five young
children. Within months, Mateo's sister Consuelo, who had migrated
from Jalisco to Mexicali to Mexico City, then after her marriage failed,
returned to Mexicali, moved from La Petrolera—another squatter settlement where she was renting a small house—onto a lot in Colonia Popular
five houses away from his. At the same time, her daughter Carla and her
husband had moved from Mexico City onto a lot in the same colonia.

Within two years doña Consuelo convinced Manuel, a married son and her next to eldest who was living in Mexico City, to come north and live on Carla's lot so that Carla could return with her husband to Mexico City. Seven years after the colonia was established, another married son, Edgar, Consuelo's eldest who was based in Mexico City as well, bought and moved onto a lot two doors down from hers with his wife and their three children. Within less than a decade the family was thus settled on 4 of the 155 residential lots making up the colonia. Family-based social capital had enabled the immigration to the colonia of family members. By 2000 another married daughter, Lorena, had acquired a house in the colonia. Meanwhile son Francisco and his wife, who had received a lot in Colonia Nueva Oportunidad through Consuelo's efforts, had sold it and with the proceeds bought a lot at the end of the same street where Consuelo lives. A niece, daughter of brother Mateo, also acquired a lot in the colonia. Thus the extended family, by 2000, occupied 7 lots in Colonia Popular. Two nieces, two daughters, and two sons married to women from the colonia thus extended affinal ties and expanded the network.

The family's community-wide social capital had been augmented in the mid-1980s as colonia members organized to press first for electricity and then for piped water. These efforts involved collective action and networking among unrelated families to take part in demonstrations and meetings at government offices. Consuelo and the president of the colonia, Socorro, became comadres during the course of these grassroots organizing events. When Socorro needed colonia representatives to go to the government offices with her, she could depend on Consuelo, and her sister-in-law, daughter-in-law, and daughters to accompany her. Women from most households in the colonia took part as well. There was constant networking among colonia families, especially though not exclusively their women, to press for services, and social capital increased community-wide, with families helping one another as they had during the original invasion. Women visited each other's houses to share a meal or a soda or a coffee and helped each other stage events, such as the Mother's Day and Día de la Virgen de Guadalupe celebrations. Neighbors were also invited to family-sponsored life-cycle celebrations.

Once services were acquired, however, factions developed, and the colonia split. Socorro stepped down from the presidency, and a woman from the dominant rival faction replaced her. One of doña Consuelo's daughters-in-law began an affair with Socorro's husband, and both eventually abandoned their spouses. Their affair created a rift between Consuelo's family and Socorro's. There were altercations among families from different factions, and the cooperation that had once been common was undermined through gossip and backbiting. In sum, over time the community-wide networking broke down, and most interactions took place among extended-family members, a few longtime friends, and people with whom family members had established ritual kinship relations at the time of their children's baptisms, school graduations, confirmations, quinceañera celebrations, and marriages.

Marriages between colonia families became, over the years, an important way of expanding family-based social capital. Mateo's eldest daughter married a young man whose mother had a lot in the colonia; the young couple eventually acquired a house lot of their own three doors north of Mateo's. His youngest daughter also married into a colonia family. Her husband's father had a green card and commuted to his work in Brawley, California, where the young man she married had been born. Eventually her husband helped her to jump the fence in Mexicali, and the couple went to live and work in Brawley. In the mid-1990s, her brother joined them there to seek work as well.

Four of Consuelo's eight daughters married into colonia families: two from Jalisco (Irma and La Muñeca), one from Durango (Lorena), and one from Sinaloa (Anamaría). Three went to live initially in their parents-in-law's houses, and one son-in-law, whose family lived directly across the street, moved into Consuelo's house. One of her sons also married into a colonia family originally from the state of Michoacán. Consuelo's sons and daughters were thus occupying or linked to households on seven other lots, and her brother Mateo's daughters were occupying or linked to households on three other lots. Family networks by 1998 thus included inhabitants of twelve lots linked by consanguineal or affinal ties. The social capital of the extended family, based on marriage, had thus expanded while that based on community organizing had diminished. The increased social capital was family-centric rather than community-centric.

The family-centric social capital began to be delocalized with Mateo's daughter's migration to Brawley. This was followed by the migration of several of Consuelo's daughters. In 1990 Irma crossed the border for the first time to join her husband Raúl. Anamaría married a man up the street from their house whose mother and maternal uncle worked in Arizona. Eventually her husband, then Anamaría herself, relocated there in family chain-migration fashion. In 2002 Consuelo finally received a border-crossing card and went to visit both Irma and Anamaría. Anamaría's brothers Edgar and Manuel are drywallers who have provided subcontracted work crews to the Plaza Cachanilla in Mexicali, the Daewoo factory in San Luís Río Colorado, the Westin Regina in Cabo San Lucas, and the Continental Plaza Hotel and Convention Center in Guadalajara. Edgar had also crossed to work, without documents, on a drywalling project in San Francisco in the late 1990s. Both he and Manuel have since acquired border-crossing cards, as have some members of their work crews, and although unauthorized to work in the United States, they have begun to bid on projects on the other side of the border.

As we have seen, Edgar has visited both his sister Irma and his sister Anamaría, and Manuel plans to visit Anamaría as well. He has had little work in Mexicali over the past year, and she assures him he can earn up to eighteen dollars an hour finishing the houses that are proliferating in this part of Arizona.

Thus Consuelo's family network, and the social capital it bears, has expanded across the border. Two of Anamaría's three children and three of Irma's five children were born in the United States and therefore are American citizens, so the family has become transnational in legality. Mateo's daughter in Brawley has given birth to all three of her children in the United States. Before her migration, Mateo and Consuelo's sibling group had only one member who worked in the United States. After receiving Special Agricultural Workers amnesty for his work in the Imperial Valley's agricultural fields, Felipe had commuted to work in a factory in Calexico from Mexicali, but he had never established a permanent residence in the United States. The likelihood he would do so diminished after he was crippled in an accident. Consuelo's paternal grandfather had crossed the border but was never heard from again.

Family members, including two of Consuelo and Mateo's brothers and three married sons and two married daughters of Consuelo, have also acquired housing in other colonias in Mexicali, spreading their family network to a variety of locations within the city. Networking among families in the colonia resulting in community-wide social capital diminished after the colonia's acquisition of services, but family-wide social capital increased once again as growing children intermarried with other families in the colonia and elsewhere. Squatter-settlement residents with green cards intermarried with families who lacked such documents and facilitated the transnational migration and job search for spouses and/or spouses of offspring.

The importance of the Rosacalba family story is that it illustrates the dynamics of networks and social capital in association with local sociopolitical dynamics and the family life cycle. It also illustrates the contrast between a community's social capital and the social capital borne by interlinked families. Social capital is not once and for all and static but can contract and expand over the life course of an individual, family, or community. Further, it is not encapsulated in one locality but may bud off to encompass several localities and become a resource that attracts even more network members and thus expands social capital in a new locale. This dynamism is augmented by the intricacies of network-mediated migration. The experience of these linked families demonstrates the importance both of a diversity of place-based network members and of the role of women, especially sisters, in facilitating transnational migration.

Transnational Migration

The question arises whether Irma and Raúl and Anamaría and Roberto, immobilized by lack of border-crossing documents, can be considered "transmigrants." As Mahler (1998) has suggested, it is necessary to approach the concept at different levels of analysis to answer the question, because it is not only countries that are linked across borders but also communities, households, and families. The theorizing of transnational migration began on a macro-level (Glick Schiller, Basch, and Blanc-Szanton 1992; Basch, Glick Schiller, and Szanton Blanc 1994): attention was directed to the way the emigrant population participated in nation-building activities in the origin state through political activity and remittances but also in the country of destination. Such analysis is outside the scope of this book, though it might be noted that the Mexican government encouraged its emigrant population to register and vote in the 2006 elections and that Mexican consular officials have constantly lobbied for the rights of Mexicans in the United States.

Later, meso-level transnational migration patterns were identified: networks of egocentric networks that often involved hometown associations established at destination and that used migrants' resources to improve living conditions in the community of origin. Much of the meso-level theorizing on transnational migration has involved looking at "transnational communities" anchored in a rancho or pueblo at origin (e.g., Guarnizo and Smith 1998; Goldring 1998; Levitt 2001; Rouse 1992; Smith 1998). Such meso-level theorizing is difficult to apply to *cities* of origin, where migrants may not have known each other before migrating. Adaptation networks therefore involve people met at destination to a greater extent than in cases of network-mediated or chain migration from a relatively autonomous small community characterized by interlocking kinship and friendship networks and intensive face-to-face interaction.

The micro-level analysis of transmigration focuses on individual, household, and family networks (see Landolt, Autler, and Baires 1999, 296, 312). It is at this level that Anamaría and Irma and their husbands can be conceptualized as engaging in a social field of transnational migration. Visits from kin based in Mexicali, including their mother doña Consuelo (who as mentioned earlier can be seen as a "connecting relative," or a "transnational link"), their brother Edgar, and soon their sister La Muñeca (who acquired her border-crossing card in November 2005 and visited Waters in 2007), make up part of their social field. Resources and news flow through Anamaría's husband's uncle Jaime and his wife, who return to Mexicali almost every weekend. There are economic exchanges during these visits, as Anamaría often sends pocket money to La Muñeca or Rosario with her mother or with Jaime, and when her mother comes to visit, she often receives gifts and money. Some members of Anamaría's and Roberto's social networks also go back and forth to Mexicali; news and sometimes goods travel through them. Furthermore, in 2006 Anamaría sent her U.S.-born children to stay in Colonia Popular with doña Consuelo for the summer.

Irma and Raúl's transnational social field is connected to both Tepatitlán and to Mexicali. Raúl's parents move back and forth between Lake Tahoe Town and Mexicali and sometimes visit relatives in the Tepatitlán area; other network members, including Raúl's uncle and some of his and Irma's compadres, move back and forth to Tepatitlán. News, gifts, and remittances flow in one direction or another. It is thus at a micro-level that Consuelo's daughters and their husbands can be seen as transmigrants—involved in transnational familial and sociokinship network relations that involve crossing borders—despite being immobilized by their undocumented status.

That they are not or not yet involved in meso-level transnational social fields may be because of their origin in cities, where focused, small-scale community projects are more problematic than in rural small towns, partly because of the lack of overlap of networks of recipients. Furthermore, doña Consuelo's daughters, their husbands, and their network members are involved in what Pessar (2003, 96) has called a "transnational cognitive space." This is shown first by their concern about family left behind—whom many mourned they could not visit because of the danger of recrossing without documents—and second by their interest in events in places where they lived before coming to the United States. Because of the presence of their sisters in the United States, Irma and Anamaría's siblings have transnational social capital and thus also participate in a transnational cognitive space.

CHAPTER 12

Conclusions

Between the 1950s, when doña Consuelo was still living in Jalisco, and 2000, when Anamaría and Irma left for the United States from Mexicali, the proportion of Mexico's population living in urban centers, defined as those with more than 2,500 inhabitants, increased from 42.7 to 74.7 percent (table 11).

Table 11. Population of Mexico and Percent Urban, 1960–2005

Year	Population of Mexico*	Percent Urban**
1950	26,282,000	42.7
1960	34,994,000	50.8
1970	50,695,000	59.0
1980	69,655,000	66.3
1990	81,249,600	72.5
2000	100,349,800	74.7
2005	106,719,000	76.0

Sources: * "Mexico: Historical Demographical Data of the Whole Country," http://www.library.uu.nl/wesp/populstat/Americas/mexicoc.htm (accessed May 10, 2005).

** World Population Prospects: The 2004 Revision Population Database. Mexico, http://esa.un.org/unpp/p2Kodata.asp (accessed May 10, 2005).

The increasing migration from urban centers in Mexico to the United States since the 1970s has been explained in terms of this rapid urbanization and the resulting saturated labor markets in the cities, as the result of both internal migration and natural increase (Cornelius 1992, 1993; Corona

Vásquez 1998; Lozano Ascensio, 2002). Structural explanations underscore the role of economic crises since 1982, which have affected the cities more than the countryside (Lozano Ascensio 2002). Structural adjustment policies leading to the withdrawal of subsidies, cuts in government employment, privatization, and openness to a foreign investment that marginalized domestically owned companies—all imposed by international lending institutions such as the IMF and the World Bank—have also played a role in reducing the quality of life in both urban and rural areas.

Despite the fact that Mexico's large urban centers today are "serving increasingly as platforms for migration to the United States" (Cornelius 1993, 335), most urban-based migrants to the United States seem to depend on rural-based networks in their places of origin (Massey et al. 1987, 99–100; Roberts, Frank, and Lozano Ascensio 1999, 15). This suggests that most urban-based migrants (or their parents) are recent migrants to the cities and strong linkages persist between them and their kin and friends in their communities of origin (Massey et al. 1987, 99). Using rural-based networks leads to the phenomenon of urban-based migrants to the United States bearing not their identity as city dwellers but "as *paisanos* from their community of origin" (Massey et al. 1987, 100). This was certainly the case with Raúl. His friends and compadres considered him to be from the Tepatitlán region, where he was born rather than from Mexicali, where he was living when he crossed into the United States. Whereas Anamaría did not use her mother's sojourn in Tepatitlán and aunts' and uncles' births in that region to establish commonalities within her network, Irma did.

When internal migrants leave home for the city, it is often because they lack the material and network resources that would permit them to risk a trip to the United States (Wilson 1993; see also Arizpe 1981; Dinerman 1982). This was certainly the case with doña Consuelo and most of her siblings. Network-mediated chain migration from a rural community to a given city is common; this pattern has been found among migrants from Tilatongo, Oaxaca (Butterworth 1962), and from Tzintzuntzán, Michoacán (Kemper 1977), to Mexico City and among migrants to a squatter settlement there (Lomnitz 1977), to a fraccionamiento in Ciudad Juárez (Ugalde 1974), to

Monterrey, Nuevo León (Balán, Browning, and Jelin 1973; Browning and Feindt 1971), and to a colonia in Mexicali (Wilson 1998b). Despite the lack of viable transnational network resources for those who move internally, transnational networks continue to develop and expand at origin, in keeping with the dynamic of cumulative causation. As immature networks mature, they may eventually come to encompass kin who stayed behind, compadres, and friends.

Offspring of internal migrants can also come to be included in this expanding transnational network at origin, whether they were born at origin and migrated internally with their parents (as in Raúl's and Irma's case) or were born in that destination city (as in Roberto's and Anamaría's case). A sister's son or daughter born in Mexico City or Mexicali is as much a nephew or niece as the boy or girl born in the rancho of origin to that same sister and as much a nephew or niece whether he or she stays at home or migrates to another town or city. These offspring of internal migrants may therefore tap kin networks in the transnational migration process from wherever they are living. It must be kept in mind, however, that as Irma and Raúl's wedding guests show, some strong ties may be weakened over the course of a lifetime, while weaker ties may be strengthened.

In the Mexican cities of destination transnational migration is facilitated in another way: networks expand through the marriage of offspring. One's children can tap the networks of their spouse's, networks that are also expanding over time to include more and more members, and these affinal kin can aid siblings of the in-marrying spouses in their own migration efforts. In summary, with reference to the increased migration from urban areas in Mexico, there are network-mediated migrations to the cities from rural communities of origin, and the offspring of these internal migrants will be included in continuing network ties with kin and friends in the community of origin. Furthermore, within the cities, networks will expand through the marriage of offspring to individuals tied into their communities of origin through parents' and their own network membership. Meanwhile, immature transnational migration networks continue to develop and expand at origin until they reach maturity, and years later, in-migrants to the city may have network members at origin who are now immersed in mature transnational networks. This explains why people who once could contemplate only internal migration can now migrate from urban centers to the United States. In other words, a family's social capital may grow even in its absence from a particular geographical locale as long as linkages are maintained—even intermittently—with kin, compadres, and friends.

Social capital can be localized or extended to encompass a variety of localities within a nation and across national borders, depending on where network members live and work. Furthermore, on all levels—individual, familial, and community—weak ties can be converted into strong ones. Network members may migrate to the same population center within that state and sometimes to the same neighborhood or colonia within that center. In the absence of a long tradition of chain migration to the United States—encompassing friends and kin who are members of a definable community and more typical for rural than for urban emigrants—network members at destination may commonly have been unknown at origin. Yet their having lived in the same city before crossing national borders may help them to establish a commonality that aids in strengthening weak ties between acquaintances.

Networks facilitating the adaptation of migrants to their new destinations can be expected to expand at destination, as weak-tied acquaintances are turned into strong-tied network members through marriage or compadrazgo (Wilson 1998a). For Irma and Raúl, friends became compadres; for Anamaría and Roberto, workmates became good friends. The establishment of ritual-kinship relationships has long been identified as aiding migrants, internal or international, in their psychic as well as their material adjustment to their new destinations (Lomnitz 1977; Nutini and Bell 1980; O'Connor 1990). Based on trust and the recognition of mutual responsibility, ritual kinship is often used to give friendship a ritual sanction, thereby honoring the strong ties that have come to prevail (O'Connor 1990, 87). Thus Raúl and Irma's shared network expanded at destination and tended to be exocentric. Roberto, not being Roman Catholic, and Anamaría, having given up Roman Catholic ritual, did not have this option, and their networks are more easily separated and more egocentric. They have expanded their networks exclusively though work-site friendships.

Doña Consuelo's history of internal migration is that of a woman whose family had neither the network nor the material resources either to stay in their place of origin or migrate to the United States. The fam-ily moved from one place to another in Jalisco, from rancho to town to small city, and when the parents separated, the mother went to Mexicali to join an aunt. Following her mother to that border city, Consuelo met a man there who took her to Mexico City. Consuelo's eventual perma-nent migration to Mexicali, the "platform" from which her daughters migrated—and from which two of her sons intermittently cross to work in the United States—was in the interest of family reunification after a failed marriage; her mother and several of her siblings had preceded her there.

The stories recounted in this book suggest the following general conclusions:

First, poor women in Mexico engage in a variety of income-producing activities in both the formal and informal economies that may involve migration to a variety of locales and—until the election of the PAN party in the state of Baja California in 1990 and to the country's presidency in 2000—also included the establishment of colonias populares to obtain plots of land for themselves or their offspring.

Second, many if not most women accept the system of male domina-tion but may opt out of an unhappy marriage if men do not live up to certain standards they consider fair. This is especially true in urban areas where women can find work. Nonetheless, even female heads of house-hold (most often an intermittent status) want their daughters to have a formal wedding.

Third, although most women migrate under the auspices of husbands or fathers, women's migration within Mexico can take place indepen-dently of males. Some parts of Mexico will release more women migrants than others, possibly because of the greater strength of neopatriarchy in the latter locations. Furthermore, women can provide important network aid to sons, brothers, sons-in-law, and brothers-in-law in the internal and transnational migration process.

Fourth, extended-family migration to a given city often also involves migration to a specific colonia or neighborhood within that city and, through colonia-endogamous intermarriage of offspring, can lead to network expansion in that locale.

Fifth, the social capital provided by networks exists on individual, familial, and community levels.

Sixth, strong ties can be either reinforced or weakened over time and the family life cycle, and weak ties can be converted into strong ties or abandoned. Individual, familial, or community social capital may therefore wax and wane in keeping with the expansion or contraction of networks. Transnational migration networks multiply in urban centers when siblings or offspring marry into families who come from different states or different population centers within the same state, with each center of origin (or residence) having its own maturation of migration networks.

Seventh, transnational migration networks can be anchored in a multiplicity of locales, including place of origin, place of anterior (internal or transnational) migration, or place of one's current residence or that of one's parents, spouse's parents, or other kin.

Eighth, adaptation networks for urban-origin migrants at destination may be, to a great extent, composed of work-site acquaintances converted into friends or ritual kin, and both friends and ritual kin may introduce migrants to future friends and ritual kin. Work-based friendships and fictive kin relationships may sometimes be alternatives and sometimes reinforcing, as a weaker tie is converted into a stronger tie.

Ninth, transnationalism involves individuals embedded in households, families, and networks who, through their ability to cross borders, provide connecting links between kin in Mexico and kin in the United States.

A number of scholars have argued that immigrants, and especially the undocumented, provide a subsidy to the capitalist system to the point of permitting the more competitive sectors of that system to persist (e.g., Castles and Kosack 1973; Gómez-Quiñones 1981; Portes 1977, 1981; Portes and Bach 1985; Sassen-Koob 1981). Adult workers provide a subsidy to the economy because the costs of their rearing and education have been borne elsewhere (Burawoy 1975; Wilson 1999, 2000) and also because, using borrowed or falsified Social Security cards, they often pay into a Social Security system they cannot later draw upon (Hayes-Bautista, Schink, and Chapa 1990). More than two decades ago Gómez-Quiñones (1981, 14) estimated that each adult Mexican immigrant worker costs the Mexican economy US$40,000 to produce; the presence of these workers thus represents a direct subsidy to the host economy. Cornelius (1989, 1998) has pointed out how important Mexican immigrants, documented or undocumented, are to the California economy, especially in small and medium-sized businesses such as construction; food processing; and shoe, textile, and electronics manufacture, as well as many other "immigrant-dependent" firms. His findings can be generalized to other states with an important immigrant presence. Motivated by economic factors, immigrants present themselves to the U.S. economy with a desire to find employment; Chavez (1992, 139) underscores "the willingness of undocumented immigrants to do any kind of job."

This willingness is apparent in the case studies presented here. Roberto has worked in a factory, in a car wash, in restaurants, and now on a public-sector construction project. Anamaría has worked in a factory, as a hotel chambermaid, and in a fast-food restaurant. Raúl has worked in agriculture and in construction and maintenance. Irma took any job she could find while Raúl was disabled, which meant primarily cleaning tourist residences. Raúl went back to work as soon as he possibly could. Roberto's mother, Miriam, was downwardly mobile in terms of job status (though not wages): her work in a hospital cafeteria in Waters contrasted unfavorably with her employment as a receptionist in a doctor's office in Mexicali.

Several migration scholars have advanced proposals to help the undocumented gain legal status or to help slow the flow of undocumented workers by offering them alternatives. Massey, Durand, and Malone (2003, 159–63) suggest, first, a temporary worker's visa that would permit immigrants to live and work in the United States for two years but not tie them to any one employer (thus avoiding some of the exploitation involved in the Bracero Program); second, providing amnesty to long-term residents without a criminal record; and third, offering tourist visas to parents of immigrants who just wish to visit their children occasionally, rather than requiring them to qualify for legal residence. Heyman (1998, chap. 7) has an innovative but rather utopian proposal. He suggests that community-based "local compacts" be formed between employers, grouped by type of business, and networks of immigrants. Both employers and immigrants (or their receiving network members) would pay for social services extended to the latter, and network recruitment, now informal, would become institutionalized. Unfortunately, employers often prefer the undocumented because of their vulnerability (Portes 1977, 1981; Sassen-Koob 1981), and marginally successful employers in highly competitive sectors of the economy may not be able to pay for social services without going bankrupt. It is often to avoid the social wage of unemployment and disability payments that employers hire the undocumented in the first place.

All the undocumented workers I interviewed hoped for an amnesty similar to that declared in 1986. Most of all they wished to be able to go back and forth across the border to visit friends and relatives and attend a quinceañera party for a niece or the wedding of a cousin. Although a limited amnesty program has been considered in Congress, it was voted down in 2007, and the legislation that passed called for building more walls and increasing the number of Border Patrol agents.

Consuelo's daughters' hopes for amnesty for themselves, their undocumented children, their spouses, and their network members seem almost futile at this point as anti-immigrant sentiment intensifies. The Immigration and Customs Enforcement (ICE), which replaced the INS when the Department of Homeland Security was established in 2002, declared in 2003 that its goal was ridding the United States of all undocumented workers by 2012 (National Immigrant Solidarity Network 2008). To that end it has carried out raids on work sites in a number of states, including Arizona and Nevada (e.g., D. González 2007). Developments in Arizona are especially pernicious for the undocumented. In 2004 Arizona passed Proposition 200, modeled on California's now-defunct Proposition 187 in its denial of all public services to the undocumented, "including public housing, food assistance, college tuition and employment benefits" (Akers Chacón and Davis 2006, 220; see also Wilson 2008b). In July 2007 a new employer-sanctions bill was passed that will close down businesses if they are caught hiring the undocumented more than once. It is to come into effect January 1, 2008. There is impressionistic evidence that the undocumented have begun moving to less anti-immigrant states (D. González 2007). A program known as Operation Streamline, initiated along part of the Texas border in 2005, had spread to the San Diego area by December 2006 and to the Tucson area by the end of 2007. Under Operation Streamline, first-time undocumented border crossers are no longer simply to be deported but will be jailed from 15 to 180 days on misdemeanor charges. Those who try to cross the border again can be charged with a felony and imprisoned for as long as two years (McCombs 2007). The program in the Del Río area of Texas and the Yuma area of Arizona has already led to a decrease in the number of undocumented immigrants attempting to cross along those border areas.

When I talked to Anamaría in the late summer of 2007, she told me that the anti-immigrant Minutemen had come to Waters and made a deal with the local police that if they stopped or picked up undocumented Mexicans in the town, they would turn them over to the immigration authorities. (Whether this is true, it is believed to be so and therefore affects attitudes and actions.) She said she and Roberto now leave their house only to go to work or for necessary chores. She quit her job in December 2007 and decided to have a fourth (and last) child. When I talked to her in February 2008 she said that when she went downtown to go shopping she did not see Mexicans anymore. I asked her if she thought they were going back to Mexico, and she replied that maybe some, but many had gone to Colorado. By April 8, 2008, a legislative committee in Arizona had approved a proposal for a guest-worker program (Associated Press 2008), showing that temporary, recurrent migration can be endorsed, while permanent settlement, involving the use of public services by immigrant families, is eschewed. The generalized anti-immigrant climate in

Nevada—including Minutemen meetings and raids on workplaces—has reduced Irma's and Raúl's visits to Reno.

We can hope that there will soon be a backlash to this anti-immigrant sentiment and that someday Anamaría, Roberto, Irma, Raúl, their undocumented children, and their undocumented network members will be able to regularize their status and return to Mexico to revisit friends and relatives. This may not occur until enough businesses go under and personal services are cut back sufficiently to make it clear that the workers from Mexico are an integral and necessary part of the U.S. economy.

Epilogue, 2009

Between the beginning of December 2008 and the end of January 2009, Roberto was laid off for a month, rehired for two weeks, and then laid off again. He and Anamaría had to borrow money to make their mortgage payments. They are thinking of returning to Mexicali.

On January 21, 2009, my dear friend doña Consuelo died in her house in Colonia Popular after months of being bedridden. Neither Irma nor Anamaría were able to attend her funeral.

Notes

Chapter 2

1. According to the leading authority on Operation Wetback, Juan Ramón García (1980, 236), the number of undocumented workers deported in 1953 was 875,318 and 1,075,168 in 1954.

2. By the end of 2008, it was estimated that from 11.4 to 12.4 million undocumented workers were in the United States, with from 6.7 to 7.3 million being from Mexico (Passel and Cohn 2008, table 1, 1; table 3, 3).

Chapter 4

1. According to the Oxford Dictionary and Thesaurus, American Edition (New York: Oxford University Press, 1996), to forage means "the act or an instance of searching for food," and foraging means "go searching, rummage (esp. for food)." Hunters and gatherers have often been conceptualized as foraging peoples (e.g., Lee 1979). As I use the concept of foraging in this chapter, it means to go searching for a livelihood in various geographical locales.

Chapter 7

1. In a study of Mexican immigrants from San Marcos, San Luís Potosí, Mexico, to Albuquerque, New Mexico, Boehm (2008, 27) has noted that "when men live in all-male apartments in Albuquerque, they take turns cooking for one another, but men virtually never cook when they return to Mexico or when their wives join them in the United States." Boehm sees this lack of cooking once women are present as part of the re-creation of masculinity in the United States. Other studies of Mexican immigrants have made similar observations. This reinforcement of masculinity may be what is happening with Roberto and Anamaría.

Chapter 9

1. Raúl tells me of other towns and cities where the owner is constructing houses. Many details are omitted here to avoid identification of the owner-employer.

2. Of six daughters and seven sons of Raúl's mother's brother, only those in the United States are included. Although all his siblings are married, only those who are or have been in the United States are shown in genealogy 3.

Chapter 10

1. Paisano ties refer to local community ties at origin, usually with the assumption that the community is rural, closed, and its members in face-to-face interaction. Paisano can also refer to someone from the same region or the same country.

Chapter 11

1. By 1992 I had twelve more interviews with women in-migrating to the state and into Colonia Popular. This chapter is based on the 1988–91 data set, whereas chapter 3 is based on the 1988–92 data set. Of the seventy-two men, fifty-seven had migrated from other states.

2. It has been noted that Mexico City–based low-skilled workers who migrate to the United States tend to tap their rural-origin social networks in the migration process (Roberts, Frank, and Lozano Ascencío 1999, 256). This is one instance of tapping networks in previous places of one's own or relatives' residence.

References Cited

Acuña, Rodolfo. 1988. *Occupied America: A History of the Chicanos*. 3rd ed. New York: Harper Collins.

Adler, Rachel H. 2002. "Patron-Client Ties, Ethnic Entrepreneurship, and Transnational Migration: The Case of Yucatecans in Dallas, Texas." *Urban Anthropology* 31 (2): 129–62.

Akers Chacón, Justin, and Mike Davis. 2006. *No One is Illegal: Fighting Racism and State Violence on the U.S.-Mexico Border*. Chicago: Haymarket Books.

Alarcón-González, Diana, and Terry McKinley. 1999. "The Adverse Effects of Structural Adjustment on Working Women in Mexico." *Latin American Perspectives* 26 (3): 103–17.

Alvarado, Rudolph, and Sonya Yvette Alvarado. 2003. *Mexicans and Mexican Americans in Michigan*. East Lansing: Michigan State University Press.

Anderson, Joan B. 1988. "Causes of Growth in the Informal Labor Sector in Mexico's Northern Border Region." *Journal of Borderlands Studies* 3 (1): 1–12.

Arias, Patricia. 1994. "Three Microhistories of Women's Work in Rural Mexico." In *Women of the Mexican Countryside, 1850–1990*, ed. Heather Fowler-Salamini and Mary Kay Vaughan, 159–74. Tucson: University of Arizona Press.

Arizpe, Lourdes. 1977. "Women in the Informal Sector: The Case of Mexico City." In *Women and National Development: The Complexities of Change*, ed. The Wellesley Editorial Committee, 25–37. Chicago: University of Chicago Press.

———. 1981. "The Rural Exodus in Mexico and Mexican Migration to the United States." *International Migration Review* 15 (4): 636–49.

Arrom, Silvia Marina. 1985a. *The Women of Mexico City, 1790–1857*. Stanford: Stanford University Press.

———. 1985b. "Changes in Mexican Family Law in the Nineteenth Century: The Civil Codes of 1870 and 1884." *Journal of Family History* 10 (Fall): 305–17.

Associated Press. 2008. "Arizona House Panel Endorses Guest-Worker Program Proposals." *Tucson Citizen*, April 26, 2008. http://www.tucsoncitizen.com/ss/local/81878.php (accessed May 3, 2008).

Ávila, José Luís, Carlos Fuentes, and Rodolfo Turán. n.d. "Mujeres Mexicana en la Migración a Estados Unidos." CONAPO (Consejo Nacional de Población), n.d. http://www.conapo.gob.mx./publicationes/migra3.htm (accessed April 24, 2007).

Aysa, María, and Douglas S. Massey. 2004. "Wives Left Behind: The Labor Market Behavior of Women in Migrant Communities." In *Crossing the Border: Research from the Mexican Migration Project,* ed. Jorge Durand and Douglas S. Massey, 131–46. New York: Russell Sage Foundation.

Barajas, Yesinia, James Besada, Elisabeth Valdez-Sutter, and Caitlin White. 2007. "Profiles of Research Communities." In *Impacts of Border Enforcement on Mexican Migration: The View from the Sending Communities,* ed. Wayne A. Cornelius and Jessa M. Lewis, 17–32. La Jolla: Center for Comparative Immigration Studies, University of California, San Diego.

Balán, Jorge, Harley L. Browning, and Elizabeth Jelin. 1973. *Men in a Developing Society: Geographic and Social Mobility in Monterrey, Mexico.* Austin: University of Texas Press.

Balderrama, Francisco, and Raymond Rodríguez. 1995. *Decades of Betrayal: Mexican Repatriation in the 1930s.* Albuquerque: University of New Mexico Press.

Barragán, María Antonieta, and Mónica León. 2007. *Hijos sí, marido no: Una nueva alternativa familiar.* Tlalnepantla, Est. de México.

Basch, Linda, Nina Glick Schiller, and Cristina Szanton Blanc. 1994. *Nations Unbound: Transnational Projects, Postcolonial Predicaments and Deterritorialized Nation-States.* Basel: Gordon and Breach.

Bean, Frank D., Georges Vernez, and C. B. Keely. 1989. *Opening and Closing the Doors: Evaluating Immigration Reform and Control.* Washington, DC: The Urban Institute.

Behar, Ruth. 2003. *Translated Women: Crossing the Border with Esperanza's Story.* Boston: Beacon Press.

Benería, Lourdes. 1989. "Subcontracting and Employment Dynamics in Mexico City." In *The Informal Economy: Studies in Advanced and Less Developed Countries,* ed. Alejandro Portes, Manuel Castells, and Lauren Benton, 173–88. Baltimore: Johns Hopkins University Press.

———. 1992. "The Mexican Debt Crisis: Restructuring the Economy and the Household." In *Unequal Burden: Economic Crises, Persistent Poverty and Women's Work,* ed. Lourdes Benería and Shelley Feldman, 83–104. Boulder, CO: Westview Press.

———, and Martha Roldán. 1987. *The Crossroads of Class and Gender: Industrial Homework, Subcontracting, and Household Dynamics in Mexico City.* Chicago: University of Chicago Press.

Berger, Marguerite, and Marya Buvinic, eds. 1988. *La mujer en el sector informal: Trabajo feminino y microempresa en América Latina.* Quito: Editorial Nueva Sociedad.

Berger, Peter L., and Thomas Luckmann. 1966. *The Social Construction of Reality: A Treatise in the Sociology of Knowledge.* New York: Anchor Books.

Betten, Neil, and Raymond A. Mohl. 1973. "From Discrimination to Repatriation: Mexican Life in Gary, Indiana during the Great Depression." *Pacific Historical Review* 42 (3): 370–88.

Blumberg, Rae Lesser. 1993. "Poverty Versus 'Purse Power': The Political Economy of the Mother-Child Family III." In *Where Did All the Men Go? Female-Headed/Female-Supported Households in Cross-Cultural Perspective,* ed. Joan P. Mencher and Anne Okongwu, 13–52. Boulder, CO: Westview Press.

Boehm, Deborah A. 2008. "'Now I Am a Man and a Woman': Gendered Moves and Migrations in a Transnational Mexican Community." *Latin American Perspectives* 35 (1): 16–30.

Bott, Elizabeth. 1957. *Family and Social Network: Roles, Norms and External Relationships in Ordinary Urban Families.* London: Tavistock Publications.

Bourdieu, Pierre. 1986. "The Forms of Capital." In *Handbook of Theory and Research in the Sociology of Education,* ed. John G. Richardson, 241–58. New York: Greenwood Press.

———, and Loïc J. D. Wacquant. 1992. *An Introduction to Reflexive Sociology.* Chicago: The University of Chicago Press.

Bradshaw, Sara. 1995. "Women's Access to Employment and the Formation of Female-Headed Households in Rural and Urban Honduras." *Bulletin of Latin American Research* 14 (2): 143–58.

Brettell, Caroline. 2003. *Anthropology and Migration: Essays on Transnationalism, Ethnicity, and Identity.* Walnut Creek, CA: Altamira Press.

———, and Patricia R. deBerjeois. 1992. "Anthropology and the Study of Immigrant Women." In *Seeking Common Ground: Studies of Immigrant Women in the United States,* ed. Donna Gabaccia, 41–64. Westport, CT: Greenwood Press.

Brown, Susan E. 1975. "Love Unites Them and Hunger Separates Them: Poor Women in the Dominican Republic." In *Toward an Anthropology of Women,* ed. Rayna Rapp, 322–32. New York: Monthly Review Press.

Browning, Harley L., and Waltraut Feindt. 1971. "The Social and Economic Context of Migration to Monterrey, Mexico." In *Latin American Urban Research,* ed. Francine F. Rabinowitz and Felicity Trueblood, 1:45–70. Beverly Hills: Sage.

———, and Néstor Rodríguez. 1985. "The Migration of Mexican Indocumentados as a Settlement Process: Implications for Work." In *Hispanics in the U.S. Economy,* ed. George J. Borjas and Marta Tienda, 277–97. New York: Academic Press.

Burawoy, Michael. 1975. "The Functions and Reproduction of Migrant Labor: Comparative Material from Southern Africa and the United States." *American Journal of Sociology* 81 (5): 1050–92.

Bush, Virgilio Partida. 2007. "Situación demográfica nacional y estatal." In *La situación demográfica de México 2006,* ed. CONAPO, 11–17. http://www.conapo.gob.mx (accessed May 28, 2007).

Butler, Edgar W., and James B. Pick. 1991. "Twentieth Century Migration to Baja California." *Journal of Borderlands Studies* 6 (Spring): 91–125.

Butterworth, Douglas. 1962. "A Study of the Urbanization Process Among Mixtec Migrants from Tilaltongo in Mexico City." *América Indígena* 22 (3): 257–74.

Bybee, Roger, and Carolyn Winter. 2006. "Immigration Flood Unleashed by NAFTA's Disastrous Impact on Mexican Economy." April 25, 2006. *Common Dreams.* http://www.commondreams.org/ (accessed 10 May 2007).

Calavita, Kitty. 1992. *Inside the State: The Bracero Program, Immigration and the I.N.S.* New York: Routledge.

Cardoso, Lawrence A. 1979. "Labor Immigration to the Southwest, 1916 to 1920: Mexican Attitudes and Policy." In *Mexican Workers in the United States: Historical and Political Perspectives,* ed. George C. Kiser and Martha Woody Kiser, 16–32. Albuquerque: University of New Mexico Press.

———. 1980. *Mexican Emigration to the United States 1897–1931.* Tucson: University of Arizona Press.

Carrillo, Jorge H., and Alberto Hernández H. 1988. "La migración femenina hacia la frontera norte y los Estados Unidos." In *Migración en el occidente de México,* ed. Gustavo López Castro and Sergio Pardo Galván, 85–112. Zamora: El Colegio de Michoacán.

Castells, Manuel, and Alejandro Portes. 1989. "World Underneath: The Origins, Dynamics, and Effects of the Informal Economy." In *The Informal Economy: Studies in Advanced and Less Developed Countries,* ed. Alejandro Portes, Manuel Castells, and Lauren A. Benton, 11–40. Baltimore: Johns Hopkins University Press.

Castles, Stephen, and Godula Kosack. 1973. *Immigrant Workers and Class Structure in Western Europe.* New York: Oxford University Press.

Caulkins, D. Douglas. 2001. "Consensus, Clines, and Edges in Celtic Cultures." *Cross-Cultural Research* 15 (2): 109–26.

Cerrutti, Marcela, and Douglas S. Massey. 2001. "On the Auspices of Female Migration from Mexico to the United States." *Demography* 38 (2): 187–200.

Chant, Sylvia. 1985. "Single Parent Families: Choice or Constraint? The Formation of Female-Headed Households in Mexican Shanty Towns." *Development and Change* 16 (4): 635–56.

———. 1987. "Domestic Labour, Decision-Making, and Dwelling Construction: The Experience of Women in Querétaro, Mexico." In *Women, Human Settlements and Housing,* ed. Caroline O. N. Moser and Linda Peake, 33–54. New York: Tavistock Publications.

———. 1991. *Women and Survival in Mexican Cities: Perspectives on Gender, Labour Markets and Low-Income Households.* New York: Manchester University Press.

———. 1994. "Women, Work and Household Survival Strategies in Mexico, 1982–1992." *Bulletin of Latin American Research* 13 (2): 203–33.

———. 1997a. "Gender and Tourism Employment in Mexico and the Philippines." In *Gender, Work and Tourism,* ed. M. Thea Sinclair, 120–79. New York: Routledge.

———. 1997b. *Women-Headed Households: Diversity and Dynamics in the Developing World.* New York: St. Martin's Press.

———, and Nikki Craske. 2003. *Gender in Latin America.* New Brunswick, NJ: Rutgers University Press.

Chavez, Leo R. 1992. *Shadowed Lives: Undocumented Immigrants in American Society.* San Diego: Harcourt Brace Jovanovich.

Chow, Ester Ngan-ling. 1996. "Introduction: Transforming Knowledgment: Race, Class, and Gender." In *Race, Class & Gender: Common Bonds, Different Voices,* ed. Ester Ngan-Ling Chow, Doris Wilkinson, and Maxine Baca Zinn, xix–xxvi. Thousand Oaks, CA: Sage Publications.

Cohen, Jeffrey H. 2004. *The Culture of Migration in Southern Mexico.* Austin: University of Texas Press.

Coleman, James S. 1988. "Social Capital in the Creation of Human Capital." *American Journal of Sociology* 94: S95–S120.

CONEPO (Consejo Estatal de Población de Baja California). 1997. *Baja California y sus municipios: Información general, cifras y datos.* Mexicali: Gobierno del Estado de Baja California.

Cornelius, Wayne A. 1989. "The U.S. Demand for Mexican Labor." In *Mexican Migration to the United States: Origins, Consequences and Policy Options,* ed. Wayne A. Cornelius and Jorge A. Bustamante, 25–48. La Jolla: Center for U.S.-Mexican Studies, University of California at San Diego.

———. 1991. "Los Migrantes de la Crisis: The Changing Profile of Mexican Migration to the United States." In *Social Responses to Mexico's Economic Crisis of the 1990s,* ed. Mercedes González de la Rocha and Agustín Escobar Latapí, 155–94. La Jolla: Center for U.S.-Mexican Studies, University of California at San Diego.

———. 1992. "From Sojourners to Settlers: The Changing Profile of Mexican Immigration to the United States." In *U.S.-Mexico Relations: Labor Market Interdependence,* ed. Jorge A. Bustamante, Clark W. Reynolds, and Raúl A. Hinojosa Ojeda, 155–95. Stanford: Stanford University Press.

———. 1993. "Mexican Immigrants in California Today." In *Immigration and Entrepreneurship: Culture, Capital and Ethnic Networks*, ed. Ivan Light and Parminder Bhachu, 329–71. New Brunswick, NJ: Transaction Publishers.

———. 1998. "The Structural Embeddedness of Demand for Mexican Immigrant Labor: New Evidence from California." In *Crossings: Mexican Immigration in Interdisciplinary Perspective*, ed. Marcelo M. Suárez-Orozco, 113–56. Cambridge, MA: Harvard University Press.

———. 2001. "Death at the Border: Efficacy and Unintended Consequences of U.S. Immigration Control Policy." *Population and Development Review* 27 (4): 661–81.

———. 2007. "Introduction: Does Border Enforcement Deter Unauthorized Immigration?" In *Impacts of Border Enforcement on Mexican Migration: The View from the Sending Communities*, ed. Wayne A. Cornelius and Jesse M. Lewis, 1–16. La Jolla: Center for Comparative Immigration Studies, University of California, San Diego.

Corona, Rodolfo. n.d. *Estimación del número de emigrantes permanentes de México a Estados Unidos, 1850–1990*. CONAPO, n.d. http://www.conapo.gob.mx./publicationes/migra3.htm (accessed April 24, 2007).

Corona Vásquez, Rodolfo. 1998. "Modificaciones de las características del flujo migratorio laboral de México a Estados Unidos." In *Migración y Fronteras*, coord. Alfredo Lattes, Jorge Santibáñez, and Manuel Angel Castillo, 243–48. Mexico City: El Colegio de Mexico and El Colegio de la Frontera Norte.

Craske, Nikki. 1993. "Women's Political Participation in *Colonias Populares* in Guadalajara, Mexico." In *'Viva': Women and Popular Protest in Latin America*, ed. Sarah A. Radcliffe and Sallie Westwood, 112–35. New York: Routledge.

Cunningham, Wendy. 2001. "Breadwinner versus Caregiver: Labor Force Participation and Sectoral Choice over the Mexican Business Cycle." In *The Economics of Gender in Mexico: Work, Family, State, and Market*, ed. Elizabeth G. Katz and Maria C. Correia, 85–132. Washington, DC: The World Bank.

———. 2004. "Breadwinner versus Caregiver: Labor Force Participation and Sectoral Choice over the Mexican Business Cycle." World Bank Policy Research Working Paper no. 2743. Washington, DC: The World Bank.

Díaz, Laura Niembro. 1988. "El papel de la mujer en la autoconstrucción de vivienda, zona metropolitana de Guadalajara." In *Mujeres y Sociedad: Salario, Hogar y Acción Social en el Occidente de Mexico*, comp. Luísa Gabayet, Patricia García, Mercedes González de la Rocha, Silvia Lailson, and Agustín Escobar, 167–80. Guadalajara: El Colegio de Jalisco/CIESAS del Occidente.

Dinerman, Ina R. 1982. *Migrants and Stay-At-Homes: A Comparative Study of Rural Migration from Michoacán, Mexico*. Monograph Series 5. La Jolla: University of California San Diego: Center for U.S.-Mexican Studies.

Donato, Katharine M. 1993. "Current Trends and Patterns of Female Migration: Evidence from Mexico." *International Migration Review* 27 (4): 748–71.

———, and Evelyn Patterson. 2004. "Women and Men on the Move: Undocumented Border Crossing." In *Crossing the Border: Research from the Mexican Migration Project*, ed. Jorge Durand and Douglas S. Massey, 111–30. New York: Russell Sage Foundation.

Dunn, Timothy J. 1996. *The Militarization of the U.S.-Mexico Border, 1978–1992: Low-Intensity Conflict Doctrine Comes Home*. Austin: Center for Mexican American Studies, University of Texas at Austin.

Durand, Jorge, and Douglas S. Massey. 1992. "Mexican Migration to the United States: A Critical Review." *Latin American Research Review* 27 (2): 3–42.

Ebaugh, Helen Rose, and Mary Curry. 2000. "Fictive Kind as Social Capital in New Immigrant Communities." *Sociological Perspectives* 43 (4): 189–210.

Ehlers, Tracy Bachrach. 1991. "Debunking Marianismo: Economic Vulnerability and Survival Strategies Among Guatemalan Wives." *Ethnology* 30 (1): 1–16.

Esteva, Gustavo. 1983. *The Struggle for Rural Mexico*. With collaborators. South Hadley, MA: Bergin and Garvey.

Faist, Thomas. 1997. "The Crucial Meso-Level." In *International Migration, Mobility and Development: Multidisciplinary Perspectives*, ed. Thomas Hammar, Grete Brochman, Kristof Thomas, and Thomas Faist, 187–218. New York: Berg.

Fernández-Kelly, María Patricia. 1983. *For We Are Sold, I and My People: Women and Industry in Mexico's Frontier*. Albany: State University of New York Press.

———. 1995. "Social and Cultural Capital in the Urban Ghetto: Implications for the Economic Sociology if Immigration." In *The Economic Sociology of Immigration: Essays on Networks, Ethnicity, and Entrepreneurship*, ed. Alejandro Portes, 213–47. New York: Russell Sage Foundation.

Fragomen, Austin T., Jr. 1997. "The Illegal Immigration Reform and Immigrant Responsibility Act of 1996." *International Migration Review* 31 (2): 438–60.

Fussell, Elizabeth. 2004. "Sources of Mexico's Migration Stream: Rural, Urban, and Border Migrations to the United States." *Social Forces* 82 (3): 937–67.

———, and Douglas S. Massey. 2004. "The Limits to Cumulative Causation: International Migration from Mexican Urban Areas." *Demography* 41 (1): 151–71.

Gabaccia, Donna. 1994. *From the Other Side: Women, Gender and Immigrant Life in the U.S., 1820–1990*. Bloomington: Indiana University Press.

Galarza, Ernesto. 1964. *Merchants of Labor: The Mexican Bracero Story*. Santa Barbara, CA: McNally & Loftin.

Gamboa, Erasmo. 1990. *Mexican Labor and World War II: Braceros in the Pacific Northwest, 1942–1947*. Austin: University of Texas Press.

García, Brígida, and Orlandina de Oliveira. 1994. *Trabajo femenino y vida familiar en México*. Mexico City: El Colegio de México.

García, Jerry. 2005. "Mexican and Japanese Labor in the Pacific Northwest, 1900–1945." In *Memory, Community, and Activism: Mexican Migration and Labor in the Pacific Northwest*, ed. Jerry García and Gilberto García, 85–128. East Lansing: Michigan State University, Julián Samora Research Institute.

García, Juan Ramón. 1980. *Operation Wetback: The Mass Deportation of Mexican Undocumented Workers in 1954*. Westport, CT: Greenwood Press.

———. 1996. *Mexicans in the Midwest, 1900–1932*. Tucson: University of Arizona Press.

Gauss, Susan M. 2006. "Working-Class Masculinity and the Rationalized Sex: Gender and Industrial Modernization in the Textile Industry in Postrevolutionary Puebla." In *Sex in Revolution: Gender, Politics and Power in Modern Mexico*, ed. Jocelyn Olcott, Mary Kay Vaughan, and Gabriela Cano, 181–98. Durham, NC: Duke University Press.

Gimpel, James G., and James R. Edwards, Jr. 1999. *The Congressional Politics of Immigration Reform*. Boston: Allyn & Bacon.

Glick Schiller, Nina. 1999. "Transmigrants and Nation-States: Something Old and Something New in U.S. Immigrant Experience." In *The Handbook of International Migration: The American Experience*, ed. Charles Hirschman, Philip Kasinitz, and Josh De Wind, 94–119. New York: Russell Sage Foundation.

———. 2003. "The Centrality of Ethnography in the Study of Transnational Migration: Seeing the Wetlands Instead of the Swamp." In *American Arrivals: Anthropology Engages the New Immigration*, ed. Nancy Foner. Santa Fe: School of American Research Press.

———, Nina, Linda Basch, and Cristina Blanc-Szanton. 1992. "Transnationalism: A New Analytic Framework for Understanding Migration." In *Towards a Transnational Perspective on Migration: Race, Class, Ethnicity, and Nationalism Reconsidered*, ed. Nina Glick Schiller, Linda Basch, and Cristina Blanc-Szanton, 1–24. New York: The New York Academy of Sciences.

Golde, Peggy. 1986. "Odyssey of Encounter." In *Women in the Field: Anthropological Experiences*, ed. Peggy Golde, 67–96. Berkeley: University of California Press.

Goldring, Luín. 1998. "The Power of Status in Transnational Social Fields." In *Transnationalism from Below*, ed. Michael Peter Smith and Luís Eduardo Guarnizo, 165–95. New Brunswick, NJ: Transaction Publishers.

Gómez-Quiñones, Juan. 1981. "Mexican Immigration to the United States and the Internationalization of Labor." In *Mexican Immigrant Workers in the U.S.*, ed. Antonio Ríos-Bustamante, 13–34. Los Angeles: UCLA Chicano Studies Research Center.

González, Daniel. 2007. "Migrants Fleeing as Hiring Law Nears." *Arizona Republic*, August 26, 2007. http://arizonarepublic/news/articles/10826sanctionsimpacto8260.html (accessed October 18, 2007).

———. 2007. "Most Undocumented Workers Watching, Waiting." *Arizona Republic*, October 8, 2007. http://arizonarepublic/news/articles/1008waitandsee1008.html (accessed October 18, 2007).

González, Gilbert G. 2006. *Guest Workers or Colonized Labor? Mexican Labor Migration to the United States*. Boulder, CO: Paradigm Publishers.

González, Manuel G. 2000. *Mexicanos: A History of Mexicans in the United States*. Bloomington: Indiana University Press.

González-López, Gloria. 2005. *Exotic Journeys: Mexican Immigrants and Their Sex Lives*. Berkeley: University of California Press.

———. 2007. "'Nunca he dejado de tener terror': Sexual Violence in the Lives of Mexican Immigrant Women." In *Women and Migration in the U.S.-Mexico Borderlands*, ed. Denise A. Segura and Patricia Zavella, 224–46. Durham, NC: Duke University Press.

González de la Rocha, Mercedes. 1988a. "Economic Crisis, Domestic Reorganisation and Women's Work in Guadalajara, Mexico." *Bulletin of Latin American Research* 7 (2): 207–23.

———. 1988b. "De por qué las mujeres aguantan golpes y cuernos: Un análisis de hogares sin varón en Guadalajara." In *Mujeres y Sociedad: Salario, Hogares y Acción Social en el Occidente de México*, ed. Luísa Babayet, Patricia García, Mercedes González de la Rocha, Silvia Lailson, and Agustín Escobar, 205–27. Guadalajara: El Colegio de Jalisco-CIESAS del Occidente.

———. 1991. "Family Well-Being, Food Consumption, Survival Strategies during Mexico's Economic Crisis." In *Social Responses to Mexico's Economic Crisis of the 1980s*, ed. Mercedes González de la Rocha and Agustín Escobar Latapí, 115–28. San Diego: University of California, San Diego Center for U.S.-Mexican Studies.

———. 1994. *The Resources of Poverty: Women and Survival in a Mexican City*. Oxford: Blackwell.

———. 1995. "Social Restructuring in Two Mexican Cities: An Analysis of Domestic Groups in Guadalajara and Monterrey." *European Journal of Development Research* 7 (2): 389–406.

———. 2001. "From the Resources of Poverty to the Poverty of Resources? Erosion of a Survival Model." *Latin American Perspectives* 28 (4): 72–100.

González-Salazar, Gloria. 1980. "Participation of Women in the Mexican Labor Force." In *Sex and Class in Latin America*, ed. June Nash and Helen Icken Safa, 183–201. South Hadley, MA: J. F. Begin Publishers.

Granovetter, Mark. 1973. "The Strength of Weak Ties." *American Journal of Sociology* 78: 1360–388.

———. 1982. "The Strength of Weak Ties: A Network Theory Revisited." In *Social Structure and Network Analysis*, ed. Peter V. Mardsen and Nan Lin, 105–30. Beverly Hills: Sage Publications.

Grasmuck, Sherri, and Patricia R. Pessar. 1991. *Between Two Islands: Dominican International Migration*. Berkeley: University of California Press.

Grimes, Kimberly M. 1998. *Crossing Borders: Changing Social Identities in Southern Mexico*. Tucson: University of Arizona Press.

Griswold del Castillo, Richard, and Arnoldo de León. 1996. *North to Aztlán: A History of Mexican Americans in the United States*. New York: Twayne Publishers.

Guarnizo, Luís Eduardo, and Michael P. Smith. 1998. "The Locations of Transnationalism." In *Transnationalism from Below*, ed. Michael Peter Smith and Luís Eduardo Guarnizo, 3–34. New Brunswick, NJ: Transaction Publishers.

Gutiérrez, David G. 1995. *Walls and Mirrors: Mexican Americans, Mexican Immigrants, and the Politics of Ethnicity*. Berkeley: University of California Press.

Gutmann, Matthew C. 1996. *The Meanings of Macho: Being a Man in Mexico City*. Berkeley: University of California Press.

Hagan, Jacqueline María. 1994. *Deciding to be Legal: A Maya Community in Houston*. Philadelphia: Temple University Press.

Haney, Jane B. 1979. "Formal and Informal Labor Recruitment Mechanisms: States in Mexican Migration into Mid-Michigan Agriculture." In *Migration Across Frontiers: Mexico and the United States*, ed. Fernando Camara and Robert Van Kemper, 191–99. Albany: State University of New York Press.

Hart, Keith. 1973. "Informal Income Opportunities and Urban Employment in Ghana." *The Journal of Modern African Studies* 11 (1): 61–89.

Hayes-Bautista, David E., Werner O. S. Schink, and Jorge Chapa. 1990. *The Burden of Support: Young Latinos in an Aging Society*. Stanford: Stanford University Press.

Hecht, Susanna. 1985. "Women and the Latin American Livestock Sector." In *Women as Food Producers in Developing Countries*, ed. Jamie Monson and Marion Kalb, 51–70. Los Angeles: Regents of the University of California.

Hernández Álvarez, José. 1966. "A Demographic Profile of the Mexican Immigration to the United States, 1910–1950." *Journal of Inter-American Studies* 8 (3): 471–86.

Heyman, Josiah McC. 1998. *Finding a Moral Heart of U.S. Immigration Policy: An Anthropological Perspective*. Arlington, VA: American Anthropological Association.

Hirsch, Jennifer S. 2000. "En el norte la mujer manda: Gender, Generation and Geography in a Mexican Transnational Community. In *"Immigration Research for a New Century: Multidisciplinary Perspectives*, ed. Nancy Foner, Ruben G. Rumbaut, and Steven J. Gold, 369–89. New York: Russell Sage Foundation.

———. 2003. *A Courtship After Marriage: Sexuality and Love in Mexican Transnational Families*. Berkeley: University of California Press.

Hirschman, Charles. 2004. "The Role of Religion in the Origins and Adaptation of Immigrant Groups in the United States." *International Migration Review* 38 (3): 1206–33.

Ho, Christine G. T. 1993. "The Internationalization of Kinship and the Feminization of Caribbean Migration: The Case of Afro-Trinidadian Immigrants in Los Angeles." *Human Organization* 52 (1): 32–40.

Hoffman, Abraham. 1974. *Unwanted Mexican Americans in the Great Depression: Repatriation Pressures 1929–1939*. Tucson: University of Arizona Press.

Hondagneu-Sotelo, Pierrette. 1992. "Overcoming Patriarchal Constraints: The Reconstruction of Gender Relations among Mexican Immigrant Women and Men." *Gender and Society* 6 (3): 393–415.

———. 1994. *Gendered Transitions: Mexican Experiences of Migration*. Berkeley: University of California Press.

Hondagneu-Sotelo, Pierrette, and Michael A. Messner. 1994. "Gender Displays and Men's Power: The 'New Man' and the Mexican Immigrant Man." In *Theorizing Masculinities*, ed. Harry Brod and Michael Kaufman, 200–218. Thousand Oaks, CA: Sage Publications.

Houstoun, Marion F., Roger G. Kramer, and Joan Mackin Barrett. 1984. "Female Predominance of Immigration to the United States since 1930: A First Look." *International Migration Review* 18 (4): 908–63.

Howell, Jayne. 1999. "Expanding Women's Roles in Southern Mexico: Educated, Employed Oaxaqueñas." *Journal of Anthropological Research* 55 (1): 99–128.

Iglesias, Norma. 1985. *La flor más bella de la maquiladora*. Mexico City: CEFNOMEX.

Inda, Jonathan Xavier. 2006. "Border Prophylaxis: Technology, Illegality, and the Government of Immigration." *Cultural Dynamics* 18 (2): 115–38.

INEGI (Instituto Nacional de Estádisticas, Geografía e Informática). 1991a. *Baja California: Perfil soiodemográfico. XI censo general de población y vivienda, 1990*. Aguascalientes, Aguas.: INEGI.

———. 1991b. *Baja California: Resultados definitivos. Tabulados básicos. XI censo general de población y vivienda, 1990*. Aguascalientes, Aguas.: INEGI.

———. 1993. *Migración. XI censo general de población y vivienda, 1990*. Vols. 1–2. Aguascalientes, Aguas.: INEGI.

———. 1997. *Mujeres y hombres en México*. Aguascalientes, Aguas.: INEGI.

———. 2001. *Industria maquiladora de exportación*. Aguascalientes, Aguas.: INEGI.

———. 2002. *Baja California. XIII censo de población y vivienda, 2000*. Aguascalientes, Aguas.: INEGI. http://www.inegi.gob.mx (accessed May 15, 2007).

———. 2004a. *Los hombres y mujeres en las actividades económicas.* Aguascalientes, Aguas.: INEGI. http://www.inegi.gob.mx (accessed May 15, 2007).

———. 2004b. "Población total por municipio de residencia actual y lugar de migración y de nacimiento, y su distribución según sexo. Estadísticas sociodemográficas. Baja California." Aguascalientes, Aguas.: INEGI. http://www.inegi.gob.mx (accessed December 29, 2004).

———. 2004c. *Encuesta nacional sobre la dinámica de las relaciones en los hogares, 2003, ENDIREH.* Aguascalientes, Aguas.: INEGI.

———. 2006a. "Hogares y su distribución porcentual según sexo del jefe para cada entidad federativa, 2000 y 2005. Estadísticas por Género." Aguascalientes, Aguas.: INEGI. http://www.inegi.gob.mx (accessed May 28, 2007).

———. 2006b. "Hogares por sexo del jefe, tipo y clase de hogar, 1950 a 2005. Estadísticas por Género." Aguascalientes, Aguas.: INEGI. http://www.inegi.gob.mx (accessed May 28, 2007).

———. 2007. "Tasa global de fecundidad, 1976–2006. Estadísticas sociodemográficas." Aguascalientes, Aguas.: INEGI. http://www.inegi.gob.mx (accessed May 18, 2007).

Jones, Richard C. 1982. "Channelization of Undocumented Mexican Migrants to the United States." *Economic Geography* 58:156–76.

———. 1988. "Micro Source Regions of Mexican Undocumented Migration." *National Geographic Research* 4 (1): 11–22.

Kandel, William, and Douglas S. Massey. 2002. "The Culture of Mexican Migration: A Theoretical and Empirical Analysis." *Social Forces* 80 (3): 981–1004.

Kearney, Michael. 1986. "Integration of the Mixteca and the Western U.S.-Mexico Border Region via Migratory Wage Labor." In *Regional Impacts of U.S.-Mexican Relations*, ed. Ina Rosenthal Urey. La Jolla: Center for U.S.-Mexican Studies, University of California, San Diego.

———. 1995. *Reconceptualizing the Peasantry: Anthropology in Global Perspective.* Boulder, CO: Westview Press.

———, and Carole Nagengast. 1989. *Anthropological Perspectives on Transnational Communities in Rural California.* Working paper no. 3, Davis: Institute for Rural Studies, University of California, Davis.

Kemper, Robert V. 1977. *Migration and Adaptation: Tzintzuntzan Peasants in Mexico City.* Beverly Hills: Sage.

Kofman, Eleonore, Annie Phizacklea, Parvati Raghuram, and Rosemary Sales. 2000. *Gender and International Migration in Europe: Employment, Welfare and Politics.* New York: Routledge.

Kossoudji, Sherrie A., and Susan I. Ranney. 1984. "The Labor Market Experience of Female Migrants: The Case of Temporary Mexican Migration to the United States." *International Migration Review* 18 (1): 120–43.

LaBotz, Dan, and Robin Alexander. 2005. "The Escalating Struggles Over Mexico's Labor Law." *NACLA Report on the Americas* 34 (1): 16–22.

Lancaster, Roger N. 1992. *Life is Hard: Machismo, Danger, and the Intimacy of Power in Nicaragua.* Berkeley: University of California Press.

Landolt, Patricia, Lilian Autler, and Sonia Baires. 1999. "From Hermano Lejano to Hermano Mayor: The Dialectics of Salvadorean Transnationalism." *Ethnic and Racial Studies* 22 (2): 290–315.

Lee, Everett S. 1966. "A Theory of Migration." *Demography* 3 (1): 47–53.

Lee, Richard B. 1979. *The ¡Kung San: Men, Women and Work in A Foraging Society.* Cambridge: Cambridge University Press.

Leobardo Arroyo, Luís. 1981. "Changes in the Non-Agricultural Employment Structure of Mexico, 1950–1970." *Aztlán: International Journal of Chicano Studies Research* 6 (3): 409–32.

LeVine, Sarah, and Clara Sunderland Correa. 1993. *Dolor y Alegría: Women and Social Change in Urban Mexico.* Madison: University of Wisconsin Press.

———, Clara Sunderland Correa, and F. Medardo Tapia Uribe. 1986. "The Marital Morality of Mexican Women: An Urban Study." *Journal of Anthropological Research* 42:183–202.

Levitt, Peggy. 2001. "Transnational Migration: Taking Stock and Future Directions." *Global Networks* 1 (2): 195–216.

———. 2003. "'You Know, Abraham was Really the First Immigrant': Religion and Transnational Migration." *International Migration Review* 37 (3): 847–73.

Lewis, Oscar. 1961. "Introduction." In *The Children of Sanchez*, xi–xxxi. New York: Random House.

———. 1968. "The Culture of Poverty." In *On Understanding Poverty: Perspectives from the Social Sciences*, ed. Daniel P. Moynihan, 187–200. New York: Basic Books.

———. 1975. *Five Families: Mexican Case Studies in the Culture of Poverty.* New York: Basic Books.

Lingam, Lakshmi. 2005. *Structural Adjustment, Gender and Household Survival Strategies: Review of Evidences and Concerns.* Ms. Ann Arbor: University of Michigan Center for the Education of Women. http://www.cew.umich.edu.

Lomnitz, Larissa Adler. 1977. *Networks and Marginality: Life in a Mexican Shantytown.* New York: Academic Press.

———. 1978. "Mechanisms of Articulation between Shantytown Settlers and the Urban System." *Urban Anthropology* 7 (2): 185–206.

Lomnitz-Adler, Claudio. 1992. *Exits from the Labyrinth: Culture and Ideology in the Mexican National Space.* Berkeley: University of California Press.

López, Henry, Rob Oliphant, and Edith Tejeda. 2007. "U.S. Settlement Behavior and Labor Market Participation." In *Impacts of Border Enforcement on Mexican Migration: The View from the Sending Communities*, ed. Wayne A. Cornelius and Jessa M. Lewis, 75–96. La Jolla: Center for Comparative Immigration Studies, University of California, San Diego.

Lozano Ascensio, Fernando. 2002. "Migrantes de las ciudades: Nuevos patrones de la migración mexicana a los Estados Unidos." In *Población y sociedad al inicio del siglo XX*, ed. Brígida García Guzmán, 241–59. Mexico City: El Colegio de Mexico.

Mahler, Sarah J. 1995. *American Dreaming: Immigrant Life on the Margins*. Princeton, NJ: Princeton University Press.

———. 1998. "Theoretical and Empirical Contributions Toward a Research Agenda for Transnationalism." In *Transnationalism from Below*, ed. Michael Peter Smith and Luís Eduardo Guarnizo, 64–100. New Brunswick, NJ: Transaction Publishers.

———, and Katrin Hansing. 2005. "Toward a Transnationalism of the Middle: How Transnational Religious Practices Help Bridge the Divides between Cuba and Miami." *Latin American Perspectives* 32 (1): 121–46.

———, and Patricia R. Pessar. 2006. "Gender Matters: Ethnographers Bring Gender from the Periphery to the Core of Migration Studies." *International Migration Review* 40 (1): 27–63.

Martínez, Oscar J. 2001. *Mexican-Origin People in the United States*. Tucson: University of Arizona Press.

Martínez Curiel, Enrique. 2004. "The Green Card as Matrimonial Strategy: Self-Interest in the Choice of Marital Partners." In *Crossing the Border: Research from the Mexican Migration Project*, ed. Jorge Durand and Douglas S. Massey, 86–110. New York: Russell Sage Foundation.

Massey, Douglas S. 1987. "Understanding Mexican Migration to the United States." *American Journal of Sociology* 92:1372–1403.

———. 1990. "Social Structure, Household Strategies, and the Cumulative Causation of Migration." *Population Index* 56:2–26.

———, Rafael Alarcón, Jorge Durand, and Humberto González. 1987. *Return to Aztlán: The Social Process of International Migration from Western Mexico*. Berkeley: University of California Press.

———, and Felipe García España. 1987. "The Social Process of International Migration." *Science* 237:733–38.

———, Luín Goldring, and Jorge Durand. 1994. "An Analysis of Nineteen Mexican Communities." *American Journal of Sociology* 99 (6): 1492–1533.

———, and Audrey Singer. 1995. "New Estimates of Undocumented Mexican Migration and the Probability of Apprehension." *Demography* 32 (2): 203–13.

———, and Kristen E. Espinosa. 1997. "What's Driving Mexico-U.S. Migration?: A Theoretical, Empirical, and Policy Analysis." *American Journal of Sociology* 102 (4): 939–99.

———, Jorge Durand, and Nolan J. Malone. 2003. *Beyond Smoke and Mirrors: Mexican Immigration in an Era of Economic Integration.* New York: Russell Sage Foundation.

Massolo, Alejandra. 1992. *Por amor y coraje: Mujeres en movimientos urbanos de la Ciudad de México.* Mexico City: El Colegio de México.

McCombs, Brady. 2007. "Jail Time in Store for All AZ Crossers." *Arizona Daily Star,* October 25, 2007. http://www.azstarnet.com/sn/printDS208133 (accessed October 26, 2007).

McWilliams, Carey. 1968. *North from Mexico: The Spanish Speaking People of the United States.* New York: Greenwood Press.

Melhuus, Marit. 1996. "Power, Value, and the Ambiguous Meanings of Gender." In *Machos, Mistresses and Madonnas: Contesting the Power of Latin American Gender Imagery,* ed. Marit Melhuus and Kristi Anne Stølen, 230–59. London: Verso.

Menjívar, Cecilia. 1997. "Immigrant Kinship Networks: Vietnamese, Salvadoreans and Mexicans in Comparative Perspective." *Journal of Comparative Family Studies* 28 (1): 1–24.

———. 2000. *Fragmented Ties: Salvadoran Immigrant Networks in America.* Berkeley: University of California Press.

Mines, Richard. 1981. *Developing a Community Tradition of Migration: A Field Study in Rural Zacatecas, Mexico and California Settlement Areas.* La Jolla: Center for U.S.-Mexico Studies, University of California, San Diego.

———, and Alain de Janvry. 1982. "Migration to the United States and Mexican Rural Development." *American Journal of Agricultural Economics* 64 (3): 444–54.

———, and Douglas S. Massey. 1985. "Patterns of Migration to the United States from Two Mexican Communities." *Latin American Research Review* 20 (2): 104–22.

Mirandé, Alfredo. 1997. *Hombres y Machos: Masculinity and Latino Culture.* Boulder, CO: Westview Press.

Moser, Caroline O. N. 1987a. "Mobilization is Women's Work: Struggles for Infrastructure in Guayaquil, Ecuador." In *Women, Human Settlements and Housing,* ed. Caroline O. N. Moser and Linda Peake, 166–94. New York: Tavistock Publications.

———. 1987b. "Women, Human Settlements, and Housing: A Conceptual Framework for Analysis and Policy-Making." In *Women, Human Settlements and Housing,* ed. Caroline O. N. Moser and Linda Peake, 12–32. New York: Tavistock Publications.

———, and Linda Peake, eds. 1987. *Women, Human Settlements and Housing,* New York: Tavistock Publications.

Mummert, Gail. 1988. "Mujeres de migrantes y mujeres migrantes de Michoacán: Nuevos papeles para las que se quedan y para las que se van." In *Movimientos de población en el occidente de México*, coord. Thomas Calvo and Gustavo López, 281–98. Zamora: El Colegio de Michoacán.

———. 1994. "From *Metate* to *Despate:* Rural Mexican Women's Salaried Labor and the Redefinition of Gendered Spaces and Roles." In *Women of the Mexican Countryside, 1850–1990*, ed. Heather Fowler-Salamini and Mary Kay Vaughan, 192–209. Tucson: University of Arizona Press.

Napolitano, Valentina. 2002. *Migration, Mujercitas and Medicine Men: Living in Urban Mexico.* Berkeley: University of California Press.

Narotzky, Susanna. 1990. "'Not to be a Burden': Ideologies of the Domestic Group and Women's Work in Rural Catalonia." In *Work without Wages: Domestic Labor and Self-Employment within Capitalism*, ed. Jane L. Collins and Martha Gimenez, 70–88. Albany: State University of New York Press.

Nash, June. 2001. *Maya Visions: The Quest for Autonomy in an age of Globalization.* New York: Routledge.

National Immigrant Solidarity Network. 2008. "1/24: WA/Info on GEO's ICE prison in Tacoma." http://isn@hsts.riseup.net (accessed January 29, 2008).

Nevins, Joseph. 2002. *Operation Gatekeeper: The Rise of the "Illegal Alien" and the Making of the U.S.-Mexico Boundary.* New York: Routledge.

Ngai, Mae M. 2004. *Impossible Subjects: Illegal Aliens and the Making of America.* Princeton, NJ: Princeton University Press.

Nutini, Hugo G., and Betty Bell. 1980. *Ritual Kinship: The Structural and Historical Development of the Compadrazgo System in Rural Tlaxcala.* Princeton, NJ: Princeton University Press.

O'Connor, Mary I. 1990. "Women's Networks and the Social Needs of Mexican Immigrants." *Urban Anthropology* 19 (1–2): 81–98.

Olcott, Jocelyn, Mary Kay Vaughan, and Gabriela Cano, eds. 2006. *Sex in Revolution: Gender, Politics, and Power in Modern Mexico.* Durham, NC: Duke University Press.

Operation Gatekeeper Fact Sheet. n.d. http://www.stopgatekeeper.org (accessed June 1, 2007).

Parker, Susan W., and Carla Pederzini. 2001. "Gender Differences in Education in Mexico." In *The Economics of Gender in Mexico: Work, Family, State, and Market*, ed. Elizabeth G. Katz and Maria C. Correia, 9–45. Washington, DC: The World Bank.

Partida Bush, Virgilio. 1994. In *Migración interna*, ed. Instituto Nacional de Estadística, Geografía e Informática (INEGI). Aguascalientes, Aguas.: INEGI.

Passel, Jeffrey S., and D'Vera Cohn. 2008. "Trends in Unauthorized Immigration: Undocumented Inflow Now Trails Legal Inflow." Pew Hispanic Center. http://www.pewhispanic.org/files/reports/94.pdf (accessed February 2009).

Peattie, Lisa R. 1975. "'Tertiarization' and Urban Poverty in Latin America." In *Urbanization and Inequality: The Political Economy of Urban and Rural Development in Latin America*. Vol. 5 of *Latin American Urban Research*, ed. Wayne A. Cornelius and Felicity M. Trueblood, 109–23. Beverly Hills: Sage.

Pessar, Patricia R. 1986. "The Role of Gender in Dominican Settlement in the United States." In *Women and Change in Latin America*, ed. June Nash and Helen Safa, 173–94. South Hadley, MA: Bergin and Garvey.

———. 1988. "The Constraints on and Release of Female Labor Power: Dominican Migration to the United States." In *A Home Divided: Women and Income in the Third World*, ed. Daisy Dwyer and Judith Bruce, 195–215. Stanford: Stanford University Press.

———. 1999. "The Role of Gender, Households and Social Networks in the Migration Process: A Review and Appraisal." In *The Handbook of International Migration: The American Experience*, ed. Charles Hirschman, Philip Kasinitz, and Josh De Wind, 53–70. New York: Russell Sage Foundation.

———. 2003. "Anthropology and the Engendering of Migration Studies." In *American Arrivals: Anthropology Engages the New Immigration*, ed. Nancy Foner, 75–98. Santa Fe: School of American Research Press.

Porter, Susie S. 2003. *Working Women in Mexico City: Public Discourses and Material Conditions, 1879–1931*. Tucson: University of Arizona Press.

Portes, Alejandro. 1977. "Labor Functions of Illegal Aliens." *Society* 14:31–37.

———. 1981. "Modes of Structural Incorporation and Present Theories of Labor Migration." In *Global Trends in Migration: Theory and Research on International Population Movements*, ed. Mary M. Kritz, Charles B. Keely, and Silvano M. Tomasi, 279–97. New York: Center for Migration Studies.

———. 1995. "Economic Sociology and the Sociology of Immigration: A Conceptual Overview." In *The Economic Sociology of Immigration: Essays on Networks, Ethnicity, and Entrepreneurship*, ed. Alejandro Portes, 1–41. New York: Russell Sage.

———. 1998. "Social Capital: Its Origins and Applications in Modern Sociology." *Annual Review of Sociology* 24:1–24.

———, and Robert L. Bach. 1985. *Latin Journey: Cuban and Mexican Immigrants in the United States*. Berkeley: University of California Press.

Potter, Brian. 2007. "Introduction: Constricting Contestation, Coalitions, and Purpose: The Causes of Neoliberal Restructuring and its Failures." *Latin American Perspectives* 34 (3): 3–24.

Pyke, Karen D. 1996. "Class-Based Masculinities: The Interdependence of Gender, Class, and Interpersonal Power." *Gender and Society* 10 (5): 527–49.

Ramos Escandón, Carmen. 1992. "Señoritas porfirianas: Mujer e ideología en el México progresista, 1800–1910." In *Presencia y transperencia: La mujer en la historia de México*. Mexico City: El Colegio de México.

————. 1996. "The Social Construction of Wife and Mother: Women in Porfirian Mexico, 1880–1917." In *Gender, Kinship, Power: A Comparative and Interdisciplinary History*, ed. Mary Jo Maynes, Ann Waltner, Birgitte Soland, and Ulrike Strasser, 275–85. New York: Routledge.

Ravenstein, E. G. 1885. "The Laws of Migration." *Journal of the Royal Statistical Society* 48:167–227.

————. 1889. "The Laws of Migration." *Journal of the Royal Statistical Society* 52:241–301.

Rivero-Fuentes, Estela. 2004. "Cumulative Causation Among Internal and International Mexican Migrants." In *Crossing the Border: Research from the Mexican Migration Project*, ed. Jorge Durand and Douglas S. Massey, 201–31. New York: Russell Sage Foundation.

Roberts, Bryan R., Reanne Frank, and Fernando Lozano Ascensio. 1999. "Transnational Migrant Communities and Mexican Migration to the United States." *Ethnic and Racial Studies* 22 (2): 1–22. http://www.migracionydesarrollo.org. See also *Ethnic and Racial Studies* 22 (2): 238–66.

Roldán, Martha. 1988. "Renegotiating the Marital Contract: Intrahousehold Patterns of Money Allocation and Women's Subordination Among Domestic Outworkers in Mexico City." In *A Home Divided: Women and Income in the Third World*, ed. Daisey Dwyer and Judith Bruce, 229–47. Stanford: Stanford University Press.

Romanucci-Ross, Lola. 1986. *Conflict, Violence and Morality in a Mexican Village.* Chicago: University of Chicago Press.

Romo, Richard. 1975. "Responses to Mexican Immigration, 1910–1930." *Aztlán: International Journal of Chicago Studies Research* 6 (2): 173–96.

————. 1988. *East Los Angeles: History of a Barrio.* Austin: University of Texas Press.

Roseberry, William. 1995. "The Cultural History of Peasantries." In *Articulating Hidden Histories: Exploring the Influence of Eric Wolf*, ed. Jane Schneider and Rayna Rapp, 51–66. Berkeley: University of California Press.

Rouse, Roger. 1992. "Making Sense of Settlement: Class Transformation, Cultural Struggle, and Transnationalism among Mexican Migrants in the United States." In *Towards a Transnational Perspective on Migration: Race, Class, Ethnicity and Nationalism Reconsidered*, ed. Nina Glick Schiller, Linda Basch, and Cristina Blanc-Szanton, 25–52. New York: The New York Academy of Sciences.

Rumbaut, Rubén G. 2007. "Ages, Life States, and Generational Cohorts: Decomposing the Immigrant First and Second Generations in the United States." In *Rethinking Migration: New Theoretical and Empirical Perspectives*, ed. Alejandro Portes and Josh DeWind, 342–87. New York: Berghahn Books.

Safa, Helen I. 1981. "Runaway Shops and Female Employment: The Search for Cheap Labor." *Signs* 7 (2): 418–33.

————. 1995. *The Myth of the Male Breadwinner: Women and Industrialization in the Caribbean.* Boulder, CO: Westview Press.

Salas, Elizabeth. 1990. *Soldaderas in the Mexican Military: Myth and History.* Austin: University of Texas Press.

Sassen, Saskia. 1996. *Losing Control? Sovereignty in an Age of Globalization.* New York: Columbia University Press.

Sassen-Koob, Saskia. 1981. "Toward a Conceptualization of Immigrant Labor." *Social Problems* 29 (1): 65–85.

Schell, Patience A. 2006. "Gender, Class, and Anxiety at the Gabriela Mistral Vocational School, Revolutionary Mexico City." In *Sex in Revolution: Gender, Politics and Power in Revolutionary Mexico,* ed. Jocelyn Olcott, Mary Kay Vaughan, and Gabriela Cano, 112–26. Durham, NC: Duke University Press.

Simpson, Eyler N. 1937. *The Ejido: Mexico's Way Out.* Chapel Hill: University of North Carolina Press.

Smith, Robert C. 1998. "Transnational Localities: Community, Technology and Politics of Membership within the Context of Mexico and U.S. Migration." In *Transnationalism from Below,* ed. Michael Peter Smith and Luís Eduardo Guarnizo, 196–238. New Brunswick, NJ: Transaction Publishers.

Staudt, Kathleen. 1999. "Seeds for Self-Sufficiency? Policy Contradictions at the U.S.-Mexico Border." In *Gender and Immigration,* ed. Gregory A. Kelson and Debra L. DeLaet. Washington Square: New York University Press.

Stephen, Lynn. 1991. *Zapotec Women.* Austin: University of Texas Press.

Stern, Steve J. 1995. *The Secret History of Gender: Women, Men & Power in Late Colonial Mexico.* Durham: University of North Carolina Press.

Stevens, Evelyn P. 1973. "*Marianismo:* The Other Face of *Machismo* in Latin America." In *Female and Male in Latin America,* ed. Ann M. Pescatello, 89–102. Pittsburgh: University of Pittsburgh Press.

Swartz, David. 1997. *Culture and Power: The Sociology of Pierre Bourdieu.* Chicago: The University of Chicago Press.

Tanori Villa, Cruz Arcelia. 1989. *La mujer migrante y el empleo: El caso de la industria maquiladora en la frontera norte.* Mexico City: Instituto Nacional de Antropología e Historia (INAH).

Taylor, Paul S. 1968a. *Mexican Labor in the United States: Chicago and the Calumet Region.* New York: Johnson Reprint Company.

———. 1968b. *Mexican Labor in the United States (Bethlehem, Pennsylvania).* New York: Johnson Reprint Company.

Thompson, Lanny. 1991. "Mexico City: The Slow Rise of Wage-Centered Households." In *Creating and Transforming Households: The Constraints of the World Economy,* ed. Joan Smith and Immanuel Wallerstein, 150–69. New York: Cambridge University Press.

———. 1992. "The Structures and Vicissitudes of Reproduction: Households in Mexico, 1876–1970." *Review* 14 (3): 403–36.

Tiano, Susan. 1987. "Maquiladoras in Mexicali: Integration or Exploitation?" In *Women on the U.S.-Mexico Border*, ed. Vickie Ruiz and Susan Tiano, 77–104. Boston: Allen & Unwin.

———. 1990. "Maquiladora Women: A New Category of Workers?" In *Women Workers and Global Restructuring*, ed. Kathryn Ward, 193–224. Ithaca: Cornell University, ILR Press.

———. 1994. *Patriarchy on the Line: Labor, Gender and Ideology in the Mexican Maquiladora Industry.* Philadelphia: Temple University Press.

Tienda, Marta. 1980. "Familism and Structural Assimilation of Mexican Immigrants in the United States." *International Migration Review* 14:383–407.

Tuñón Pablos, Julia. 1999. *Women in Mexico: A Past Unveiled.* Austin: University of Texas Press.

Twinam, Ann. 1998. "The Negotiation of Honor." In *The Faces of Honor: Sex, Shame, and Violence in Colonial Latin America*, ed. Lyman L. Johnson and Sonya Lipsett-Rivera, 68–102. Albuquerque: University of New Mexico Press.

———. 1999. *Public Lives, Private Secrets: Gender, Honor, Sexuality and Illegitimacy in Colonial Spanish America.* Stanford: Stanford University Press.

Ugalde, Antonio. 1974. *The Urbanization Process of a Poor Mexican Neighborhood.* Austin: University of Texas Press.

Uzzell, Douglas. 1976. *Ethnography of Migration: Breaking Out of the Bipolar Myth.* Houston: Rice University, Program of Development Studies.

Valdés, Dionicio Nodín. 2000. *Barrios Norteños: St. Paul and Midwestern Mexican Communities in the Twentieth Century.* Austin: University of Texas Press.

Vargas, Zaragosa. 1993. *Proletarians of the North: A History of Mexican Industrial Workers in Detroit and the Midwest, 1917–1933.* Berkeley: University of California Press.

Vélez-Ibáñez, Carlos G. 1983. *Rituals of Marginality: Politics, Process and Cultural Change in Urban Central Mexico, 1969–1974.* Berkeley: University of California Press.

———. 1996. *Border Visions: Mexican Cultures of the Southwest United States.* Tucson: University of Arizona Press.

Whetten, Nathan L. 1954. *Rural Mexico.* Chicago: University of Chicago Press.

Wiest, Raymond E. 1983. "Male Migration, Machismo, and Conjugal Roles: Implications for Fertility Control in a Mexican Municipio." *Journal of Comparative Family Studies* 14 (2): 167–81.

Williams, James D., and Clyde Eastman. 1994. "The Changing Population of Labor Force Ages Along the U.S.-Mexico Border." *Journal of Borderlands Studies* 9 (Fall): 23–46.

Wilson, Tamar Diana. 1986. *Chain Migration, Household Sustenance Strategies, and Kinship Networks (A Study of Zacatecans in Los Angeles).* Applied Anthropology Demographic Project. University of California, Los Angeles. Los Angeles: Department of Anthropology/University of California, Los Angeles.

———. 1992. *Vamos para buscar la vida: A Comparison of Patterns of Out-Migration from a Rancho in Jalisco and In-migration to a Mexicali Squatter Settlement.* PhD diss., University of California, Los Angeles.

———. 1993. "We Seek Work Where We Can: A Comparison of Patterns of Transnational Outmigration from a Rancho in Jalisco and of Internal Migration into a Mexicali Squatter Settlement." *Journal of Borderlands Studies* 8 (2): 33–58.

———. 1994. "What Determines Where Transnational Labor Migrants Go? Modifications in Migration Theories." *Human Organization* 53 (3): 269–78.

———. 1998a. "Weak Ties, Strong Ties: Network Principles in Mexican Migration." *Human Organization* 57 (4): 394–403.

———. 1998b. "Micro-, Meso-, and Macro-patterns of Women's Migration to Colonia Popular, Mexicali, Baja California." *Journal of Borderlands Studies* 13 (2): 63–82.

———. 1998c. "Approaches to Understanding Women in the Informal Sector." *Latin American Perspectives* 25 (2): 105–19.

———. 1999. "Anti-Immigrant Sentiment and the Process of Settlement among Mexican Immigrants in the United States: Reflections on the Current Wave of Mexican Immigrant Bashing." *Review of Radical Political Economics* 31 (2): 1–26.

———. 2000. "Anti-Immigrant Sentiment and the Problem of Reproduction/ Maintenance in Mexican Immigration to the United States." *Critique of Anthropology* 20 (2): 191–213.

———. 2002. "The Masculinization of the Mexican Maquiladoras." *Review of Radical Political Economics* 34 (1): 3–17.

———. 2003. "Forms of Male Domination and Female Subordination: Homeworkers vs. *Maquiladora* Workers in Mexico." *Review of Radical Political Economics* 35 (1): 56–72.

———. 2004. "Wage-Labor Migration and Class in Jalisco and the United States." *Latin American Perspectives* 31 (5): 100–117.

———. 2005. *Subsidizing Capitalism: Brickmakers on the U.S.-Mexican Border.* Albany: SUNY Press.

———. 2006a. "Strapping the Mexican Woman Immigrant: The Convergence of Reproduction and Production." *Anthropological Quarterly* 79 (2): 295–302.

———. 2006b. "Crossing the Border from Jalisco, Mexico: Network-Mediated Entry into Micro-Labor Enclaves." In *Labor in Cross-Cultural Perspective*, ed. E. Paul Durrenberger and Judith Martí, 283–306. Lanham, MD: AltaMira Press.

————. 2008a. "Economic and Social Impacts of Tourism in Mexico." *Latin American Perspectives* 13 (3): 37–52.

————. 2008b. "Research Note: Issues of Production vs. Reproduction/Maintenance Revisited: Towards an Understanding of Arizona's Immigration Policies." *Anthropological Quarterly* 81:713–18.

————. 2009. "The Expansion of Immigrant Networks at Origin: A Case Study of a Rancho in Jalisco (Mexico)." *Research in Economic Anthropology* 29:283–303.

Ypeij, Annelou. 2000. *Producing Against Poverty: Female and Male Micro-Entrepreneurs in Lima, Peru.* Amsterdam: Amsterdam University Press.

Zahniser, Steven S. 2000. "One Border, Two Crossings: Mexican Migration to the United States as a Two-Way Process." In *Immigration Research for a New Century: Multidisciplinary Perspectives*, ed. Nancy Foner, Ruben G. Rumbaut, and Steven J. Gold, 242–76. New York: Russell Sage Foundation.

Zamora, Emilio. 1993. *The World of the Mexican Worker in Texas.* College Station: Texas A&M University Press.

Zavella, Patricia. 1991. "*Mujeres* in Factories: Race and Class Perspectives on Women, Work, and Family." In *Gender at the Crossroads of Knowledge: Feminist Anthropology in the Postmodern Era*, ed. Micaela de Leonardo, 312–36. Berkeley: University of California Press.

Zúñiga, Víctor, and Rubén Hernández-León, eds. 2005. *New Destinations: Mexican Immigration in the United States.* New York: Russell Sage Foundation.

Index

www.ingramcontent.com/pod-product-compliance
Lightning Source LLC
Chambersburg PA
CBHW020702270326
41928CB00005B/228